OUR CHICAGO CUBS

Our Chicago Cubs
Inside the History and the Mystery
of Baseball's Favorite Franchise

RICK PHALEN

Foreword by JONATHAN WINTERS

Diamond Communications, Inc.
South Bend, Indiana
1992

OUR CHICAGO CUBS

Manufactured in the United States of America

Diamond Communications, Inc.
Post Office Box 88
South Bend, Indiana 46624-0088
(219) 299-9278
FAX (219) 299-9296

Library of Congress Cataloging-in-Publication Data

Phalen, Rick, 1937-
    Our Chicago Cubs : inside the history and the mystery of baseball's favorite franchise / Rick Phalen ; foreword by Jonathan Winters.
      p. cm.
   ISBN 0-912083-60-3 : $22.95
    1. Chicago Cubs (Baseball team)--History. 2. Baseball players--United States--Interviews. I. Title.
GV875.C6P43 1992
796.357'64'77311--dc20
                                      92-24663
                                         CIP

CONTENTS

FOREWORD vii
INTRODUCTION ix

THEY PLAYED IT AS A GAME
Billy Jurges 1
Augie Galan 5
Claude Passeau 8
Hank Wyse 13
Andy Pafko 19
Bill Nicholson 26
Hank Sauer 30
Frankie Baumholtz 42
Roy Smalley 49
Jerry Kindall 56

BROADCASTERS
Jack Brickhouse 61
Vince Lloyd 69
Jack Rosenberg 75
Arne Harris 78
Harry Caray 86

THE FOURTH ESTATE
Mike Royko 90
George Will 98
Dick Dozer 101

IT CAN DRIVE YOU CRAZY
Herman Franks 109
Lou Boudreau 111
Dallas Green 117

THE BIG EXPERIMENT
Elvin Tappe 125
Charlie Metro 129
Bobby Adams 135

EXALTATION, DESPAIR,
BEWILDERMENT, & OTHER
ASSORTED FRUIT
Dick Selma 137
Ferguson Jenkins 148

Don Kessinger 153
Glenn Beckert 158
Ron Santo 161
Billy Williams 165
Mark Grace 169

OVERACHIEVERS
Gary Woods 171
Mick Kelleher 181

SHOW BIZ
Tom Dreesen 187
Elmer Bernstein 193
Jim Belushi 196

BEHIND THE SCENES
Ned Colletti 198
Dick Balderson 206
Billy Harford 211
Paul Gerlach 217
Frank Maloney 222
Frank Capparelli 228

IT'S NOT JUST THE GAME
—THE FANS
Dan Peterson 231
Sam Sianis 237
Palmer Pyle 240
Tom Morrison 244
Mike Murphy 248
Marge Meyer 258
Jerry Duncan 264
Fred Speck 269
Marc Janser 274
Jeff Harris 278
Mary Francis Veeck 283
Tina Phalen 288
Tom Clarke 290

To my dad, who was
always available for a
game of catch.

——Acknowledgments ——

This book was made infinitely easier to write with the help of Vicki Pietryga who works for the Cubs. She never failed me. Mick Kelleher gave encouragement and assistance that was invaluable, proving again he is one of the truly nice people around. Mike Murphy, one of the original Bleacher Bums, for putting me in contact with some of the old Bums. Mike Royko, who after his interview, volunteered that he thought this book "was a good idea." That went a long way. To everyone I spoke with for their enthusiasm and cooperation for the project. Finally, to Alice Vazquez who was always there with her support and fine work.

My father was not interested in baseball. Therefore, I didn't get an opportunity until later on in my childhood to see some games. For instance, there was American Legion ball—I think the only thing he knew about the American Legion was they had some slot machines and it was a place to get a drink.

It wasn't until I got to be at least 10 or 12 before I saw my first game in Cincinnati. I can remember going down there and seeing Frank McCormick and Ernie Lombardi, Lonnie Frey, Ival Goodman. Players not unlike the famous Gabby Hartnett, whom I always remembered as a kid, and certainly later on Ernie Banks.

I was a fan. The only opportunity I got to see Cincinnati play was usually once a year and that was opening day. Something I looked forward to all fall, way into the winter, and, when spring arrived, my stepfather would say, "Kid, let's go on down to Cincinnati and see the Reds play."

Fortunately, I think a lot of us are old boys. I know I'm an old boy. I have baseballs that are signed by Joe DiMaggio, and I have a baseball signed by Ted Williams, Johnny Vander Meer—who pitched the only back-to-back no-hitter—a Cincinnati guy.

I remember my glove. I've still got my glove from when I was a kid, believe it or not. This outsized mitten with Walker Cooper on it, who I think played for the Cardinals. And I was able to save my glove and, boy, I used it a lot.

It's never over until it's over. It's not over 'til the fat lady sings. Don't hit those showers too early, you might be sorry. How many times have you gone to Wrigley Field, the Mets pounding us, it's the Dodgers, it's St. Louis, no matter who it is—we might as well leave. Hey—it's the eighth inning. Let's go. Only to reach the parking lot and hear a tremendous roar... what happened? Somebody like Ernie Banks hit the long ball. And the game was 9-8. And the Cubs came out on top.

I hate to leave a game. I guess that's the little boy in me. I've stayed in football games where it was 45-3. My mother once said, seeing a small collegiate team, Whittenberg vs. Otterbien, "It's already 50-3. Why are we staying?" I said, "You never know."

I am a baseball fan. I said I was a Cincinnati fan. But I am a Cubs fan, too. An interesting thing about Chicago and its Cubs and guys like Rick and all the guys that are included in this book—players and managers and coaches and sportscasters alike—whether you're a Cubs fan or not, when you read this book you realize the hunger people in Chicago have...it's like a fantastic disease, but this time it's a good disease.

Because it's not like all of us out there that didn't grow up in Chicago or in the area, that we've dumped our allegiance to our teams. I think that everybody today, through those long years of drought—that basically...deep down inside of him, whether he's a little boy or an old man...he's pulling for the Cubs now.

I think very honestly there are more fans out there like myself that would shelve their teams...maybe I'm out of line in saying this. I think that there's a thing that's running through the country. The Cub fans and the Cubs themselves are due. I think before too long you're going to see the Cubs not only win the pennant and their division but very possibly the World Series.

Jonathan Winters
Santa Barbara, California

INTRODUCTION

The last time the Chicago Cubs won a World Series was in 1908. They beat the Detroit Tigers four games to one. Teddy Roosevelt was President, Ronald Reagan was not born, World War I was still six years away, and the automobile was just gaining popularity.

The franchise has played some of the worst baseball in the 20th century. The Cubs have sustained respectability only twice: the period from 1906-1911 and from 1929-1938.

Why then are the Cubs the most popular baseball team in America? Why do fans in airports and hotels mob the team? Why, no matter the caliber of baseball they are playing, will Wrigley Field be sold out for every game? Why are they the best drawing team on the road in the National League?

Our Chicago Cubs addresses this phenomenon and many other aspects of the Chicago Cubs through interviews with individuals who have witnessed and participated in events surrounding the Cubs. This oral history consists of interviews with past and present players, a former general manager and managers, front office and field personnel, broadcasters, writers, entertainers, and fans, and even a past batboy and minor league umpire.

Many subjects, opinions, and points of view are covered when you speak with 55 individuals. Each interview is unique and covers many topics.

Working on this book has given me the opportunity to revisit my youth when I dreamed of playing in the major leagues. As my father used to say, "Many are called, but few are chosen." I wasn't chosen—hell, I wasn't even called—but for those who were chosen, and played for the Cubs, it was something none of them have ever forgotten. Every Cub I spoke with loved playing for Chicago.

I found it particularly enjoyable speaking with the Cub players of my era as a youngster, the mid-'40s to the mid-'50s. Many times I finished an interview with tears in my eyes—remembering them as "the Boys of Summer" and now advancing on the long surrender to old age.

One interview I found very sad. Bill Nicholson, the Cubs' home run hitter of the '40s, said no one knew he played major league baseball where he lived and thanked me for taking the time to talk with him. Thousands still remember him as someone who brought excitement into their lives. This is a gift few possess.

My interest in the Cubs began one Sunday in August 1948 when my dad took me to see the Cubs play the Boston Braves in a doubleheader. The Braves were clearly the better team and would win the pennant that year, losing to Cleveland four games to two in the World Series. But for some strange reason the Cubs, who would finish last that year, won two that day and I was forever hooked. It has definitely been a bittersweet experience since.

That Sunday afternoon many years ago still lives with me. Phil Cavarretta hit a ball into the ivy in left center near the 368-foot mark with the bases loaded. The Braves' left fielder, Jeff Heath, could not find the ball in the ivy. Everyone in the park knew that Heath was faking it because Cavarretta had circled the bases for an inside-the-park home run and if he could not find the ball it would be called a ground rule double. Heath fooled the umpire and Cavarretta was called back to second. Only two runs scored, not four. All hell broke loose. The fans threw everything but their money on the field. Play was delayed and Charlie Grimm, the Cubs' manager, was apoplectic. It didn't matter, the Cubs won and also took the second game.

Driving home with my dad after the game I was overawed. Big crowd, excitement, controversy, and two wins. Unfortunately, there have been too few afternoons like this since that warm day in 1948.

But I continue to be drawn to them. Considering some of the teams they have fielded, it is not rational behavior. But being a Cub fan obviates rationality.

This book attempts to explain their appeal. This tangible and intangible attraction they hold on many of us.

In any event, I hope you learn something new about the Cubs and possibly about yourself. I did.

THEY PLAYED IT AS A GAME

———— BILLY JURGES ————

He was playing shortstop in the '32 World Series when Babe Ruth supposedly "called his home run" against Charlie Root of the Cubs. According to Bill, he didn't.

His only regret is that he did not accept the manager's job offered to him in 1938 by Phil Wrigley. He recommended Gabby Hartnett to Wrigley instead and the next season Bill was traded to the New York Giants. Makes you wonder.

I came up in 1931...they had a great ball club, of course. They still had Cuyler in the outfield. They had Hack Wilson, Gabby Hartnett, and Charlie Grimm at first base, and Woody English playing third.

It's a different baseball game today. It's entirely different. Everything is pitching today. You have specialists. After all, it's tough hitting in the major leagues today, because of the specialists they have. They have a starter, they have an in-between guy, and they have a finisher, and they have five or six fellows in the bullpen. Years ago, they only had one or two fellows in the bullpen and they would finish up. The pitchers years ago started a ball game, they expected them to finish the game. But today, it's altogether different. It's all pitching.

You were fortunate your first full season in '32, you went into the World Series. That's a very memorable World Series. You were at shortstop when Babe Ruth supposedly called his home run off Charlie Root.

It's a good story, but I'm relating what Gabby said. After all, Gabby was right up there. Babe used to do that over in the American League. He used to motion to the opposing ball club in the dugouts it's only two strikes. And this is what he did this time. He said, "It's only two strikes." The Cub bench, they were on the Babe. They were kidding him along and so forth and the Babe gestured that this is only two strikes and that's what he said. That's what Gabby said he said. "That's only two strikes." So, he hit the ball, and the ball, if I remember correctly, Charlie Root was pitch-

1

ing, and it looked like the ball went between Charlie Root's legs and wound up over the center-field wall.

As far as you're concerned, he did not call his shot?

No. Mark Koenig was with us at the time. He was from the Yankees and he said that Babe used to do that over in the American League. So, you can just take it from there. But it's a good story and I shouldn't even touch on it, but that's the way it...

What do you remember of the "homer in the gloamin'"— the '38 game? Mace Brown was pitching. You were playing Pittsburgh. It was a big game and Hartnett hit that ball over the left-field wall.

Well, it was dark and the previous inning, the umpire said this is going to be the last inning. And the game was going to be called. Mace Brown hung a high curveball and Gabby hit it. It was dark and I was on my way up to the clubhouse because there was two strikes on Gabby and, you figure, well the game's going to be over, and he hit it.

You were offered the manager's job in 1938 but turned it down.

I was called downtown to Mr. Wrigley's office and I didn't know what they were going to talk to me about. As I walked into his office, there was three or four other gentlemen there, and he said before I sat down, "Bill, we want to make you manager of the Cubs." And I was so shocked I fell back in my chair. I said, "No, you don't. After all Gabby Hartnett's been here for 15, whatever it was, 15 years and he's entitled to a shot at it." So I said, "I can't take it because of that. Otherwise, I would take it." So that was that. That's the reason I didn't take it, because Gabby was entitled to it. I'm second-guessing myself on that. The reason I second-guess myself on that because I was the first one to be traded after the World Series in '38.

We played the Yankees in the World Series of '38 and I was living in New York at the time. After the ball game, the fourth ball game, the Yankees beat us badly. I went up to Gabby, and I said, "Gabby, I hope to see you next year." He said, "Bill, as long as I have the baseball club, you'll be with me." So, I was the first one to be traded.

Comes the 1939 season, of course, the Cubs traded me for Dick Bartell. The first series we played in New York, Dick Bartell came up to me and he says, "Bill, how about that son of buck Terry?" I said, "Well, what happened?" He said, "Well, after we played the last game in 1938 I was with Bill Terry and I wished him well, that he would have a good winter and so forth, and he told me as long as he had the ball club I'd be the shortstop." So, we had a big laugh about it. So, that was that. It happened to Dick Bartell and it happened to me.

I took it in stride 'cause baseball being what it is, you don't expect to stay with a ball club all your life. Some ballplayers do, but I didn't expect to.

From '39 through '45 you were with the Giants. What was wartime baseball like?

It was a good brand of baseball. It was really good. After all, it wasn't tops, but it was good. It's better than what they're playing today.

Expansion's a bad thing. After all, it's gonna be thinned down again. Baseball fans really don't know what the hell a major league ballplayer should do. They're not well educated. Years ago, they had a fellow by the name of Red Barber and he educated the baseball fans in Brooklyn. And they knew what was goin' on. For example, if Pee Wee Reese was up there hitting and a hit-and-run was in order, he would educate—tell the fans about it—what was going to happen. And this doesn't happen today. A few of them do it. A few of the commentators do it, but not very many, and so consequently, the baseball fan today isn't educated. For example, if there's 40,000 people out at the ballpark, about 5,000 of the fans would know what the hell's going on. They wouldn't know that the shortstop's moving around, the outfielders are moving around in different positions, and the pitcher's trying to set up the hitter and things like that. They don't know anything about that.

What was your reaction, Bill, being traded back to the Cubs in 1946? You had two more years with Chicago, '46 and '47. Were you happy to come back?

Yes, I was happy to come back. I liked Chicago. Chicago is a great town and they're great fans. They're wonderful fans.

Fans today in Chicago—they're a younger group. They're younger fans and they're enthusiastic and Harry Caray does a hell of a job keeping them alive. He's a great announcer.

Of course, different towns have different groups. They have

3

older people at some ballparks. For example, in Cincinnati. Cincinnati has an older group of fans, I think. They relate to the game differently.

Is the ballplayer of today different than your day?

There's no question about it. Years ago, the ballplayers played for the fun of it more or less. Today, they're for the money and so forth and they don't give 100%. They don't give out. Years ago, the pitchers used to run about two hours a day to keep in shape and all you see today is a pitcher running around the ball field once and he thinks he's in good condition. And that's one of the reasons they don't finish ball games. They're not really in top shape.

Anything you would like to do differently?

Yeah. The thing I'd like to do over again would be to say "yes" to Mr. Wrigley in 1938.

You wish you'd taken that job.

Yes. After being that I was traded—yes.

Do you think Hartnett did it deliberately because he knew you were offered the job?

Well, years ago they used to say about managers that ballplayers on the ball club that were in line for the manager's job, they would get rid of them. So I don't know if that was in Gabby's mind or not, but he got rid of me.

───AUGIE GALAN───

Played for the Cubs from 1934 to 1941. He had a lifetime batting average of .287 and was a solid performer. Playing during the Depression with Chicago, he had to buy most of his equipment. He had to live on his baseball earnings through the year because he couldn't take another person's job during the off-season.

In 1935, I will never forget we had a tremendous ball club and to win 21 games in a row to win the pennant—that was one of my biggest thrills in baseball.

Charlie Grimm was the manager.
Well, Charlie was, what do you call him, "Jolly Charlie." Actually, he was a very good manager to play for. He knew baseball and we had a ball club that knew how to play baseball and he turned a lot of the game over to us. Oh, he was real good.
When I started out I made $4,000 a year. Eventually, after '35—I made $7,500. And the end—I made $9,000.

Your last year with the Cubs was in 1940.
Yeah. Then I went over to Brooklyn.

$9,000 was considered a pretty good salary in the Depression.
Well, I guess so. But nobody realized it. You know, we paid for almost everything ourselves. We had to buy our shoes and gloves and almost everything else. The only thing the club gave us those days was the uniform and sweatshirts. We paid for everything else.
Actually, everybody don't realize we'd go home in the winter time when things weren't good and we could not get a job, being a ballplayer, and take somebody's job away from them. We couldn't do those things. So, it wasn't as good as everybody thought it was.

You played under Gabby Hartnett.
Well, Gabby was probably the best catcher in baseball as far as I'm concerned. He played 16 years in the major leagues and only dropped one pop fly and he challenged them all. Come out to the

pitchers mound and, when he'd holler, "I got it," everybody scattered because he was going to get it. And, not only that, but he used to...be a man on first base and two outs and, you know, when a game is close, and he'd holler to the pitcher, "Let him go, I'll get him." And, by God, he'd throw him out. Oh, he had a great arm. And he threw a lightest ball, you know. He threw like a bullet but the ball was light to catch. He was great. A great receiver and a pretty good hitter, too.

Billy Jurges was my roommate. Mr. Wrigley called Jurges into his office and offered him the manager's job and Jurges says, "No, Gabby is your man," and that's the way Gabby got the job. I said, "You're stupid. You'll probably never get another chance." Gosh sakes. I told Bill...we were really close, you know. I told him definitely, "Gosh sakes, you shouldn't have...when they offer you a job, you take it."

What was your reaction, Augie, being traded from the Cubs to Brooklyn in 1941?

Well, that's when I was hurt. I was getting over a knee injury where I injured myself in 1940 where I hit the concrete wall and didn't know whether I could play again. The doctors said I'd never play again, so I worked, and worked it hard. It took me almost a year to get back where I thought I might be able to play. So, the Cubs did promise to keep me if I just could pinch-hit and then about six or seven weeks to go, they said I was going to Los Angeles. I said, "No, I'm not." I mean, they promised me and I went to see Judge Landis and he told me, he says, "Hey, you're not going nowhere. You're going to stay right here with me 'cause I see something's wrong here."

And, in the meantime, the Dodgers found out about that and they contact the Cubs and the Cubs says they had to contact L.A.— you know the Angels in Los Angeles. In the meantime, they got ahold of them and they made a trade and I became property of the Dodgers.

And you had some big years for Brooklyn.

Oh, fantastic. All that time I had the bad knee, but they had a trainer—he fixed up a steel brace for me for my left knee. With the hinges in it. I could play ball then. I wore it for five and a half years.

Made the difference. I mean, every time I hit the base it would hurt, but with that protection the pain would go away until I slid in again. After five and a half years I hit the base awfully hard one afternoon and it didn't hurt, so I threw the brace away.

What was your biggest thrill playing for the Cubs?

Well, I guess the thrill was being up there all the time and then the 21 straight games. To win the pennant—that was a big thrill for me. And I guess another thrill was when I went 154 games and didn't miss a game or an inning and didn't hit in a double play. And how lucky can you get.

In '35 I didn't hit in a double play. I think I went 198 consecutive games before I hit in a double play. It's a National League—it's baseball's record. I'm lucky because the only thing they can do is tie it—they can't beat it.

The Cubs were always a great team. As far as I'm concerned they were great—the fans were great. I loved Wrigley Field. I loved everything about it and it was my first love.

You know, things change. You gotta go along with the times. What can you do? The only thing, I was born too early. But that's progress in the good old USA and things are going to happen—I guess they're going to continue. The only thing is you're just happy for the players when they make more money.

I enjoyed every minute of it. It was great. I only wish I was playing today.

———Claude Passeau———

A mainstay of the Cub pitching staff from 1939 to 1945. He pitched a one-hit masterpiece in the third game of the 1945 World Series, winning 3-0. Was later hurt in the sixth game, which threw the pitching rotation for the seventh game out of whack.

A very tough competitor, he pitched with three-days rest. He completed what he started; of 331 big league games in which he started, he completed 188—a 57% completion mark. One tough cookie.

I was one of those pitchers. I just happened to be one of them that, whenever I pitched, it was always a pretty hard game. Of course, I pitched some terrible games, too.

Back in those days, we pitched with three-days rest. Say you pitched today, rest three days, and pitch the fourth day. You go back and look at my record. I pitched about five or six years in a row—18 complete games. And one year I had 24.

You pitched 188 complete games in the major leagues.

Somebody sent me something a few years ago. And—well they were just talkin' about how many complete games they don't have now. But Hartnett told me one time, he says...Hartnett was my manager then...he told me, he says, "One thing we bought you for, traded for you, is you could beat Brooklyn, New York, Cincinnati." I believe it was pretty regularly when I was with the Phillies.

How was Hartnett as a manager?

He was a swell fellow. He got along well with his players and I liked him very much.

Who caught most of your games?

Well, Scheffing caught some. Livingston caught some and McCullough caught some.

I didn't have any real preference. I liked McCullough for the simple reason he had a good arm and he could throw. And one thing that—I had to laugh—I was lookin' at a talk show one night

8

and they were interviewing McCullough after I retired. And they asked McCullough, "McCullough, you caught some mighty good pitchers. How about so-and-so and so-and-so?" and they named me. He said, "Well, I don't know whether Passeau was the best pitcher I ever caught. But I say one thing, he was the meanest son of a bitch I ever saw."

If you would go back and look at my averages—I didn't hit very many fellows. But I came so close they thought they was hit—so that kind of helped me out a little bit. I was mean when I played between the lines.

What was your best pitch?

I only had one. See, I couldn't throw a curveball. And my fast-balls sailed and I threw it 90% of the time.

I belonged to Detroit at one time. And they took me to spring training and they were going to teach me how to throw a curveball and all that kind of stuff. And they were trying to change my stance on the mound and all this, that, and the other, and I was wild a little bit. They finally just gave up on me after sending me to several minor league clubs. And they couldn't change me either. I never got a chance to set—usually when they changed me from one club to another, they already was established, you know, and I didn't get much chance to pitch. They say if you can't throw curveballs you'll never make it, so they released me. So that's the way I finally went to Des Moines and won 20 and Pittsburgh bought me.

Pittsburgh bought me and they had a crew of pitchers and they were going to send me to Louisville. So they made a trade for two catchers—Earl Grace and Al Todd. And after it was all over with, the Phillies called and said, "How about throwing somebody else in that trade that we just made last week and we'd prefer a pitcher." Well, they were figurin' on sending me out, so they called them back and said, "We've got just the fellow you need." So they sent me to Philadelphia. They didn't trade or nothin'. They just gave me to Philadelphia.

Were you 4F during the war?

Well, see, I got shot through the hand. I had a crippled left hand when I was 14. And then I had a bad knee that eventually I had to have operated on. Take the cartilage out. Then I had a bad back and I had to have my back operated on. So the combination of everything—I was examined four times, but they told me that I could never carry a pack. I wouldn't be worth a damn.

What was wartime baseball like?

It was a whole lot better than they're given credit for. I think the pitching was really good—a whole lot better than it is now, I believe. 'Cause we were going eight and nine innings a game where these fellows are going four and five now.

Some think with expansion that the caliber of major league baseball was better during the war than it is now.

I think so. For the simple reason during the war, we had anywhere from six to eight starters—major leaguers. But some of the ball clubs they've got now, they don't have over four or five. And then they're gettin' worse. There's just not enough ballplayers, that's all there is to it.

The caliber of ball was pretty good during the war?

I thought it was excellent.

What do you remember about the '45 season?

Well, we were beatin' the teams that we knew to beat. If you go back and look, we had a lot of complete games pitched that year. And, I always asked to pitch the second game of a doubleheader, especially in Chicago 'cause I loved to pitch in Wrigley Field. I was an inside pitcher. I pitched inside to righthanders and inside to lefthanders. And then that's the longest part of the ballpark.

They're not going to pull it.

That's right. And I just like to pitch there, that's all. I pitched them on the handle part of the bat all the time.

They couldn't get any wood on it.

That's true—they'd hit the doubles, alright. They got a lot of hits. Some fellow I talked to not very long ago says that, "Well, you gave up more hits than innings you pitched." I says, "Yeah, but I didn't walk very many. I was on that plate all the time."

The third game of the 1945 World Series you pitched a one-hitter.

Well, the worst thing I remember—Rudy York hit the ball. He

was my ex-roommate. And he told me the next day, he says, "Roomie, if I had known..." What it was was my fastball sailed. And he swung at the ball and then he saw it started sailing so he kind of held up. He just did pitch the ball over the shortstop's head. I was in and out and my fastball was sailing. See I only pitched to 28 men. So I was around the plate. I pitched all on the black most of the time.

You got hurt in game six. You got hit by a line drive.

Well, it was a semi-line drive. And again, that was from my neighbor that lives pretty close to where I live now. Jimmy Outlaw. It just jammed him. The ball was on the trademark and inside and it came back at me as a knuckleball. And I just grabbed at it quicker than I should have and it got me right on the end of my ring finger on the right hand.

I tried to pitch but my fingers were so stiff I couldn't. So I left with a 6 to 1 or 2 lead in about the sixth inning. We had to go 12 innings before we won the ball game, but I didn't get credit for the game. That messed up our pitchin' rotation and we didn't have a pitcher for the seventh game.

Borowy came in, was the winner, and started game seven.

Yeah, he won that 12-inning game. The fellow wasn't too strong. He was a very good pitcher—about a six-inning pitcher, but he's just a fellow that couldn't throw it every day. He didn't weigh but about 165-170, I guess, at the most.

We should have won the thing, but when I got hit on the finger, that just messed up the deal.

You pitched for the Cubs in '46 and '47.

Well, you see I had my back operated on in '46. February 17th. And so I really didn't...I wasn't going to go back. And they told me to come back and just fool around in the bullpen and kind of work with the young pitchers and things like that. I shouldn't have been up the last two years.

Did you retire after the '47 season?

No, I managed. I worked for the Cubs. I went on the road and when we'd have a ball club going bad, I'd go and work with that ball club. I don't know what year it is now—'48 I guess it was—I went down to Centralia, Illinois, and worked with that ball club. In '49, I went to Visalia, California, and we just had terrible young boys, that was all. Wasn't a prospect in the bunch.

The Cubs had a bad minor league system.
That's true. And the thing that almost all major league clubs do, they try to get local boys to bring in attendance, I'm sure. Instead of looking for talent, they were looking for attendance, maybe. They just weren't there, that was all there was to it.

So the Cubs were signing some Chicagoland ballplayers that just didn't have it?
Right. I'm not second-guessin'—I was just one of the Cubs.

Claude, what was the most money you made playing for the Cubs?
I made $20,000 one year. I'd say '40, '41, something like that. I was born 60 years too early. I'm 82 now.
When I went out to pitch, I really enjoyed it. I always thought I was going to win. I've often said that the highlight of my baseball career was when I was traded to the Cubs.

They were nice fans, weren't they?
They are. They were nice people. The people that ran the ball club were really nice, too. I just wish I'd have been born later.

So you'd make more money?
Right. I don't know what I'd do with it, though. I have a good time now. I have a good business. I've been in the John Deere business—tractor business since 1940. Even when I was with the Cubs—I had somebody else running my John Deere business. I gave the business to my son about 12 years ago.
I'm around the shop. But I go fishing practically every day I can.
I just wish I could have done better...we could have won more.

———— HANK WYSE ————

*The ace of the 1945 pennant-winning Cubs with a record of 22-10
and an ERA of 2.68. A workhorse, he started 34 games in 1945
and completed 23. In other words, he completed 68% of his starts.
Two years later he hurt his arm and finished his career in the early
'50s in Class D ball at Tyler, Texas.*

What are your recollections of 1945?

Well, I know I got awful tired. I had 10 days off and then I
pitched that first game and I won. And then three days later I
pitched again. Three days later I pitched again. Two days and I
pitched again. And they sat down with me and talked with me and
said they was going to try to win the pennant and wanted to know
if I could pitch on two-days rest and three-days rest and would like
to get Hank Borowy from the Yankees. Said they was going to get
him, but they had to get him through waivers and it would take a
little time. So I pitched—I don't know—how many games now
right offhand—I don't remember. But I pitched with three-days rest
and pitched with two-days rest. And on the days I pitched with
two-days rest, I was tired all over, not just my arm, but all over. I
think what I ought to tell them I can't throw today, I don't feel good,
my arm's dead. That day I'd shut you out. And three-days rest I'd
feel strong and I'd have to struggle to win.

Nobody had pitching coaches then. But Roy Johnson was my
manager in Tulsa and he used to be a pitcher—so he helped most
of the pitchers.

I finally quit after a while from pitching two days. We got to
first place and I got out of two days and three days every time. I
never got no four or five.

If it rained on my fourth day...the day I was supposed to pitch,
I pitched the next day. I missed some turns.

Did Borowy help?

Yes, he did. He won, oh, four or five in a row before he got
beat. He won 10 or 11 and lost one, I think, for us. He took the
pressure off some of us.

You started the second game of the '45 Series and lost to Virgil Trucks, 4-1. What's your recollection of that game?

Well, the biggest recollection after we warmed up, a TV guy come down and asked us would we shake hands. I made a mistake —I'll never do it again.

Why?

Well, he pitched a no hitter at me in the Texas League and I throwed a one-hitter at him.

So, I went and wished him good luck. I made a mistake. He beat me again.

I made Greenberg look bad a couple of times. But Jim Tobin, that used to be with the Boston Braves, was sittin' in the stands with glasses and he was calling pitches.

Sittin' out in center field somewhere and callin' pitches.

How was he getting it to the batter?

Oh, I don't know how he did that. I just knew he was gettin' it from the catcher. I made Greenberg look real bad on curveballs about three-quarter delivery and I decided he hadn't seen my good curve and I come overhanded and hung it high inside and he stepped back like he knew what was comin' and hit the ball in the bleachers.

They were a pretty good hitting team.

What was the best salary you made playing for the Cubs?

$12,500. There was a lot of guys that didn't make that. They couldn't give us raises then. Salary was frozen.

I did make a little bit more money then. They had ways of gettin' around it. They gave my wife $2,000 to go home. They gave me $4,000 to sign a contract before I went home and give her $2,000 to go to spring training and things like that. Then they paid her expenses.

It's 1946, the ballplayers are back from the war. Did the pace pick up?

I think it probably started in '48-'49. Probably '49 before it really picked up.

Why did it take that long?

Well, Musial and guys like Ted Williams and all of the good

guys, they was coming back then. I think it made a little difference. There were some 4F players during the war that—they were good ballplayers, but they weren't the same players that the stars were.

What happened to the Cubs after 1946?

I don't know what it was. I think the salaries went up real good and Wrigley wouldn't go out and buy no players and they wasn't producin' nothin' in the minors. I guess that's the only reason I can think of.

Did you like playing for Wrigley?

I never met the guy but once. He never come down on the field.

He was up in the press box. He was up in the press box or had his own box or something. He never would come down on the field and talk to you. But he would come to the clubhouse. We'd have a meeting on the road after a game—night game—after we went to bed, they'd go down to the diner and stay all night and try to make deals and things. That's about all I ever saw of him.

What were some of the highlights of your career?

Well, all of it was a highlight for me. I was havin' a good time. I was winning and we was winning and I was thrilled. I was pretty happy. Seemed like all of us was. I was elected on two All-Star Games. I didn't get to play. I throwed battin' practice in one of them, but I was thrilled about that and thrilled about gettin' to play in the World Series. But I enjoyed it all. I really...I think anybody who plays in the big leagues is lucky anyway.

I had two brothers better ballplayers than I was. They played semi-pro ball. One of them when he was 17 got to pitch a double-header and hurt his arm and the other one got married pretty young —he was a catcher. He could have played in the big leagues. Both of them were better ballplayers than I. My dad was a good ballplayer, but he just played semi-pro. He helped us kids. Played ball every time we got a chance to play and wanted to know what we wanted to play—why he wanted to play. He didn't want no foolin' around. He wanted us to play right. And I guess that's where we all learned it.

The coaches in the minor leagues. I was lucky. I played in the Ban Johnson League in Kansas City and there was an old pitcher,

Roy Sanders, that played with Pittsburgh. And he managed the Golden Jewelers and we won two or three years in a row—the pennant in the Ban Johnson League. He helped me and then when I signed a big league contract, I got to Tulsa, well Roy Johnson was there. And he helped me. When I got to Tulsa, they sent me to Moline, Illinois, for a while and I got down there and Mike Gonzalez was the manager and he was taking a shower one day and he thought everybody was gone from the ballpark and he was talking to himself. We'd lost about five or six in a row. He said, "I wonder who I'm going to pitch tomorrow." And I said, "You're going to pitch me or I'm goin' home." He said, "Who said that?" I told him I did and he said, "You mean that?" And I said, "Yeah, I come down here to play baseball and I want to play." He said, "I'll pitch you."

Next day I won. And every day for, I don't know, a week or two, every day we was home, why he was at the ballpark making me throw curveballs, sliders, we'd throw them outside, inside, high, and low, every day. And, one day I was in the theatre and they had a double feature. I think I gave a quarter to see two westerns. He come in and paged me. And I come outside and he said, "Pack up. You're going back to Tulsa." I said, "You're kiddin' me." He said, "No. They called and asked for my best pitcher. I'm sendin' you." He started to walk off and he said, "Hey, Wyse." I said, "Yes, sir?" And he said, "You're not my best pitcher. They asked for the best pitcher and I'm sending you. You've got the best chance for the big leagues first. When you get down there, you do the same thing that you're doing here and you'll make it."

I really had good people work with me that helped me and when I got to Tulsa I got the same thing from Roy Johnson. He'd take me out there. He'd run with me after a ball game and tell me all about it. So, he kept me pretty clean and taught me how to pitch. I went up in '42 and he (Johnson) come up in '43.

Only regret I have is when I hurt my arm. They was having trouble. Guys wasn't gettin' in shape. We had some bad weather coming north and we was in Dallas or Houston—I forgot which—Houston, I believe. Cavarretta and McCullough and Merullo—all of them —the good hitters wanted some extra battin' practice and I asked Roy Johnson, I said, "Where you goin'?" He said, "They want some extra battin' practice." I said, "Can I go along?" And he said, "Sure." Of course, Roy couldn't throw very hard and his curveball's just a spinnin' and I said, "Do you care if I throw battin' practice? They want to hit some good hard stuff, curveballs, sliders, and everything. I'll throw them." I just kept throwin', they just kept playing, and he said, "Hey, you better quit. You've been throwin' for 30 minutes." And when the ball game started, Grimm told me to go down and warm up and I told him I couldn't throw. My arm was drawn up and stiff. They sent me to the doctor and he found chips in it, so that was the end of my career—1948.

About two days before the season started, they sent me to Shreveport in the Texas League.

Well, they never really did tell me what was wrong with my arm. They never told me to put it in a cast and then they told me I was going to Shreveport. I never heard from them anymore. Didn't get it checked.

They promised me when they sat down with me and talked to me about pitchin' with two-days rest and three-days rest and asked them, "Well, that's going to be pretty rough on me. I might hurt my arm." And Grimm told me, he said, "Don't worry about that. Mr. Wrigley will take care of you for life." Grimm never talked to me since.

He was the best clown I ever played for. He kept you loose and laughin'. He was funny.

Did you like playing for him?

Yeah, I did. He never did talk to you.

Wilson was there when I first come up. He was a lot stricter than Grimm was. He had curfew and everything. Grimm never had no curfews. He didn't say nothin' if you stayed out all night. He never did say nothin'. He might have had a coach come talk to me, but he never had no bed check or anything. Wilson did. Day and night both.

You finished your career in the minor leagues.

I went from the majors to the Texas League and from there to the Athletics and then back...Washington sold me to Kansas City and I wouldn't sign with Kansas City and I went to Beaumont in the Texas League. And I wouldn't play with them the next year. I was supposed to go out on a two-year manager job and that club folded up.

You finished in Class D in Tyler, Texas.

Well, I thought I could manage it because I thought I was a pretty good teacher. I helped some young players in the league when I was playing and some of them went to the big leagues and they give me credit for helpin' them pitch. I don't believe in everybody pitchin' the same way. I believe in what you feel comfortable you do. Throwin' the ball hard ain't going to win. You gotta learn how to pitch. Set up hitters and things. That's what I tried to do and since I didn't get the managin' job, nobody offered me a coachin' job, why I decided just to stay here and I put all my tools in that navy bag and hung it up on the wall.

I guess it was June, I come in one day and it's about 110 here. I'd been workin' outside all the time. I parked the car and opened the garage door, went inside, and took the duffle bag and emptied it out in the middle of the floor and my wife comes through the kitchen door into the garage, and she said, "Yeah, that's what I thought. I didn't think you'd quit." I just put it all back in there and hung it up. And I said, "Well, I don't know what the hell I was doin'." And she says, "What do you mean?" I says, "I don't know what I got that down for. I'm going to quit." But I must have missed it pretty bad.

We didn't lose that World Series. Grimm did. His pitchin'. He didn't use them right.

Erickson went up the last day—went up to the office and asked to start. And Hy Vandenberg should have started or I should have started. He knew or he should have knew that Borowy should have had four or five-days rest. Got five runs off him in the first inning.

Who do you think Grimm should have thrown in that seventh game?

Hy Vandenberg.

He (Borowy) had a tough ball game that day that he won it. He had a tough time then.

I'd have used the last guy in the bullpen before I'd have used him.

——————ANDY PAFKO——————

A tremendously popular Cub. He always gave 100%. Consistent, reliable, with a great attitude. On June 15, 1951, he was traded to the Brooklyn Dodgers. It still hurts thinking about it.

All he ever wanted to do was play baseball. Thank God he did, for there were few more gifted ballplayers than "Handy" Andy Pafko.

You came up in 1943 at the end of the season and played in 13 games.

I came from L.A., I had a real outstanding year. I played in the Pacific Coast League. I led the league in hitting. I was voted the most valuable ballplayer. And I think we won a pennant by 21 some ball games, we got in the playoff and we lost four straight. And, of course, it was very bad, but on the other hand, it was a break for me, 'cause like you say, the Cubs had 13 games left to play in the '43 season.

I joined the ball club and I'll never forget I walked in the clubhouse and the first guy I ran into was Stan Hack, the famous third baseman of the Cubs. And he said, "Andy, I heard you were coming. Welcome to Chicago." He made me feel like I was part of the ball club immediately. That particular day was kind of rainy and I was hoping to get rained out, to kind of get my feet wet a little bit, to get acclimated to the conditions of the big leagues. We did play the ball game and I'll never forget my first two times at bat. I got two base hits and I knocked in four runs. And to me that was a real great start in the big leagues and in 13 games I hit about .370 or .380, so that was a great start for me as a Chicago Cub.

We were playing against Philadelphia and the pitcher for Philadelphia that particular afternoon was big Bill Lee...and he was a former Cub, by the way. He was a big, strong guy. And he hung a curve up near my eyes and I hit it to left field and knocked in two runs. So, I broke in with a bang, so to speak.

What was the caliber of play during the war? As bad as many have said?

Well, maybe it was overdone somewhat. I mean, there's a lot

of guys that were in the service. Guys like Johnny Mize and Enos Slaughter and Stan Musial—some of the great names of the past, but it was still big league baseball, so I considered it a big thrill just to be in the big leagues. I still considered it the big leagues.

I mean, guys like Harry Brecheen and Howie Pollet and Max Lanier. I think the caliber of the pitching was up but maybe some of the guys were a little bit older and they didn't move as fast in the infield or the outfield. But the pitching was still up there.

The Cubs always drew real well. I mean, no matter what, if you were a Cub fan, I mean, you'd never pull for the White Sox. I mean, you're either American League or National League and the Cubs always had a great following and I still think we had great crowds. Maybe not like today, because, it's a different era. But I still recall we had great crowds. The center-field bleachers were open in those days and they were always filled up. That's where a lot of the guys used to like to sit to watch the ball game from center field.

We enjoyed the train travel. We were more of a family. We stayed together and we used to enjoy each other's company. We got aboard the train and we had a lot of time to talk about baseball. Not like today. Get on a plane and you're there in a couple of hours. Well, we used to travel from Chicago to St. Louis, St. Louis to Boston...of course, that was an overnight trip. And you could just sit around and talk baseball. We enjoyed it. I tell you, there was more camaraderie in our days.

You're one of a few guys that can say they played for the last Cub pennant winner.

It was still during the war, and we thought we had a pretty good year. That's the year we had pretty good pitching. Hank Wyse, I remember he was our mainstay. I think he won over 20-some ball games. And then we had Claude Passeau—he was one of the older guys. He was more of a steadying influence on the younger guys. We had Paul Derringer, Hy Vandenberg, and some of the older guys. It was an older pitching staff, but we battled the St. Louis Cardinals that particular year...right down to the end.

Here, I'm in the big leagues my second year and I'm still more or less a rookie and I find myself in the World Series in Detroit. It was quite a thrill for me because I'd never saw a World Series before. And here I'm in one myself, and playing against Detroit.

I'll never forget the first ball game. My biggest game of all-time —I played in four World Series beyond that—but that first ball game, I got three hits off of Hal Newhouser. Newhouser was voted the most valuable ballplayer that year. I think he won about 26 or 27 ball games and here I get hits off the great Hal Newhouser—to me that was a big thrill.

My younger brother was stationed in Europe at the time and he heard the World Series ball games by short-wave radio and he was telling all the guys, "that's my brother playing with Chicago." And he had a hard time convincing all his buddies over there that that was his brother playing in a World Series.

That year we got Hank Borowy from the Yankees and he won 10-11 ball games for us. Unfortunately, he came up with a blister on his hand and he couldn't quite cut the mustard. He had a problem with that during the summer. He just had a soft hand and he gripped the ball too tight and, unfortunately, he came up with a blister and that took care of him for the rest of the Series. I mean, he just couldn't throw it. I'm sure that cost us the World Series, because he was our mainstay. He was our stopper. We just didn't have anybody else to do it for us.

Claude Passeau got hurt.

Yeah, he got hit by a line drive—by somebody—I forget who the hitter was, but he got hit on his pitching hand and, unfortunately, that didn't help us either. So, we had a lot of bad breaks as far as pitching was concerned.

After 1945 things started to go downhill. Why?

I've been asked that question many times. Why...how come the Cubs never could compete with the other ball clubs?

I'm certain our scouting system wasn't up to par with the other ones. That's the only thing that I can come up with, because we never came up with any young ballplayers. We always had to go via the trade route and we always got some older fellows. So, I'm sure the scouting system wasn't up to par. That's the only thing that I can think of, really.

We had a great manager in Charlie Grimm. Everybody loved to play for him. Of course, then after Charlie gave up the reins, then we came up with Frankie Frisch—he managed us for a while. Of course, Frankie—under his regime I was traded away in 1951 to the Dodgers.

What was it like playing in Wrigley Field?

We had people sitting in the center-field bleachers. I remember we were playing against the Cardinals one day—and I forget who our pitcher was—but anyway, Johnny Hopp, a Cardinal outfielder, got hit in the head that day and I thought that he was almost gone. He didn't wake up until they took him to the hospital. And then shortly after that I think Cavarretta, or somebody, went to the front office and told them that "you better cover that section or do something 'cause someone's going to get killed out there," and I guess a year or so later, they roped it off and ever since then nobody has been sitting in the center-field bleachers. On a hot day, naturally the people came out with their white shirts and the white ball coming out of those white shirts was tough to pick up.

It was one of my favorite ballparks. It was fair for the hitter. Fair for the pitcher. If you hit a ball real well, it went out the ballpark.

But I think the most vivid memory playing center field is...I made a catch out there which the umpire said I trapped the ball. This is against St. Louis. I think we had a one-run lead going into the top half of the ninth inning at Wrigley Field...and we had two out, and there was a man on first base—I think it was Slaughter. Rocky Nelson hit one of those little short Texas Leaguers in short left center and I dove for the ball for the third out and I start walking off the field, but I didn't realize that Al Barlick, who was umpiring behind second base, said I trapped the ball. But, before I realized what was going on, Nelson and Slaughter they were rounding third base. In the meantime, Peanuts Lowrey, who was playing left field, said, "Andy, throw the ball, throw the ball." So I threw the ball in desperation. I think I hit Rocky Nelson in the back and we got beat by one run. And I argued with Mr. Barlick for what seems like eternity. But I definitely caught the ball.

June 15, 1951. Brooklyn was in town and you were told to pack your bags and go across to the other clubhouse. You had been traded. Was this a surprise?

Well, the way it came about...we had a three-game series in Wrigley Field, June the 15th. That's the trading deadline. We'd already played one game with the Dodgers the day before and we're having batting practice. We're standing around the batting cage and then all of a sudden the Dodgers come out of the dugout.

I remember distinctly Don Newcombe came out of the dugout and he's yelling over toward the Cubs where we're standing around having batting practice. He says, "Hey, Pafko, you're gonna be a Dodger tomorrow." I said, "Well, my goodness." I didn't hear anything. There was no rumors around Chicago. Apparently there must have been something said around—maybe around New York —that maybe the Dodgers were trying to get Pafko from the Cubs.

But lo and behold, we played that particular ball game and the game was over and I went back home—I lived in Chicago and my wife made dinner. We'd just sat down to eat and the phone rings and sure enough, it's Wrigley Field—the front office calling. It's Wid Matthews. And he said, "Well, we made an eight-player trade, Andy, and you were one of the guys involved." Well, that was quite a shock to me. I mean, I don't think I finished my dinner. My wife started to cry. And we had one more game to play so I went out to Wrigley Field the following day, and I took all my belongings out of the Cub clubhouse and now I'm over to the Dodgers' side and I'm playing against my former teammates the very next day. So, it was quite a shock to me, but there was nothing mentioned in the Chicago papers that I was going to be traded.

It turned out, I think, for the best because I went from a ball club that was not in contention and I went to the Dodgers and here they were scheduled to win the pennant. But, unfortunately, they got beat that year. Remember, Bobby Thomson hit that memorable home run—"the shot heard 'round the world." I think I had the best view of "the shot heard 'round the world," 'cause I was playing left field that day.

Well, I don't know if you've ever been in the old Polo Grounds in New York. I think it was about 279 right down the left-field line. I would say maybe it went about 300-some feet. It was a line drive. Had it been hit in Brooklyn I might have had a shot at it. But it landed maybe about four or five rows above the 300-foot mark.

That would have been a line drive out at Wrigley Field?

Oh, definitely. Definitely. But, you have to give credit to Thomson. He hit it at the right time, at the right place. I was part of history, I guess.

I can still see you with your back to that wall.

I used to get photos from fans all over the country and they used to say, well, could I have your autograph on this one. I know it was not a pleasant memory, but as years went by, I mean, I almost forgot about it.

Were you shocked at being traded?

Well, I just don't know how to answer that. I was shocked at the beginning. I mean, I didn't know what was going to happen to me. We'd just bought a home in Chicago. We thought we'd be here for a few more years—but we had no control over that. But, I was kind of upset. I thought I was having a pretty good year. I was one of the better players they had here in Chicago. But I guess that the trade...that wouldn't have happened unless I was included. But the way things turned out, I was happy after a while. I guess I was the one that they really wanted in the trade.

Well, I played, naturally, with the Cubs my first time in the big leagues, then I went to the Dodgers for a couple of years, then I finished my career with the Milwaukee Braves. I still consider myself a Cub. I live in the Chicago area. There's a lot of great fans here and wherever I go, I mean, if I go to a football game or any place that a lot of people are gathered, they still recognize me and they still see me as a Cub and my favorite team is Chicago. I think I'll always be a Cub, I guess, at heart.

What was your greatest thrill?

My greatest thrill...well, I've had a lot of them. I played in four World Series, four All-Star Games—but I think the biggest thrill that ever happened to me when I was a member of the Cubs back in 1945—there was about a month left of the season. My mom and dad never saw me play a big league game and a group of my friends in Chicago got together and they brought my mom and dad to Chicago, to Wrigley Field, to see me play. And I'll never forget —it was just like today—I was playing against Pittsburgh and I came up to the plate for the first time. The bases were loaded—two out—and I'm the hitter and what do you think I did?...I struck out. Oh, boy! What a beginning. This is going to be a long, long day. But, I don't know. I guess God was on my side.

The same thing happened about three innings later. The same situation. Bases loaded, two out, and I came up to the plate again and this time I hit a grand slam home run off of Preacher Roe, who later became my teammate with the Dodgers. And, we often talked about that when I became a member of the Dodgers and he brought that particular hit up—when I hit that home run in Wrigley Field with my mom and dad. And my mother didn't know too much about baseball, because they came from the old country. My dad got up and started applauding. But she didn't know what happened, so they had to explain to her that your son just hit a home run and that's the best thing that a hitter could do in baseball. So, she finally got up and started applauding and I guess she started to cry.

My mom and dad never wanted me to play baseball, anyway, because it was a tough profession. They didn't know too much about the game. They just wanted me to stay close to home and get a good job. But my high school coach, he encouraged me. He said, "Andy, I think you've got some baseball ability. I think you should try out for baseball." Which I did and they were kind of sad when I left home. But, fortunately, I made the grade and then eventually they were happy for me because I did make the grade. But in the beginning, they were against baseball. They didn't want me to play games. Get yourself a decent job, you know, and be close to home.

I don't know what I would have done had I not been a big league ballplayer. I mean, my heart was set. I enjoyed the game. I started playing back on my parents' farm in Wisconsin. I remember I used to play with my brothers. We had two families that made up the ball club. I just wanted to play baseball so bad I could taste it and I never thought I would get that big—I just wanted to get the opportunity to play the game and, fortunately, I made it. So I was very happy about it, but I don't know what I would have done. I had my heart set to become a ballplayer.

——— Bill Nicholson ———

The Cubs' long ball hitter in the '40s. Led the National League in home runs and RBIs in 1943 and 1944.

He hated hitting against the white shirts in the center-field bleachers before it was blocked out. He considered himself lucky to have gotten out of Chicago alive because of this hitting disadvantage. Still he loved being a Cub. After the interview, Bill told me no one where he lived knew he played major league baseball. He thanked me for talking with him. It was sad.

What were you making your first year with the Cubs?

Well, the first half a year, I got $800 a month. And the next year I got $5,000 for a little while and then they said...they told me when I signed that if I was a regular, come back and they'd give me some more. Well, I took 'em up 'cause I was playing regular and I got an extra $1,000. Yeah, 1940.

I played right field...I might have played two or three games in left field. They were good fans out there. They didn't give me any trouble. But, the fans had, you know, as soon as the weather warmed up, had the white shirts and that was a thing they could have avoided.

They did afterwards, they blocked that out.

After about 10 years they did. They didn't do it in my 10 years. Jim Gallagher said it was all in my head. It wasn't...but I've got a knot on my head today where I got hit in 1947 with a fastball that a fellow didn't throw at me. Just didn't realize I couldn't see at all.

He was a relief pitcher in New York. It was a 1-0 game. We were ahead and they took Schumacher out and put in a pinch hitter for him and they were having just as much trouble as we were. But I know I went up there and he threw me a fastball, I guess. I couldn't tell what it was, 'cause I never saw it. But, I did see it just as it went in the catcher's glove...out of the corner of my eye and then he threw me another one and it was the same thing. He was a relief pitcher and threw about 90 miles an hour then. Ace Adams. He played in the Southern League when I was down there. He wasn't throwing at me. I never saw any pitch...I mean all that time at bat.

At that time you didn't have batting helmets. Did you have liners in the caps?
We had a little piece of cardboard in it. Of course, I got hit in the forehead. If I'd of seen it, it might have killed me, 'cause I might have turned my head. It hit me in the forehead and I still got the little knot today.

You played during the war years.
I wasn't 4F...I tried to get in the Navy before that and they turned me down 'cause I was color blind. And the Army just...they waited on me and they finally took me right there near the end...I mean in '45, early in '45. But it appeared the war was just about over, so I never did go.

What do you remember of the caliber of play during the war years in the National League?
Well, it did definitely take some quality players away. Musial didn't go right away. He went at the last. And a few more of them. They were top notch players, but there were still a lot of stars left in our league.
I believe it was acceptable. It definitely wasn't as great as it was before the war, and maybe not quite as good as after the war, but today...it looks to me like it was better quality than is spread out today, of course, they've got a lot more teams.

You think that the quality was better during the war than with expansion.
I believe so. Well, I might be wrong.

You lead the National League in home runs and RBIs in '43 and '44.
Well, they never gave me any credit for that during the war years, but there were still some good...a lot of good ballplayers and damn few weak pitchers. There were pretty good pitchers at that time.

You think the pitching held up.
Yeah, I do. Of course, I was playing in Chicago and that was a

handicap right there, we had a terrible background. Ted Williams played there after the war in the All-Star Game and he commented on it. So he didn't see too good either. In fact, he was probably the greatest hitter in my era.

What do you remember about the 1945 team?
Well, we had some weakness, but we had some pretty good pitching, too. I guess the whole league was a little bit weaker and maybe we were fortunate.

What do you remember about the 1945 World Series?
Well, I didn't hit very well. I didn't hit too good the whole season. I was way off. And, I went to the hospital right after the Series. They had good pitching, but I'd hit those fellows before and I had pretty good luck with them. Like Trucks and Trout, but I didn't hit them in the Series. I hit Newhouser better than I did anybody else and he was a lefthander. I hit him better than I did the righthanders. It was my feeling that I had to hit Trout and Trucks and try to get him. They had real good pitchin', but they had some weak spots. Hank Greenberg was playing, but he was near the end of the line.

I hadn't hit well the whole season. And they took me to the hospital and later I found out I had diabetes. So I wasn't up to par. I went down with it bad in '50, but I didn't realize... I knew it was something.

The Cubs declined after 1945... what happened?
Well, I guess the other teams brought up some pretty good young ones and probably we didn't. We didn't have anything in the farm system that would replenish our spots we were weak in.

What was your greatest thrill with the Cubs?
I guess that time in New York when I hit a home run the last time up on Sunday and I just...well, as far as performance, it was a great thrill to me. And the next Sunday I hit three in a row and then I guess I got a walk and a couple outs. In the second game I popped up and then I singled and then I hit another home run. And later in the game, they were four runs ahead of us and I came up with the bases loaded and Mel Ott walked me intentionally. So I guess, for performance, that August was about as good as I could...that was 1944.

I think I could have done better if I hadn't of had diabetes and hadn't hit out of that white background the whole 10 years I was in Chicago. That white background in there stopped a lot of them.

Did a lot of the players go to Jimmy Gallagher and say, "Do something about that"?

Oh, yeah. We used to go. Billy Herman, of course, he was a hell of a second baseman. He only stayed a little while after I was there and he was up there all the time to the office. Even before Gallagher, I guess. 'Cause he was scared he'd get killed up there.

Well, I was fortunate to get out of there with my life. Vander Meer, when he came up, of course he threw those two great no-hitters in 1938 and that was just before I got up there. And, he could really burn me. I just...I don't know what he was throwing, but he was as fast as Feller. And one day in Chicago, he was wild and he had the bases loaded and I was up there hittin' and he got me 3 and 2 and he reared back and threw and I didn't see the ball to this day. And he just missed the top of my head as it went by. So, I guess I'm lucky in being here today.

He just ticked the back of my head and he didn't let up. And I guess that's the reason they stayed with him when he was wild.

I loved Chicago...if they'd done something about that darn glare...but they did do something about it as soon as I left. I guess Jim Gallagher—he hated me for complaining about it. I was glad to have a job, but, damn, I hated...I lost a lot of balls out of that darn glare. And I guess I was lucky to come away. It finished Hank Leiber—his own roommate hit him. Cliff Melton—he roomed with him when he was with the Giants, and he was pitching this day and he just came in high inside on him and he hit him side the head. That finished Hank.

Why did they call you "Swish"?

The Brooklyn fans named me "Swish." I don't know. I just relaxed waiting for the pitcher to get through his motion and stuff...a couple of them did quick-pitch me, but I got around that. But I moved my bat a couple of times, just to relax, and the fans got so— in Brooklyn—they started...they'd say "Swish" every time I moved my bat. Well, it was only a few fans that started that but then it got so damn near the whole stands doin' it.

───── HANK SAUER ─────

The Mayor of Wrigley Field. Forty years ago he was baseball in Chicago. They idolized him in the left-field bleachers—they were not yet known as the Bleacher Bums. Big, likable—he was revered in Chicago. He understood Cub fans—hustle for them and they will love you.

"People in Chicago were so good to me. That's what you call my hometown. Frank Sinatra said it right. I loved it."

June 15, 1949 I was traded to Chicago with Frank Baumholtz. I was traded to Chicago for Harry Walker and Peanuts Lowrey.

I went over to Chicago and, boy, it was a bad flight. The both of us got sick. I got to the ballpark just in time to play and Frisch happened to be the manager at that time. So he called me into the office and he says, "Hank, I got you over here for two reasons. To drive in runs and hit home runs." He says, "I want you to forget everything they said to you over there (Cincinnati)." Well, I went wild from then on. I hit over 30 home runs that year and I'm not sure if I drove in 100 runs or not that year, but it was pretty close. From June on—so I had a pretty good year.

That was '49. '50 I had a good year—I hit over 30 home runs. '51 I hit over 30 home runs. '52 was my big year.

That's when Cavarretta had it. They fired Frankie Frisch in '51 —the middle of the year. Then Cavarretta took it over. I'm having a pretty good year. One time Frankie Baumholtz and I were in New York, playing a doubleheader—it was hot. So he and I decided to go to a show to cool off. Then we got to the train about— this was when we were going on trains—we got to the train about 12:30 and our trainer said, "Boy, Hank, you boys are in trouble." I said, "What for? All we did was go to the show, why are we in trouble?" He said, "You weren't in at curfew." I said, "Curfew on a train? I've never heard of it. Never heard of curfew on a train." So I said, "Wait a minute." I got Cavarretta out of bed and I said, "What is this?" He said, "You guys, you're my buddies. I loafed with you when I was playing with you, and now you're the guys that are screwing up around here." I said, "I'm not screwing up, we went to a show to cool off after the doubleheader and this is what happens."

So he changed. "Well," he says, "I'm not going to fight it," he says. "But I thought you guys would be the last guys to come in late." I said, "We only come in late for one reason. We were tired and we went to a show that was air-conditioned and we stayed there until 12:00."

Hank, would you say in all your years of playing ball that '52 was your biggest year—your most enjoyable year?

It was what I call one of the best steady years I've ever had in baseball. I hit 41 home runs...it just seemed like everything happened every day good. What happened, happened right.

I think the reason I got the MVP that year...over Robin Roberts is because I hurt him. I think I got two home runs off of him that broke up one game he was shutting us out. I hit a home run to beat him, 1-0. Then I beat him another game, a couple of games like that and I think that's what did it.

I remember that year '52—I think it was against the Cardinals—and you hit three home runs, the Cubs won I think, 3-2. Do you remember that game?

Right.

Then Stu Miller pitched the next day and said you'd never see one of his fastballs because he didn't have one.

He never had one—you kidding? You know where I tried to hit Stu Miller? Into the right-field dugout. That's exactly what I tried to do. The first time I faced him, Eddie Stanky was the manager of the Cardinals. And I walked up and said, "Eddie, who's pitching for you?" He pointed to that guy—he pointed over there. "Over there —that kid over there." I said, "Aw, come on, that's a bat boy." "That's the pitcher, he's pitching today." And it was Stu Miller. He looked like a bat boy. Well, we had four hits off of him. I got three of them. You know, they played me around, nobody played second base. Three of the hits I hit got as far as second base and just spun in the dirt and hit right off the end of the bag. I laughed and I said, "Hey, kid, I hit it just like you threw it."

The 1950 All-Star Game. There was a furor when Burt Shotton, who was the manager of the Brooklyn Dodgers, didn't want to start you in left field. All Chicago was up in arms.

Well, it kept getting worse, getting worse...and I was leading the ballots. Finally, he come out and he says, "Well, I'm not going to play him in center field." I played center field just as good as anybody else. I couldn't run as good as anybody else, but I could have played out there. In fact, that's the easiest place to play. You do a lot of running out there, but I didn't mind that. So, he says, "I'm going to put Snider out there." So I blasted him in the paper about it. I says, "If they don't play me, I am not going to report to the All-Star Game."

In fact, I'm going to tell you who told me to say that. Frankie Frisch. I admired Frankie Frisch. I liked him a whole lot. He always was truthful with me. We got in our arguments, but he was always truthful with me. He says, "I always liked you, Hank, because you had the guts to talk back to me. The rest of them don't say anything to me. They haven't got the guts to say anything to me. But you do." He says, "Don't go." That's exactly what he says. "Don't go." So I just told the newspaper guys, "If I don't play, I don't go." Now it goes to the commissioner. The commissioner says, "He was voted in and he is going to play." And that's the way it went.

So I started. So Enos Slaughter said, "What's wrong with me playing center field? I play center field. Let Hank play right field and Kiner can play left." Well, that's the way it started. So, the first time up, I had a line shot out to right field. I drove in the first run in 1950.

What do you remember of the '52 All-Star Game? You won that with a home run?

Well, I know it rained like mad. Jocko Conlan was the umpire at third base and I said, "Hey, Jocko, call this damn game." I said, "Look at this." And I just reached down and scooped the water right off. He said, "It's nice and dry in here, Hank."

We're going to the fifth inning and Stan Musial's the first guy up. And, I don' recall—I think it was Raschi pitching. And he throws the ball and hits Musial. Now they take the pitcher out, they bring Bob Lemon in. So he comes in and he hangs me a curveball. That's the one I hit out of the ballpark. Over everything. And that put us ahead, 3-2.

And Juny Hillerich...you know Hillerich and Bradsby...he was leaving the ballpark. He was going up that street and he said he saw the ball hit the street and bounced up by somebody's porch. The guy run down and picked the ball up. So he stops the car and gives the guy $5.00 for that ball. He says, "Can I have the ball, I'll give you $5.00 for it." "Sure, here, take it." He gave him $5.00 for the ball 'cause he was listening to it on the radio. Then two days later he says, "Hank, here's the ball you hit out of the ballpark." And about two weeks later I got a letter from the Hall of Fame at Cooperstown. They asked me if I wouldn't give them the ball. So I sent them the ball. That ball's at Cooperstown now. I want to give that bat to Cooperstown, too. That's the one I hit the home run with. I told my kids if anything happens to me, I said I want that bat to go to Cooperstown.

After the game was over, I go out and there's a gas station right around the corner by the ballpark. I'm going out to the gas station to get a cab to get to the airport so I can fly home to Chicago with my family. As I'm standing there, I heard someone behind me. "You big bastard. You're the luckiest guy that ever lived." And I thought somebody's going to hit me from behind. I've gotta get out of here. I looked back—it was Bob Lemon. And he started laughing. He says, "Did you ever see a better pitch in your life?" I said, "It was low and outside off the black." He said, "It was right down the middle—it was a hanging curveball." It was.

In 1953 they give me a day. That was my worst year. 1953 was my worst year. I broke two fingers and broke my hand. I think I only hit 19 home runs that year. I didn't have a great year. And that's the year they give me the day. And they gave me a barrel of sauerkraut, and they give my wife furs, and they give me a car, and when I go out to the outfield, they had to halt the play over an hour to pick up the tobacco out there. We got over eight bushel baskets full.

I chewed it—but I can't chew that much. See what happened, Yosh Kawano—he chewed all the time. From then on he never had to buy any more tobacco. The years I was there he never bought tobacco. I said, "Yosh, the guys chew this stuff. Don't let it lay around." What's left, take home, 'cause I never chewed it in the wintertime.

In 1954, I went out and hit 41 home runs, drove in over 100 runs and I said, "Well, maybe I'll get a $5,000 raise or something, or $6,000 or $7,000 raise." I'd had a pretty good year. So, here comes the contract...$1,500 cut from Wid Matthews. I sent the contract back, I wrote back to him, I said, "Hey, you sent this contract to the wrong guy, didn't you? I'm the guy who hit 41 home runs for you guys last year." He says, "No, I sent it to the right guy." I says, "I thought I had a pretty good year. I think I deserve at least a $5,000-6,000 raise." He says, "You're not going to get it." I said, "I'm not going to sign it. Trade me." He says, "No, we're not going to trade you, either." I said, "Well, I'm not going to play for that kind of money with you people." "Well, then," he said, "stay home."

Then he flew out to Los Angeles. He talked to me out there. In fact, when he went to the bathroom, his wife said to me, she says, "Hey, you better sign. He's pretty hardheaded." I says, "I'm not a Dutchman for nothing. So am I." I says, "I think I had a pretty doggone good year. I think I deserve a raise." So, then he comes out, he says, "Well, this is going to be it, Hank." I says, "Not for me." I says, "Just trade me. Or just release me." He says, "We can't do that." I says, "Well, I'm not going to sign for this kind of money." "Well, then," he says, "I'm leaving."

So he left, went back to Chicago. He says, "OK, I'll tell you what I'll do, and this is going to be it. I'll give you the same salary back, $37,500, and that's going to be it. Don't send the contract back because you're not getting it back. You can stay home for the rest of the year." So I signed the contract.

See we had to go from year to year. Our contracts run from year to year. The only thing I regret more in my life is I didn't keep the letters from Warren Giles and the letters from Wid Matthews. I had letters telling me, if you don't sign, stay home. Today, I'd like to see some of these kids getting letters like that. If they got letters like that today, they'd be free agents.

I thought I had some pretty good years. They talk about today. These salaries. Well, here's a consistent hitter. He's hit 20 home runs, four out of five years. Hell, I did that for 30 home runs.

Well, if McReynolds from New York, is getting over $3 million for hitting consistently .280, .270, and hitting 20 home runs, he's making over $3 million, I think I'd be making that at least.

I think it's going to escalate to the point where the owners are going to try and get rid of the ball clubs. Because even the money that they're getting from CBS—I think it was $1 billion or $2 billion—they're asking for some of that money back, you know. "Hey, we're going broke, you people are going to have to pay us some of that money back." Well, that's paying their salaries now— over $33 million in Oakland. Over $33 million. That's got to be pretty tough to do.

I don't know who's going to pay the salaries. Like Canseco, like some of those players, who knows if Canseco is going to be able to play?

And just like our ball club, it's gotten to the point where it's tough. And I don't know if Bob Lurie can afford to pay them, how long can you go in the hole? There's no better guy around than Bob Lurie. He's one of the nicest guys in the world. But how nice can you keep being? And paying these guys this kind of salary. Sure, they're good ballplayers. Sure, they deserve raises. Sure, they deserve the money. It's money we never got and I'm glad to see them getting money. But this is getting out of hand now.

You were in spring training in 1956 and ready to break camp at the end of March, and you were traded to St. Louis.

It was an off day. It was Good Friday. And I'm playing golf with Paul Richards and we'd played 36 holes already. So he said, "Come on, we can play nine more, Hank." This was when he was managing Baltimore. "Hot damn," I said, "I've got a feeling something's happening today." He said, "What do you mean?" I said, "I think they're going to trade me today. For some reason I'm thinking they're going to trade me." He said, "Aw, baloney, they're not going to trade you. They never said anything to me about it. I'd know something about it." "Alright we'll play nine more."

I went back in there and there was a note in my box to see Wid Matthews right away. So I go in and he says, "Hank, you've got two choices. Either you go to Los Angeles and play out the season and we make a manager out of you and we want to keep you in the organization, or..." And I says, "What is the 'or'?" He says, "Or you can go to St. Louis. They want you in St. Louis." I says, "I want to go to St. Louis. I wouldn't trust you beyond no means. I would not trust you." I said, "I don't know what's going to happen to you. I'll go over there with Frank Lane. He's the one that started me in the big leagues in the first place." So I went over there with Frank Lane and I played that year out.

A funny thing happened that year too. When I go over there, Stan Musial is my roommate. When I go over, Stan says, "Hey, Hank, you're my roommate." I said, "Who said so? I don't know if I want to room with you or not." I wanted to all along anyway. I said, "OK, we'll be roomies." So I was his roommate and I'm having a pretty good year that year. Hit right around .300 that year. And Stan is hitting pretty good. He hit .318.

So at the end of the year, Frank Lane comes up to me and says, "Hank, we're going to have to let you go." I said "What! I had a pretty good year." He says, "Yeah, you had a pretty good year, but that roommate of yours had a lousy year." "What do you mean?" I said, "He hit .318." "He's not supposed to hit .318, he's supposed to hit .330." So, that's how I got away from St. Louis.

So then the Giants picked me up. I got bigger raises with the Giants than I ever got playing with anybody else. Other than my MVP year, I got a pretty good raise that year. I got a $5,000 raise with the Giants. I had a pretty good year in 1957.

So in 1958, we come out here. I'm negotiating with 'em. I says, "Hot damn, I think I had a pretty good year with you guys." They offered me three. I said, "I think I should at least get five." He says, "Nah, we can't give five, Hank, we haven't got that kind of money." I said, "Chub, just one time give in to me. Let me say I was a winner." He says, "Alright, I'll give you $5,000." That's how I got a $5,000 raise. That's one of my biggest raises in baseball, other than the MVP.

What was the most you ever made playing for the Cubs?

...$37,500 was my biggest.

I personally did not think Matthews was a good GM...he'd never tell you the truth, as far as I'm concerned. He never told me the truth. That's when I told him, when I had a choice, I told him, "I don't trust you." He said, "I was told—I was told by Mr. Wrigley that you will not leave Chicago. You are going to be with us for the rest of your days and you are going to be in our organization. You are going to be one of our organization men." I said, "That's fine." The very next year, he lets me go...he lets me go in 1956...

In 1957 he was fired for letting me go. That was it. Wrigley says, "Hey, you've made too many bad deals. You let this guy go. He was the mayor of Wrigley Field. He did a good job for us and I wanted him and you let him go anyway."

Hank, you played for Frankie Frisch, Phil Cavarretta, and Stan Hack. How would you rate them?

Well, you know a lot of people didn't like Frankie. Frankie Frisch was tough. Kids today could not play for him because he was really rough. And he'd swear more than anybody you ever saw in your life. He's the kind of guy if you wouldn't talk back to him, wouldn't say anything to him, he had you. I got a couple of arguments with him and he and I was—we were pretty good friends. In fact, when they fired him, I saw him in Philadelphia—that's where they fired him, in Philadelphia. He was walking up the street and I said, "Hey, Frank, what's up? What's wrong with you?" I knew there was something wrong. He said, "Aw, they fired me." I said, "What do you mean they fired you? How could they fire you." "Well, those kids. They told them they can't play for me. I'm too tough on them." Well, he was tough, I'll have to say that. And I liked Frank. I thought Frank was a good manager.

And Stan Hack was one of those kind of guys that—he's just levelheaded and not tough, would not swear, would not do nothing. He was alright.

Cavarretta was one of those kind of guys, more on the Frisch side. He get to telling you, "Don't step on my bunions. I don't like it," and stuff. And he was tough.

I would say the one I liked more than anyone else was Frank Frisch. As tough as he was, he was honest with you and many a times he'd sit on the bench and look up—he'd be reading a book on the bench. He'd be reading a book on the bench and all at once he looks up, he says "What's the score, guys?" They say, "It's 1-0." He says, "That figures." Then he'd look up and saw a guy on third base and say, "Well, what's going to happen this time?" Well, a guy would pop up in the infield. "Well, that figures too."

I had some pretty good years for Frank. I went over there, like I said, in '49 when he come in. I finished up great for him. The next year I had a good year for him. I hit over 30 home runs again for him. Then after I cornered him in Philadelphia, I says, "Geez, I'm sorry to hear that, Frank." He said, "Ah—I only had one ballplayer —that was you. The rest of them were just...belonged in the minor leagues." Which isn't true, but that's the way he felt about it.

A lot of people don't remember that your brother, Ed, played for the Cubs in '43-'45, during the war. In fact, he was in the '45 World Series.

Yeah—his experience with the Cubs was just the opposite of me. See Gallagher was the general manager there for him. He didn't treat Ed like he treated me. Ed kept saying, "Boy, I hated that guy. I didn't like him at all. Boy, he treated me lousy." I said, "Ed, I can't say that about the guy. He's treated me good. I can't say anything bad about him." He says, "I don't blame you. Sure he's treating you good. He's treating you good 'cause you're having pretty good years." He says, "I had a pretty good year." He did. He said, "Why they send me out?" Today he would have been in the big leagues a lot earlier. He'd have been playing in the big leagues 10 years.

He was 16 months younger. And he was a line drive-type hitter. And they wanted power, this is what I produced for them. But he wanted power and Ed was a line drive-type hitter. In fact, when Peanuts got out of the service that year, 1945, Ed was hitting over .300, well over .300 with Chicago. As soon as Peanuts got up, he threw Peanuts right out in the outfield and Ed had to go to the bench. Well, that kind of hurt him. And I think if they'd have traded Ed, he might have stayed in the big leagues. He could run; he could fly. And had an excellent arm. He was a good line drive-type hitter...hit to all fields.

He loved Chicago. Oh, he liked Chicago. He told me, he says, "Hank, if you ever get to Chicago, this is a great town." He says, "The people are great. Just give them 100%..." The only guy they ever really booed badly, and you'll recall that, is the shortstop.

Roy Smalley?

Roy Smalley. He loafed to first base one time and they never let him up.

That was I think the biggest reason they had to get rid of him. He was done. Why he could stand at home plate, throw the ball in the center-field bleachers. No one had a better arm than him.

Who used to do that? Smalley and Jeffcoat?

That's right. I saw both doin' it. Both of them standing right at home plate, just get up to home plate, throw it right in the center-field seats. They had great arms.

Who was the best pitcher you ever faced?

I've gotta say that Koufax was one of them. This was later on. But the one that was tough for me was Drysdale. He was tough.

What about Ewell Blackwell?

When he was in Cincinnati, two years in Cincinnati, he was

unbeatable. If he could have lasted 10 years-15 years in the big leagues, there's no doubt in my mind he would have had 270, 280 wins and been in the Hall of Fame.

Did you ever get in any fights in the big leagues?

Remember Del Rice? You know Frank was a funny guy. Get a guy on third base, he wants you to steal home. So one day I'm up there and two guys stole home. Didn't make it, but stole home. The next guy that stole home was...I think was...Jeffcoat. He stole home. I think he made it. And he took the ball and just pounded it right into his back. Well, Jeffcoat didn't see it. So I walked right up and I says, "That wasn't necessary. Why did you do that?" He says, "I'm tired of these guys stealing home." I said, "Well, ...why don't you go pound on the manager? Don't pound on the guy that comes in. He's doing what the manager tells him to do." And then he started swearing at me. Now, we're going at it. So then we got into a fight. Didn't last long. Poor Del, I could have probably crushed him. Of course, he was as big as me, but I felt that I could hurt him. But the one that really caused problems was Poholsky. Tom Poholsky with St. Louis.

The last day of the season I'm up there hitting. I've been hitting them pretty good. And Tom Poholsky's pitching. The first time, they've got a man on second base. And instead of walking me, Stanky says, "Don't walk him. Hit him. You might get him out of the game." Well, this was going on all year. They hit me over 10 times that year. I mean really hit me.

No helmets. I never wore one in my life. I wore that insert, but never wore a helmet. Well, anyway, after the first out, the guy...he drilled me. Boy, he hit me right in the kidney. I couldn't hardly talk. I staggered out to the mound. There was no way I could get in a fight because I couldn't do nothing. I was hurtin' so bad. And I walked up to him, Poholsky, and I said, "Okay, you've got three more shots at me. This is my first time at bat. You've got three more shots at me. If you hit me one more time, I'm going to get out here before anybody else gets out here and I'm going to kill you. I'm going to break every bone in your body." So, the next three times up, I'm walked three times in a row. He never even come close to home plate. 'Cause he knew I would have. But in those days, I'd fight at the drop of a hat.

After Pafko, I had nobody behind me. Bill Serena—he could tell you those stories. He says, "I don't want to hit behind him.

Don't let me..." Well, Pafko didn't want to hit behind me either. 'Cause every time I'd hit a home run they'd knock you down or they'd hit you. They'd get Pafko because Pafko couldn't get out of the way of the ball. "These guys hitting me—every time he hits a home run I go down." Then they put Serena behind me. Then Serena says, "Why do you want to knock me down? I'm a .220 hitter. Knock the guy down that's hitting the home runs." He'd scream that at the pitchers. "What are you knockin' me down for?"

When I first went up in the big leagues, they would knock you down and tell you they were going to knock you down from the mound. We were playing in Chicago and Claude Passeau's pitchin'. The first ball he throws I hit into the center-field seats. As I'm runnin' to first base, he says, "Hey, Busher, let's see what you look like the next time up there." Now, as I'm hittin' third base he's walking toward me. It looks like I'm going to have to fight my way home. So he says, "In fact, let's see what you look like the next three times up there." Well, the next time up there he says, "Here it comes, Busher." Swoosh...right by me. And you know it's hard to see in Chicago. It was hard to see. I don't remember what happened the next three times up, but I know every time I went up there, he told me, "Hey, Busher, here comes another one. And you might get another one after that, too."

I've accomplished almost everything I wanted to do in baseball. Only one thing is my regret. I never played in a World Series. The Giants win the World Series and I got a ring with the ballplayers. I didn't feel like it belonged to me because I didn't have nothing to do with it. But like Bob [Lurie] said, "You had a lot to do with it. Some of these ballplayers are yours. You taught them their hitting, and you talked to them about hitting. So you did deserve it." But that was my only regret. Not playing in the World Series.

What do you do for San Francisco?

At first when I started I was the cross-checker for the whole country. I cross-checked all the ballplayers. Then from there as Hubbell got a little older, I kind of handled...more or less handled the minor league system. I'd weed 'em out and bring the guys up and send them to different ball clubs. They'd have good years. I'd bring them up a couple of steps or a step, wherever I thought they could play. Then I handled all the minor league training camps, which we have about five or six of them. Then it got to the point where I said, "Well, I just want to knock a lot of this off." So the last five or six years now, I've been a major league scout. I go to Oakland...I don't travel all over the country. I go to Oakland...scout the American League and I go to Candlestick to scout the National League. And that's my job now. I enjoy it and I still have my hands in it, but it's getting to the point where I think that I may have to give the whole works up and take my wife away sometime. She likes to travel.

So I may retire. There's a good chance of it, yes.

──Frankie Baumholtz──

A solid performer who was a rookie at age 28 due to four years at Ohio University and five years in World War II. A lifetime .290 hitter, he always gave his best. He loved playing in Chicago.

Frank, you were traded with Hank Sauer on June 15, 1949 from Cincinnati to Chicago. What do you remember about that trade?

Well, I tell you, my wife and I were in a movie. And about 10:00 at night, a short while before the movie ended, Bobby Adams, who I used to room with, came in the movie and I said, "What are you doing here, Bob?" And he says, "Well, I came to see you and say goodbye to you." And I says, "Where are you going?" He says, "I'm not going anywhere. You are." And I says, "What are you talking about?" Well, he says, "You and Hank Sauer were sold to the Cubs for Harry Walker and Peanuts Lowery. And you're supposed to go to Crosley Field and get all your gear together and you're catching the real early plane to Chicago, cause they promised that you and Hank Sauer would be there."

Well, we were supposed to get on the midnight train, but no way could I get our gear until the next morning, so a plane took the both of us to Chicago and it was the most horrendous ride—I don't think I ever got over it. It was the bumpiest and scariest plane ride I ever had. As a matter of fact, I was scared to death for about the next five years of flying in a plane. Just from that one flight. And, we both got to Chicago in time. Hank started and I pinch-hit in the game.

I'll tell you what, it's the most enjoyable years I ever spent in major league baseball. Right there in Chicago. I always thought it was the greatest ballpark in the country to play in.

You were 31 when you were traded to the Cubs.

Well, you see, I spent four years in college and five years in the war. So, when I came out, I was already past, what in those days, what the guys should be playing in the big leagues. I was just starting when most players were through.

Was that hard economically for you?

Well, yes, it was. My first big league baseball contract was for $4,000.

Oh, well, you know, today they get...when a first-year player gets what—over $90,000. I'll tell you what—even my highest salary—starting salaries today are almost seven, eight times higher than what I made.

I think the biggest salary I had—it's hard for me to remember— something like $16,500. That was after I hit .325 in '52 and they offered me a $500 raise.

How was Frisch as a manager?

Frank wasn't my type of guy, personally. And apparently I wasn't his type of guy. The chemistry between us wasn't very good. He just chose players to play that I thought were inferior to me.

Who did he start instead of you?

At this late date, I can't even remember. I know they had guys like Carmen Mauro, three or four other guys there, and when we were on Catalina Island, I don't think he liked the fact that Hank Sauer and I were such close friends. We were always together.

He did say to me one day, just before I was left in Los Angeles, we were on Catalina Island, "There's only room for two Germans on this ball club and you're not one of them."

That was in the spring of 1950. He dumped me in Los Angeles when they broke spring training.

So you played that whole year—1950—in L.A.

As a matter of fact, it was one of the most enjoyable years I've ever had.

Normally, for September they usually call players back. But he refused to call me back.

You came back in '51 and had a good year. You hit .284.

And I played regular.

Frisch was fired and replaced by Cavarretta.

Well, Phil and I—we were friends from the time I went to the Cubs. So was he with Sauer and there was five or six of us that were pretty close. As a matter of fact, Phil was the best manager I ever played for. He had a rough temper, but not as far as the ballplayer is concerned. He always spoke his piece. But he knew baseball.

He was your best manager?

I thought he was. Of course, I didn't have that many. I had Grimm for a few days. I had Frank Frisch for a short while and I had Johnny Neun for a year and a half in Cincinnati. I had Bucky Walters for a very short while. Bucky was instrumental in Sauer and I getting traded, I think. And then when I left Chicago and went to the Phillies, Mayo Smith was the manager.

Stan Hack was the manager after Cavarretta. Stan was a very nice guy. Stan Hack was a super gentleman.

Warren Giles traded Hank Sauer and I to the Cubs. I ran into Warren Giles some years later on the street in Cincinnati when he was running the league—president of the league—and he said, "Frank, worst thing that ever happened to me in my baseball career was the trade I made of you and Sauer for Harry Walker and Peanuts Lowery."

1952 was your best year in the big leagues.

That's the year I finished .325. In '53 I had .306. But in '52, that's the year I was second to Musial and that's the year they offered me a $500 raise. Later my wife and I used to talk about it.

Wid Matthews sent me a contract for a $500 raise and I stuck it in the dresser drawer and one day my wife says, "What are you going to do with that baseball contract?" I says, "Nothing. I'm not going to sign it." She says, "Why don't you send it back?" So I sent it back. And he called me up—Wid Matthews called me up and he says, "Hey, you sent me your contract back unsigned." I said, "Well, I can make more money selling men's clothes in the May Company Department Store than what you're offering me." And he says, "Well, I'll send you another one." So, about three days later I get another contract in the mail from him and it was for a $1,000 raise. I stuck it in the drawer and let it sit there. And my wife said, "What are you going to do?" I said, "If that's all that hitting .325 is worth to them, I'm going to quit. I'll just stay here and go in the clothing business." She said, "Well, you do what you have to do."

And about three days before spring training started, the phone rang. And it was Wid Matthews. He was calling me from Jackson, Mississippi. That's where he used to live. He says, "You didn't send the contract back." And I says, "No, it's sitting in the drawer and I'm not going to send it back." He says, "Why?" I says, "Well, if that's all it's worth to you, as I told you before, I can make more money selling men's clothing." And he says, "What do you want?" I says, "If it's not worth at least a $5,000 raise, forget it." So he said, "You've got it. Come on down to spring training." I said, "You son of a gun. Making me go through all of that."

1952 is a hell of a season for you. You and Musial were neck and neck for the batting title.

Oh, there's a good story there. Near the end of the year we were still down the wire and we had about four off days after a doubleheader right at the end of the season with the Cardinals. We had a great series and they went on to Cincinnati. And when they left Chicago on Sunday, there was 1,000th of a percentage point difference in our batting averages. Well, they went on to Cincinnati and beat Cincinnati, I think, three games and Musial got eight or nine hits over there. But during the interim, they were planning on Musial pitching to me in St. Louis the last day of the season. And we didn't know—the Cubs didn't know anything about it.

So on Saturday night, we get on the midnight train and we go to St. Louis, it arrives probably 10:30, quarter of 11:00 on Sunday and you know there's always a bus waiting to take you to the ballpark. And we go to the ballpark and when we walk out on the field to take our practice, there's about 20,000 people in the stands. And they're in the second division and so are we and we're wondering what the heck brought them to the park. And unbeknownst to all of us in the previous day's paper was announced that Stan Musial would pitch to me.

I was the leadoff hitter with the Cubs and Jocko Conlan was the plate umpire and in those days you couldn't start a game on Sunday 'til five minutes after 2:00 because of the blue laws or something. And just before the game was to start, Stanky, who was their manager, ran out and called time and Jocko Conlan wanted to know what he was doing out there calling time when the game hadn't even started yet. And, he called time and he walked out to the mound and Harvey Haddix was the pitcher. So, he sent Haddix to center field and brought Musial in and Musial was warming up on the mound and me, being a left-handed hitter, I was standing there and watching Stan warm up and Cavarretta was our manager. He ran out of the dugout. And he said, "Frank, Stanky's trying to make a fool out of you." And I says, "What are you talking about, Phil?" And he says, "Well, you see what he's doing. He brought Stan Musial in to pitch to you. What are you going to do?" I says, "Well, if Stan Musial pitches to me, I'm going to bat right-handed." He said, "You're going to bat right-handed?" Oh, and incidentally, the third baseman that day was Solly Hemus. And he says, "You're going to bat right-handed?" And I says, "Yeah!" He says, "Did you ever bat right-handed before?" I says, "Phil, I gotta tell you the truth. I never swung a bat right-handed in my life." So, Jocko calls "Play Ball" and I went around the other side of the plate and Musial threw one pitch and the ball was right over the plate and I swung as hard as I could and it's the best ball I ever hit in all the time I was in the big leagues. That ball hit Solly Hemus on the shins and went down into the left-field corner. I wound up on second and they put an "E" on the board. Solly Hemus never had a chance to move and I never knew how in the heck I could hit the ball that hard.

Anyway, Musial got a couple of hits in the game and I got a base hit off of Harvey Haddix, but he was already four or five points ahead. After the inning, he called the press box and he told them, "If I ever saw a base hit in my life, that was it." That little tidbit was in *Ripley's Believe It Or Not* about six months later.

So I went in the record books as a switch hitter and Musial went into the record books as first baseman, outfielder, pitcher.

Before they blocked out the bleachers, did you have a hard time hitting in Wrigley Field?

Well, I'll tell you. When I was with the Reds and we went into Wrigley Field, everybody sat out there. And they had white shirts on and stuff. And I never crouched in my life except when I was in Wrigley Field in those days. I crouched down so I could see the ball. As a matter of fact, I think every ballplayer that came in there and played in those days had to do something that would make it more comfortable to play. But after I got to Chicago they changed all that. They blocked that all off.

The greatest place in the world to play for me was Wrigley Field. You know, despite the fact that I played center between my buddy Hank Sauer and Kiner, that wasn't a bad outfield. Hank Sauer was a great left fielder and they had to have Sauer play right and that put him out of position. So, throughout the years when Garagiola was broadcasting he used to, about every six weeks, he'd bring that up.

He would say, they would hit the ball in right center or left center and, you know, I'd go after the ball and Joe Garagiola would say, "Well, there goes a line drive out in left center and there's Kiner hollering, 'Go get it, Frankie, go get it.'" And the same thing would happen on the other side, you know, when the ball would be hit in right center.

An old friend of mine who played first base for the Yankees, Tommy Henrich—after baseball, we got to be real good friends and he had a little radio show in Canton, Ohio. And he says, "I saw Frankie Baumholtz the other day and he was walking on his knees. That was from playing center field between Kiner and Sauer."

We had some great people out in right center and left center. I had a crew out there in right center that talked to me during the whole game. They were super. These were people that went to the games every day. They were there every game.

The best thing that I remember about Chicago is the fact that I was playing with the Cubs in Wrigley Field and I enjoyed playing there more than in any other park and I made some very, very fine friends in Chicago. As a matter of fact, one of them, I got to work for his company after I was through playing baseball.

Used to have a place that I always went to eat, you know, after the games, we used to call "The Cottage." Where a lot of the ballplayers used to go. A friend of mine by the name of Freddie Hattonberger ran it and owned it and a number of us, Sauer and myself and others, used to go down there and eat our dinner there and it was quite an enjoyable place.

I went to Ohio University in Athens, Ohio, as a basketball player. We almost won the National Invitational Basketball Tournament in 1941. It was THE tournament in the country. And I was named the Most Valuable Player in the NIT tournament and then I became a baseball player after World War II and I was the first guy that played professional baseball and professional basketball at the same time.

I played the first year of the NBA with the Cleveland Rebels. It was called the Basketball Association of America. And the year before that I played in the old National Pro League with the Youngstown Bears. And then I...well, I was very fortunate. The time came when I had to make a choice which I was going to do, because both games broke into each other's seasons and I had to make a choice.

So, when I was at Cincinnati, Warren Giles called me in the office and said, "I don't want you to play professional basketball next year." And he handed me a check. And when I saw what was on the check, I said, "You just talked me out of playing." It was very fortunate because Cleveland sold the franchise to Providence, Rhode Island, and then I would have been away from home totally.

The greatest thing that ever happened was the fact that I had an opportunity to go to Ohio University. I played basketball and it just so happened that I played baseball on the university baseball team and through that I received a contract from the Cincinnati Reds and received a $1,000 bonus, which I carried around with me for ages. And Ohio University gave me the opportunity to do all these things and that's where I met the young lady who later became my wife. All my kids went to Ohio University. And my associations through-out all the years have been tied in with Ohio University. I was nine years on the board of trustees of the university and for the past few years, I've been on the Ohio University Foundation Board of Trust-ees. Spend most of my extra time in Athens at Ohio University helping out.

I've had a very, very great and fruitful life in sports and it's just sad that the times were then when ballplayers weren't paid the kind of money that...well, nowhere's near the kind of money that's being paid today. As a matter of fact, I think in those days ballplayers used to lie about the kind of money they made. They would have been embarrassed to tell somebody they were only making $16,000. But I wasn't embarrassed. It was a lot of money to me.

───── Roy Smalley ─────

In 1948, at the age of 22, Roy was the starting shortstop for the Cubs. He had a gun for an arm, with a quick release. But during his time with the Cubs, 1948-53, he did not achieve the stardom many had predicted. By spring training 1954, he lost his job to Ernie Banks.

We discussed how Mike Royko has been a critic over the years of Roy's play at shortstop. He handled this with grace and charm, saying, "Mike Royko has not been a fan of Roy Smalley, but Roy Smalley has been a fan of Mike Royko."

At the end of the interview I asked Roy if he had any regrets. He said..."I'd like to do it over again. I mean, I'd like to try to be better than I was...wish I could have been."

I signed with the Cubs in 1944 and had come to Los Angeles to be with the L. A. Angels. That was a World War II year and a lot of the Pacific Coast League players were in the service and that was the justification, I suppose, for a kid who was 17 years old—18 shortly after the season started—to stay with the Coast League, the Triple-A club, all year. But I did stay with them all year. California was greatly different in those days. We trained in Anaheim. Anaheim was just a little town surrounded by orange groves.

I probably made the mistake of—I made some people think I might be a budding DiMaggio. At one of our first exhibition games I hit a home run over the 420-foot center-field fence and probably raised expectations unreasonably high. But I was with the Angels that year. We won the pennant and then I went in the Navy. Got out in '46 and played a couple of months in the lower minor leagues in the Cub organization and 1947 in Des Moines in the Western League and then went to the Cubs in 1948.

What were the Cubs like in '48? It was a last-place team. You were a rookie. You were, I think, 22 years old.

Charlie Grimm was the manager and I have very fond memories of him. In retrospect, I don't think Charlie was the great manager—if the criteria are what they would be today about Tony

49

LaRussa or Gene Mauch, or say Alvin Dark back a little farther—
some of those kind of people. But Charlie was great for a young
guy to come up to. I mean, Charlie was so even tempered, he was
really "Jolly Charlie." He was a great guy and just pulled for everybody on his ball club.

As a manager, his philosophy—again, in retrospect—seemed
to be give 'em a bat, a glove, and a ball and let them go and there's
not too much that's cerebral about it. If you try to think too much,
you're going to get yourself into trouble. I go back and forth on that
because it's like my golf game, sometimes I think he's right. You
either have the talent or you don't and thinking about it may not do
that much good. I don't really think that. I mean, I think there's a
lot to think about and the people who think the game better are
usually the better players. But on the other hand, there really is no
substitute for talent.

But that was a fun club for me to be with. You know, it had
players like Eddie Waitkus and Bill Nicholson. Second baseman I
played with was Hank Schenz. Stan Hack was gone, but Andy
Pafko played—I think played third part of that year. Hal Jeffcoat
was a rookie. I played with Hal a couple of years previously in the
minor leagues. So, it was a fun ball club to be with from the standpoint of the people who were on it. What wasn't fun was that we
were a last-place club and couldn't win.

*Gene Mauch was on that team and is your brother-in-law. Did
you play in many games together?*

Yeah, quite a few actually. Gene came over to us from Brooklyn—in those years, we were getting a lot of players from Brooklyn.
You know Brooklyn had that great club and a great minor league
organization and they were producing a lot of ballplayers and very
few of them could crack that big club, so a lot of them came to the
other clubs in our league and the Cubs got quite a few. Gene was
one of them and when he came to us, he was assigned to be my
roommate and we became friends. Not that that made any difference to him because he thought himself primarily as a shortstop in
those days and he was going to try to win a job. And he played
shortstop in some games when he came over. I think I'd hurt my
ankle or something and he played well. And Gene was a fiery
player. He was a very heady player as you know from knowing
him as a manager. But, he was—admittedly, he was a little short

on physical ability and that was a handicap to him, so he couldn't quite achieve what he wanted to, which was to be the Eddie Stanky-type ballplayer in the major leagues. So, Gene's career in the major leagues mainly was, it turned out, preparation for his managerial career. But we played together some. We really had a lot of fun doing that. We felt like we could really turn those double plays. And we did. We turned a few.

Was he your brother-in-law at that point?

No, I met Gene's sister—my wife—as a result of my friendship with Gene and so—Gene and I met in '48 and Jolene and I got married in 1950.

What was the caliber of play in the National League in the late '40s?

I think it was extremely high caliber. Sadly, there were a few ballplayers who did not come back from World War II and not all of them were casualties. I mean, some of them didn't come back because they had aged in the meantime and couldn't resume careers, but most did and I don't think any of them that I saw had suffered from the experience. They came back as good or better than ever. I thought the caliber of baseball in those years was very high.

You were with the Cubs from '48 to '53. What are some of your fondest memories?

Well, the fact of playing baseball in Chicago is one fond memory. You know, even though there were times when there were fans that gave me a bad time—I always enjoyed playing there and daytime baseball in Wrigley Field—I mean, it just had no equal, I felt. I think that everybody who's ever played in Chicago for the Cubs, who's experienced that, had that same kind of feeling.

I think the fans who gave me a bad time weren't without some justification for it in that I didn't demonstrate the consistency that they wanted to see and along with the fact that the club was not a good ball club, and because we didn't win, I think it was kind of natural that they would look for somebody to blame and I deserve a share of that blame. Unfortunately, when things like that happen, the positive contributions that you make tend to get overlooked. But they weren't overlooked by everybody, there were people who liked me a lot and I certainly appreciated that.

51

You had a great arm.

Probably right there with Carl Furillo—I don't know which would have been the strongest.

Marty Marion told me one time that I had the best arm he'd ever seen on a shortstop. And that was high praise coming from that guy, 'cause he was one of my heroes.

What was your greatest thrill as a Cub?

You know, I think about some of the good days that I had that were a tremendous amount of fun. There was one time—I believe it was in 1950—when we were playing the Cardinals and the Cardinals had a very good ball club with Marion, Stan Musial, with all those guys, and one time in a doubleheader I hit for the cycle in the first game and I hit another home run in the second game. To do something like that is a heck of a lot of fun.

On the other hand, there were some wins that were just tremendous fun. I remember one series at the end of the 1949 season when the Cardinals came into Chicago and needed two games to clinch it and we beat them three of four games—we beat them the first three and knocked them out of the pennant. Well, it's not that we wanted to spoil it for the Cardinals, we just wanted to beat whoever we were playing and that's the way the chips fell. So there was a lot of satisfaction in that.

I remember a game in Boston, in Braves Field in 1949—no, I think this was in 1950—against Johnny Sain who had been a tough pitcher for the Cubs. Sain wasn't throwing quite as hard in '50 as he had thrown in '48. He had become more of a curveball pitcher and he had remained a winning pitcher. You remember the old saying—"Spahn and Sain and pray for rain." Of course, in '50 they had Bickford, who had a good year, too. But anyway, in this night game in Braves Field in Boston, Sain was pitching and my game plan was to look for a curveball. And in hitting when you go up and look for a pitch—and this is a Ted Williams' approach—and I didn't fancy myself to be Ted Williams—but this is a real fun part about hitting: that you go up and look for a pitch, the pitch that you think you're going to get. You try to study the pitcher and know him and know what he's going to try to do to get you out and what pitch he's going to throw in your strike zone. And then you lay off anything else until you get two strikes. And then when you get two strikes you get defensive and get the bat on the ball.

Well, my game plan was to lay for the breaking ball. He threw curveballs—two or three speeds—and even mixed in a slider and then an occasional fastball. Well, at this particular time I was hitting the ball well. The first time up I got a curveball and hit a towering flyball to left field that came down almost vertically—it came down glancing against the left-field fence and bounced away from Sid Gordon, the left fielder, and I got a triple by the time it was retrieved. Nobody on base as I remember. It was a close game and nobody else on our club was doing much with Sain. So my hitting was sort of wasted, but second time up, I stayed with my game plan, laying for the curveball, got a curveball, hit it off the center-field fence for a triple. Third time at bat, I'm staying with the plan even though you would wonder—well, if you hit the curveball that well twice, maybe he will change on you—I'm looking for the curveball—he threw me a fastball. But I was hitting the ball so well, staying back so well—I hit it over the center-field fence. The game going into the ninth inning, they're ahead of us and we get the bases loaded, as I remember, with one out. I come up with the bases loaded and we're behind and I stay with my plan. I look for the curveball. I get a good curveball to hit. I hit a ball that may be the hardest ball I hit. One hopper to the shortstop—double play—game's over—we lose, but maybe the best night I'd ever had in my life just from the standpoint of how well I hit the ball and how well my plan worked.

Frisch took over from Grimm in 1949. What was he like?

Frankie was a little bit arrogant and he was a little bit impatient with...particularly with veteran players. He chewed me so that I could hardly walk one time in Chicago when we were playing the Giants. I hit a towering pop fly into short right field behind Eddie Stanky. This must have been right after Frisch joined the club in '49. And I kind of lost the ball off my bat—it was a bright day. And I didn't run hard to first base and Stanky stumbled around and let the ball drop and I could have been standing on second base had I been running hard. And he just gave it to me unmercifully in the clubhouse after the game. I'll tell you this, I never let that happen again—ever. But I like Frank, mainly because or partly because he liked me. It's hard to dislike somebody who likes you. There were people who didn't like Frank.

He was replaced by Phil Cavarretta in the summer of '51.

Phil was easy to play for. His main requirement, as you might suspicion, is that you give it 110%. Phil would be in your corner until the cows come home if you put out for him and worked hard for him and gave it everything you had. And he would be very patient. I like Phil a lot personally, and I liked playing for him.

You lost your job in '53 to a Hall of Fame shortstop—Ernie Banks. What do you remember about that? When he came up, did you say, this guy is special?

Yeah, there wasn't any question about it. He had this nice, easy, effortless swing and the ball just jumped off his bat. And you only see that with great hitters. He also was a good enough short-stop. He was smooth and could get the job done. But, of course, the bat was the main thing. But in the circumstances of his taking over, I mean, Phil Cavarretta was very loyal to me and I was going to play until I played myself out of a job and I had toward the end of the '53 season. It was just when Ernie joined us, I had pulled something in my ribs and it was very painful to play, but I played until I just couldn't. Everybody knew that Ernie was going to be great. But when I couldn't play, Ernie started playing and I think that was the last that I played. Went to spring training with the Cubs the following year in 1954 and Ernie was just—you know—he was on his way to the Hall of Fame. Spring of '54 they traded me to Milwaukee for a right-hand pitcher.

What's the difference between your era of the '40s and '50s and the players in the '80s and '90s?

Well, one difference, of course, is that there has been expansion. Another difference is that there has been this tremendous growth of the other major sports and some minor sports in popularity and all of these competing sports have, I think, well, unquestionably, have siphoned off a lot of talent. You know, when I was a kid —and that's going back a lot of years now—but, it seemed like there was a minor league club in every town in the country. And the other sports had not become major sports. You know, pro football was nothing. Pro basketball, I mean, to the people who were in it, it was something. But I mean as a major popular sport, they had not done it. And so baseball was it. And the really good athletes were going into baseball. So, my feeling is that the quality of the game over all has been diluted and that it is not at as high a level as it was then. That's not to say it's not good now and I do think that the really good athletes in baseball now are as good as any of them ever were.

I think there has been a difference in attitude because of the money. It's a different game today. And that's not to say that there are not ballplayers in the game today who would go out there and grind it out and be professional about it whether they got $500 or $5 million. There are those kinds of players and I think my son was one of them. I think the quality level is not quite as high overall and I think the contribution to that is the attitude of the players brought about by the presence of so much money.

I really enjoyed the game. My career in it. I enjoyed it as a player. I enjoyed it as a minor league manager. You know, I've made great friends. I met my wife. Gave my son a career. So, you know, I'd like to do it over again. I mean, I'd like to try to be better than I was...wish I could have been.

A Cub infielder from 1956 to 1961. A journeyman ballplayer who, after his big league career, became one of America's top college baseball coaches at the University of Arizona. Speaking of Wrigley Field, he said, "It's a magic place to me to this day."

You played for the Cubs in the late '50s and early '60s. What are your memories?

Our Chicago Cubs were not challenging for the pennant in those years, but we were featured, of course, by some outstanding players—notably Ernie Banks. I count my four and a half years with the Cubs as one of the real memorable times in my life because of my contact with Ernie. Ernie was, and he is, one of the truly great people in baseball. Not only was his performance of an all-star type, but his personality and his friendliness and his genuine interest in all his teammates was of that kind also. He's Hall of Fame in every area, as far as I'm concerned.

I remember the first day I reported to the Cubs after signing the contract from the University of Minnesota. It was July 1, 1956 that I reported for a doubleheader with the Milwaukee Braves. And one of the first people to introduce himself to me and make me feel at home in the clubhouse was the old catcher, Clyde McCullough. And Clyde was very, very friendly. Very helpful and invited me to warm up with him before pre-game infield that Sunday morning and kind of shepharded me through the doubleheader. And then we were leaving that night for a long train ride out east to go to Brooklyn, New York, Philadelphia, and Pittsburgh. And he wanted to know if I played cards. I said, "No, I don't." He said, "Come on the train tonight and we'll teach you how." Well, then my good friend, Yosh Kowana, the clubhouse man, got me aside and he said, "Kid, don't play cards with those guys. They'll take all your bonus money." It was good advice and, although Clyde McCullough I still count as a friend, I never did get into a card game with him.

I thought the best manager I've had in all 10 years of professional ball was Lou Boudreau. Lou, of course, was an infielder, shortstop, and that was my position. So he understood my defensive needs and what I was responsible for as a middle infielder. He seemed to be a jump ahead of most managers in plotting his strategy during the game. Lou did not have a great deal of talent to work with in that year. But, boy, he really worked and managed hard. And he was very, very helpful to me and I appreciate that. And I see Lou from time to time and I'm quick to tell him that I still regard him as the best manager I played for in the big leagues.

Charlie Grimm was the manager coming out of spring training that year and actually I was sent down—that was 1960 —and I was sent down to Houston in Triple-A ball just before we broke spring training camp. And Charlie was still the manager. And then they got to Chicago, as people will remember, and about three weeks into the season Lou Boudreau and Charlie changed places. Lou came from the broadcasting booth at WGN and Charlie replaced him doing the color for the baseball broadcasts. And, right away, Lou Boudreau called me back from Houston and put me in at second base with the Cubs. So I appreciate his confidence in me to begin with, and then all of the help he gave me that year.

What do you remember of the College of Coaches?
I think in theory, the College of Coaches was a good idea. In practice, however, it was just too cumbersome. It didn't work. People need a leader and the team needs a leader. A recognized, acknowledged, single leader from whom they take their orders and from whom they follow the strategy and so on. And the College of Coaches was a very noble effort to diminish the blame that was placed on the manager...for failure. And, it didn't work. We went from one head coach to another head coach and they were rotated in and out of the job—these were good men, too. These were men who knew baseball. I remember Grady Hatton. And Charlie Metro. Vedie Himsl and Elvin Tappe. These guys all knew baseball. But they were so different in personalities that the transition from one to the other was so dramatic that it had the players in confusion and turmoil rather than achieving the end and that was to keep harmony and to have a better team.

It wasn't workable at the big league level. Because these men —and even today in the modern baseball era—these players need a man on whom they can depend for authority and direction and leadership. Not a group of men, but *a* man.

Many believe the period from 1947 to 1957 produced some of the best baseball ever.

Extraordinary. The National League was peopled then by Jackie Robinson, Roy Campanella, Duke Snider for the Dodgers, Willie Mays for the Giants, Ernie, of course, with the Chicago Cubs. Roberto Clemente, Elroy Face, Bob Friend with the Pirates. These players are legendary and rightly so. They were extraordinary ballplayers. And I think today there are extraordinary ballplayers also, but I feel very privileged to have played in '56 and '57—to see these great players like Jackie Robinson. He was at the tail end of his career, but nonetheless, what a fantastic talent he was. And how I'll forever be grateful that I got to play against him and to bat against Robin Roberts, Curt Simmons for the Phillies, Sandy Koufax, Don Drysdale. It was no picnic. Warren Spahn, of course, of the Braves. It was a great privilege and thrill—although I didn't realize it so much at that time. But now I look back on it as one of the real privileges in my life.

I think when we take the All-Star teams from the two leagues now—in the '90s—that they're comparable to the All-Star teams in the '50s and '60s because there are still the outstanding performers. I believe that today the baseball players are stronger. They are faster— as a group. And they are better conditioned with the advent of weight training and better nutrition. I think today's physical abilities are as great as they were back in—maybe even a shade better—than they were in the '50s and '60s.

Now, a lot of my friends—we old-timers—a lot of them don't share that feeling. But I've watched very closely the players coming out of college because that's my bag now and on into the big leagues and they are very, very fine athletes. Now, I need to temper that with —how shall I say—there are so many players now that run the gamut from the extraordinary player—like Ricky Henderson and Dave Winfield—all the way down—and you see the lower level has expanded so much more with expansion. So there are guys now advancing to the major leagues that in the '50s and '60s would have been in Double-A ball, and spending a lot of time in the minor leagues before they were equipped to go to the major leagues. So that lower level is much more diluted now. But the extraordinary performer is still there.

Do multi-year contracts hurt a player's performance?

I think some do—regrettably. Human nature being what it is,

when there were not the multi-year contracts and the huge amounts of money back in the '50s and '60s that we see now, the guys were on the edge every day. Every game was crucial that they perform well, and that they hang onto their job. Of course, the guys like Ernie Banks and Willie Mays and Mickey Mantle, their jobs weren't in jeopardy, but the great majority of us, they were. Our jobs were in jeopardy. And so we had to be ready and play hard every day in order to stay in the big leagues.

Because you were on one-year contracts?

One year contracts and not a great deal of money. Now with the multi-year contracts, I wonder if some of the motivation isn't less today than it used to be.

What was the most you made with the Cubs?

Oh, with the Cubs...I think...probably about $12,000 or $13,000 was the most I made with the Cubs. But I need to point out that I was a bonus player and I received a nice check for signing my name to a contract in 1956. I was very well compensated. The bonus money was $32,000. In addition to the $32,000 was a three-year contract at the minimum at that time which was $6,000. So it was a package of $50,000 for three years. It was very good money. More than I deserved.

You're one of the premiere college coaches. Is the approach to the game different now than it was when you were playing?

Not at the college level at all. The college game remains consistent and it is for the love of the game and there's so much energy and so much enthusiasm at the college level today that also existed back in the '50s when I played at the University of Minnesota. So, I don't see any different motivation or different kinds of spirit in college now than I did back in the '50s. There are expanded programs. There are better ballparks. There are greater schedules. There's better equipment. And there are better techniques. But the spirit is the same now as it's always been.

Who are some of the ballplayers that you managed that went on to the big leagues?

Oh, we've had a good many. Right now, Jack Howell is one of our guys. Joe Magrane from the Cardinals. Casey Candaele from the Houston Astros. Craig Lefferts, pitching with the Padres, was with the

Giants and the Cubs before that. Scott Erickson, who's doing so well with the Minnesota Twins. I counted last year at one particular time in the season there were 11 of our Wildcats playing in the big leagues.

Would you entertain an offer to go to the big leagues as a manager?
No. Not anymore. There was a time when I was coaching—oh, about 15 years ago here at Arizona—when I received a tangible offer. But, no, at this point I'm 56 years old next month and I feel I belong in college. This is where really I'm the happiest. I'm finishing my 19th year.

I feel very much blessed to have had a career in professional baseball for 10 years and then to be equipped by virtue of my college education to go right into something I'd always wanted to do and that was coach college baseball. If you're at the University of Arizona, I can't think of a better place to coach baseball.

I think my greatest thrill was in 1960, shortly after Lou Boudreau called me up from Houston and put me right in at second base...and I played virtually all year at second. Was playing the position behind Don Cardwell's no-hitter. Don had just been traded from the Philadelphia Phillies to the Cubs. I think, indeed, it was his first start as a Cub. And it was a Sunday afternoon, second game of a doubleheader in Wrigley Field, and he beat the Cardinals with a no-hitter. And, late in the game I made several nice plays to preserve the no-hitter, and to be part of all of that drama, and play a key role in something so exciting as a no-hitter, was I think my biggest thrill.

I still regard the Cubs as my favorite team. I saw my first big league game in Wrigley Field when I was in high school. I saw the Dodgers play the Cubs and, from that moment on, I dreamed of being a Cubbie.

And I then signed with the Cubs on June 30, 1956 and every time...literally, every time I took the field at Wrigley Field as a starting player in those four and a half years I was there, every time was a special thrill for me.

It's a magic place to me to this day. And it's one of those historic parks that has so much charm and tradition that I hope that they never tear it down like they did Comiskey.

BROADCASTERS

———— JACK BRICKHOUSE ————

*He started doing the Cub games on television in 1947 and contin-
ued for 34 years, retiring in 1981. Always did a professional job
and was a great salesman for the Cubs and baseball. Was elected
to the Hall of Fame.*

When did you start broadcasting sports in Chicago?

1940. Bob Elson got me my job as a staff announcer here at
WGN and sports assistant. It was better than half a century ago
and I'm still around. In those days, even a big station like WGN
did not have certain departments. It was not as categorized or de-
partmentalized as broadcasting facilities are now. You did everything. You were a staff announcer. You did it all and also you did
a sports assistant's job. Even Elson, who was the No. 1 sports
broadcaster in town, did the same thing I did. For example, emcee
a couple of shows here and there, do a man-on-the-street now and
then, do the dance band pickups. We all worked at all of them.
That's the way it was in those days. When Bob went away to service, I finished up the 1942 season and then I did the whole 1943
season by myself.

This is on WGN? For the Cubs?

Yes. Cubs and the White Sox in those days. We took the
team that was in town, or if we had to do one that was out of
town, we did those wireless-ticker report games. And those were
fun. I remember having a wonderful conversation with Ronald
Reagan about that because he used to do the same thing in Des
Moines, Iowa, when he was a sports announcer there. He did the
Cubs games and we had a lot of stories to exchange about experiences when that wire goes kaput.

Anyway, in '44 I went away to service. Then I came back—I
beat Elson back. So in 1945, and by this time WGN had given up
baseball broadcasting in favor of being a good team member of the
Mutual Network and doing the kid shows. You couldn't deliver
the kid shows to Kellogg or Post Toasties or whoever, unless, of
course, you could deliver the second biggest market in the country
at that time. The ball games used to start around 3:00 in the after-

noon, so you can tell that would be a conflict. So WGN gave up baseball at that time.

The Cubs went to Ralph Atlas at WIND and the White Sox to WJJD. At that time WIND had Bert Wilson, so when I came back I did the White Sox on WJJD and the reason I'm mentioning that is because that was the year the Cubs won the pennant, the last pennant they had and I did the White Sox exclusively that year! So, I'm still waiting for my first Cub pennant, believe it or not!

'46 Bob Elson came back from service and got the White Sox job. So, now I'm, as they say, at liberty and I auditioned and won the Giants' broadcasting job in New York City and did a season there. Word is that I was sent there by the Cubs to put the Giants in last place and I managed to do it.

Then I came back here in '47 because television was coming along. And, to be honest about it, I got in a little bit of a salary dispute with the Giants about what the job was really worth and I guess I'm more of a midwesterner than a lot of other people. So, I came back here. At that time, Joe Wilson had done the Chicago Cubs on television for WBKB, the only television station in town at that time. The next year they asked Joe and me to team up together and do the Cubs games, which we did in one of the most delightful years I've ever had in my life. Joe and I got along like Damon and Pithias.

What year?

'47. Then in '48, Channel 9 went on the air, WGN Television, and they called me and asked me if I would come back. Well, I was on an indefinite leave of absence, actually, from GN. I never did really quit or resign. They were nice enough to let me still do a lot of shows over here in the off-season. So I was still identified with the place in radio. So, when they decided to go into television, they asked me if I would come back and I came back with a dual capacity. I wore two hats in the place. I was their sports broadcaster, but also their manager of sports, which meant that I was management and helped negotiate contracts and things like that. Worked out very well.

What year did you start a full season of Cubs games on Channel 9?

1948. I was the first voice on Channel 9. That's what we did that year—the Cubs. At that time, there were three stations doing the Cubs games. Ours and WBKB with Joe Wilson and WLS used,

I think it was Vince Garrity and Rogers Hornsby. There the three of us were at the ballpark and then the next year, the other two dropped and we wound up with the exclusive contract for the Chicago Cubs television.

What was it like back then?

It was very interesting because in those days, there were very, very few sets in the market compared to what we have now. There were maybe 10,000 sets in Cook County. And about 8,000 of them had to be in bars. So that meant then, that your percentage of viewers per set was very, very high. In other words, you're liable to have a 30-point viewer per set whereas now, what have you got, 1.2 or 1.3 viewers per set because of the number of sets in use. So in those days, you had not only 30 to 50 people watching each set, but they were in bars and because of the room noise and so forth and so on, we found that a lot of people were turning on the radio in these bars because we took the position from the beginning—look, let the picture do the work—don't talk as much as you do on radio. But then we found out that they're turning in radio and turning off the sound of the television set because they're getting more information on radio. Well, the minute we found that out, we started to talk a little more on television. Until the number of sets in homes began to increase and therefore the viewers per set decreased, so when you got to around four viewers per set and that sort of thing, we started to get those letters saying, "Hey, don't talk so much. I'm not a moron. I can see. Keep your mouth shut. Stop doing a radio broadcast." So, that's when we started to, again, decrease the wordage of our broadcasts on television.

And, of course, that's the way it is right now. And we have done such things as simulcast, too. As a matter of fact, that's not completely out of the picture right now. They did basketball simulcast here in Chicago this last year. I don't agree with it. I think it makes sense for each media to do its own particular type broadcast.

One of the things you did well was to stay on the fence. That fine line of not being a "homer," but being objective.

You just touched on something that has been a very important part of my philosophy of broadcasting and my approach to the job. From the very beginning, I took the position, and we found it out in our mail and in our conversations with our listeners and viewers and phone calls and that sort of thing, that the majority, the vast majority of your audience at the local level, would like to have the announcer kind of root for the home team and be with them. Now, this is not true with the World Series or an All-Star Game or a network feature. I've done several World Series. I've done several All-Star Games, so I know a little about that. No, on that basis you take a strictly neutral approach as they do today. But, from the beginning I took the position that if the vast majority of our people would like to have us kind of root for the team with them and be part of the family with them and be their guy with them, alright, I'm all for that. However, how do you do this and maintain reportorial integrity? And my position was, the big trick is to give plenty of credit to the opposition. Give them all the credit they have coming. If a man does a great job out there, give him credit. And I've assumed this very simple attitude that if, on that basis, you beat the opposition then it makes your victory all the sweeter if you beat a great team. A great effort. On the other hand, if you lose to them, it's no dishonor to lose to a great performance. And this was the simple approach that I've taken all these years.

You were, for lack of a better word, a good salesman for the sport of baseball.

I would like to think so. One of the most flattering things I ever heard was Phil Wrigley referring to me as the best salesman baseball had. Not just the Cubs. But baseball. Because another position that I've taken all these years is that my job as a broadcaster is to sell tickets, sell the game, sell merchandise, move merchandise off those shelves, and if there's any time left over, you now have the luxury of selling yourself. So that's the package.

What was it like covering some of those poor Cub teams?

Well, for one thing, I'm a fan. You and I are fans. Maybe sometimes too much of a fan. But, by golly, that's the way it is. That's the way we're made. To me, those people out there are heroes until they prove otherwise. There are 650 guys in major league uniforms, okay? To me, the 650th man in the major leagues had to have certain unique specialized skills in order to get there and because he is in a major league unit of 650 people, in a world of several billion people, he has my respect until he proves otherwise. And there have been very few of them who have proven otherwise. Some, yes. But for the most part, that's the way they've looked to me.

So, I'm a rooter and so even though they were losers, and I think this has been characteristic of both the Cubs and the White Sox in this town where I believe we have the fairest-minded fans in the world, that even though they have not won the games they should have, there's still been plenty to root about and cheer about from the standpoint of some individual performances, plus what wins we have had. It's still major league competition.

Who is the greatest Cub player you ever saw?

That's a tough one. I suppose my favorite Cub, if you want to put it in that basis, would have to be Ernie Banks. Because Ernie not only hit those 512 home runs, but he was MVP a couple of years and hit all those home runs with ball clubs that weren't exactly the greatest ball clubs in the world. So, consequently, he had to do a lot of it himself, plus the fact that off the diamond, out of the ballpark, he's one of the greatest, single, goodwill ambassadors baseball has ever known. Ernie has the unique talent of making a little boy or a little girl really believe that the reason Ernie came to the ballpark today was to meet you. And, you know kids are a lot smarter than we give them credit for. Kids, whether they know it or not themselves, have an instinct for when an adult really likes them and when they're faking it. And you could tell, they loved Ernie. They were on the same level, 'cause they just knew he loved them.

Who do you think was the best manager the Cubs had during the time you covered them?

Cubs have had some very good managers. I would have to kind of divide that one up, I think. I suppose I'd have to go with Charlie Grimm. I would have to go with Scheffing—I thought Scheffing did a very good job one time when he took them into a tie for fifth. That may not sound like much, but this was a pretty unfortunate ball club. I thought Herman Franks was a very good manager. Very few guys smarter than Herman.

Durocher?

Well, let me tell you about Leo. Leo, for one year, did a great job with the ball club. But he had a ball club to do it with, too. Just one year he had talent. And yet, that particular year—the '69 season—Leo mismanaged that ball club toward the end of the year. Now, in his day, Leo Durocher was as sharp and as good a manager as ever lived maybe. He had the instincts of a riverboat gambler. Nobody had to tell him this guy's thrown 88 pitches now in only six innings, so forth and so on. He didn't have to have that. He could watch this guy. And he could tell. And he went against the book a lot. But that was before he got to Chicago.

Now he got to Chicago and he had a little tough luck at the beginning but then the ball club began to really put together a heck of a season. You talk about the personnel of that '69 ball club. You're talking about some talent. Here's Randy Hundley, Ernie Banks, Glenn Beckert, Don Kessinger, Ron Santo, Billy Williams, Jim Hickman, and, of course, several guys in center field, including the unfortunate youngster, Don Young. Now you take the pitching staff—Fergie Jenkins, Billy Hands, Holtzman, guys like that. This was a good ball club.

What did Durocher do at the end of the season?

Well, now this is not my original thinking, but it's thinking with which I agree. I talked to experts, or guys I regard as experts. The old-timers. The pros. And this is probably one of the advantages that I have that the fan doesn't have and that is that I have accessibility to these people.

These guys, and some of the players, too, even though they may not want to be named, admitted that Leo mismanaged the ball club the last month because he had a tired ball club. They were exhausted. Poor Kessinger was dragging that bat behind him walking up to the plate sometimes. Yet, if you were to put these men on a lie detector and ask them did they give their best effort, the answer would be "yes" and they would pass the test because that's what they did. But they were simply tired out. Well, as a lot of these guys would tell you, these old pros who've been around a long time, other managers, scouts, other players and so forth—real veterans of the game—there comes a time when you have to use the guys on that bench and rest some of those regulars. Especially in those hot days of August and September and Leo didn't do that. He didn't do that.

What was your biggest thrill?

It's so tough to answer because I've been on the scene for so long. Eight no-hitters, you know. Any one of those is something to take to your grave with you. The first World Series I ever did. The Banks 500th homer. Watching Musial get that 3,000 hit. Watching Pete Rose out here when he was managing the ball club.

You can talk about Pete all you want, but I know he showed me a touch of class. Competitive class when he was managing the Cincinnati ball club. What was it—4,190 hits—number 4,191, I think it was, going to tie Ty Cobb's record? It was the last game before they hit Cincinnati and they were kind of hoping that they could save it for Cincinnati so he put himself on the bench. But now came a situation at Wrigley Field when Pete needed a base hit. He put in the best man he had, Pete Rose, and Pete came through with that hit and tied that game and stayed in the game and went into the 10th or 11th inning, came to bat again, and, if he had gotten that hit that would have broken Cobb's record, so be it. To heck with all such things as celebrations in Cincinnati. I want to win this game. Well, he tried, but he grounded out. But the point I make is, for that minute, Pete Rose was one of the great class competitors.

Same way when Musial got his 3,000th. Freddie Hutchinson was trying to save him for St. Louis where they were headed right after this Cub game. They wanted that 3,000th at St. Louis and Stan wasn't even on the bench. He was out in the bullpen sunning himself with the pitchers. All of a sudden, Hutch needs a base hit. In came Musial. Sure enough. Base hit off Moe Drabowsky. That was it.

What was your biggest disappointment?

Well, biggest disappointment I guess I'd have to say was losing that '69 season. Because they had that eight-and-a-half game, nine-game lead in the middle of August—still blew it. And not only that, but they blew it by eight games. It wasn't even close before it was over. The Mets stepped out and won that thing as well as the Cubs losing it.

Your last game—do you remember it?

Oh, yes.

What was that like?

Kind of a numbing experience. Kind of walking in a dream. "Is this really happening?"-type feeling. When those 1,000 or more people gathered outside the Pink Poodle and below the Pink

Poodle, below the ramp there in the inner part of the ballpark, the mall there, and kept yelling, "We want Jack! We want Jack! We want Jack!" That grabbed me. It really did. It grabbed me.

I suppose if you talk about the biggest personal thrill, I suppose this has to be true of any broadcaster, or any ballplayer—was when I went into Cooperstown. I'll never forget. I got the notice of this in January and the ceremony was in the latter part of July. So I had all those months to know it. And yet, I guess I didn't really fully realize what it was all about 'til the night before.

First of all, a little while before the ceremony, I got a personal handwritten note from Ted Williams, an old friend. You know, to get a handwritten note from a guy like that saying, "Congratulations. I've always considered you a good friend and I'm happy for you." That's a keeper.

Now the night before, I was standing on the patio there of the hotel where *The Sporting News* was having a cocktail party and I was talking to Joe DiMaggio. And a fellow came up and asked Joe for his autograph and Joe obliged him and then said, "I'm sure you'd also like the autograph of another Hall of Famer, Jack Brickhouse." And that's when it hit me. My God! I hit my hand against my forehead. I'm in the same lodge with guys like this. It finally hit me. And even though it's the media wing and the Frick Award, and a separate part of Cooperstown, nevertheless, it's still in the Hall of Fame building and it's Hall of Fame recognition and I have to say that is one of the great thrills anybody could have.

Any regrets?

Yeah, I regret that I haven't seen more pennants. The only pennant I ever actually saw was the '59 pennant when I worked the White Sox. And I worked that World Series, Vinnie Scully and I worked it. It was a great Series. But, I would have to say the lack of pennants and not seeing the Cubs in a World Series, ever. 'Cause in '45 I was working the White Sox.

I've always said my biggest ambition was to have the White Sox play the Cubs in a World Series. Be assigned to the broadcast. Have every game go at least 15 innings. Seven of them. And in the last one have Ernie Banks come out, even if they had to put him in a wheelchair, get up, and hit one out of the ballpark and put them back in the ball game and then after that, I don't care what happens!

───── VINCE LLOYD ─────

Veteran Chicago sportscaster. Likeable and easy-going, he always made you feel very comfortable—not an easy thing to do.

I went to WGN in September '49. Actually, when they brought me up, they were just starting to televise...they had been, I think, on baseball maybe a year or two, but they were planning to do Big 10 football that season. They wanted me to do that. And then they had boxing and wrestling after baseball, and some college basketball. And when the baseball season came around the next year, I was not in the booth during the game—I'd be down on the field doing interviews either before or after the game, sometimes both. Originally, I was there just to do television. But they had some labor problems and a couple of people in the station wanted me to do some radio work also and I did. And then...that got the president of the company very upset when I refused to continue working. Some of the other guys were threatening to go on strike.

What do you remember of the interviews at Cubs park?

I remember one with Danny Murtaugh, manager of the Pittsburgh Pirates and a wonderful little guy. He looked like one of those little coal miners who'd meet you in the bar sometime and whack you silly if you so much as looked sideways at him. Danny I don't think ever used a swear word, including "damn"; his worst habit was chewing tobacco. And I'd do an interview with him and about three days later I'd get a letter from a woman who is absolutely furious with me because I have permitted this uncouth man to continue to spit chewing tobacco into her living room.

I got tricked one time into doing an interview with...oh, what was his name, pitcher with the Brooklyn Dodgers, who as it turned out, knew about five words of English and never wanted to use any one of them. And one of the guys on the ball club, it might have been Duke Snider, had told me, "You gotta interview him. He's great." That was the longest 15 minutes I've ever endured in my life.

Television, about all you have to do, I felt, was embellish the picture and maybe talk about things other than what the fan obviously could see, to augment what he was seeing. And in radio, it was always my philosophy that I had to be the eyes for the listener. That was brought home to me by a man down in Peoria, a veteran who had lost his sight and he ran the newsstand at the city hall. I got to know him. He was a good baseball fan. In fact, we were up at Wrigley Field watching a game one day and he said, "I want you to sit with me." We had gone up on a train caravan. "I want you to sit along side me during the game." Which I did. And he said, "Tell me what this guy looks like." And I would. And he said, "When a batter swings, if he hits the ball, you don't have to say anything. I can tell from the crack of the bat whether or not he hit it solidly or where it might be going...left or right." Which was true and it just amazed me. He then told me, "Don't forget, when you're broadcasting, all your listeners are like me. They can't see." And I never forgot it.

The toughest years were when you left training camp and you knew you had a lousy ball club. You were going nowhere. And how do you keep up interest?

Well, it came home to me one day and, very fortunately, about the second year that I was doing them. I had left the ballpark one day. We had gotten our brains beat out again. Looked terrible. And just as I'm getting about 15 feet from my car, a kid about six or seven years old stops me, got a program, wants an autograph. Well, I stopped and I signed it for him. And he said, "Gee, Mr. Lloyd, wasn't that a beautiful game. Ron Santo hit another home run." You know, for those people who had a chance to go to a ball game, just being there made maybe the week, maybe the month, maybe the summer for them.

The worst playing I think was done the year that Mr. Wrigley decided to go with the rotating managers. All the confusion and dissension that season—it was just impossible. Oh, just unbelievable.

During your time, who do you think was the least equipped manager to lead the Cubs?

I'm going to forget those rotating coaches. There's a couple of them that left an awful lot to be desired. Elvin Tappe was a super guy, but he was not equipped nor prepared to manage at that time. I think that probably Jim Marshall got in way over his head when he was made manager. I like Jim personally.

Who do you think was the best manager?

Oh, I'd have to go with Leo. Yeah, there's no question about it. Regardless of what you felt about him personally, he was an outstanding baseball man.

Santo, for example, they had a hell of a shouting match in the clubhouse one day. It was a tough deal, the guys tell me in later years, to restrain both of them. I mean they had two and three guys holding Leo back and two or three holding Santo back and one of them would have been knocked out and I know it would have been Leo.

Don Young in '69 dropped two flyballs in a key game against the Mets. And Santo really berated him because Young left the clubhouse long before any other player did and ducked all of the press. Got out of there in such a hurry, nobody saw him. Santo really leveled him with the press. So did Durocher. Got all over him. Now, here's the odd thing. The next morning, Santo called a press conference at the hotel. We were staying at the Waldorf Astoria. He apologized to Young in front of all the press. When he got to the ballpark, he apologized to Young once more in front of the whole team. He was continuously...I'd say the rest of his career, criticized by the public for that tirade against Don Young.

Durocher never apologized. And he was just as tough on Young, if not tougher than Ron was.

You did the Cubs and the Sox. It's a Cubs town...why?

I wish I could really understand it. I think there are several reasons for it. One of them, I think, has to go back to the convenient location of Wrigley Field. You can get to it on public transportation. The "L" stops right there and so many of the buses. That's one thing. Also, daytime baseball is another. I think (also) the fact that Wrigley back in the 1920s instituted the idea of Ladies' Day at the ball games.

That started women coming and they could bring their little ones with them. They had a babysitter at the ballpark. That has carried over and I think that's one of the big reasons the Cubs up until now have so many women fans.

But you have to remember, too, this goes back even before lights. It was still a Cubs town for the most part.

We found this out in 1959. The Cubs I think were either last or next to last in their league and were that way almost from the beginning of the season. The White Sox had a great team, with a lot of colorful ballplayers on it...Sherm Lollar, Looie Aparicio, Nellie Fox, great pitching staff, Jim Rivera, Jim Landis, and they won the American League pennant. Our ratings consistently, all year long, would have a higher rating on a weekend when we'd do a Cubs game than we would have on a weekend when we did a White Sox. We were just confounded. We could not believe it. We consistently had higher ratings on Cubs telecasts than we did on White Sox telecasts. How do you explain that?

I was amazed when I first started traveling in '65 to all the National League cities. My heavens, in L.A., we'd get to the hotel and that lobby would be jammed. We could be getting in there at 11-12 o'clock at night and the lobby would be jammed with Cubs fans. And the next day, anytime you'd go down, they'd be down there waiting for autographs. They'd be at the ballpark, they'd want to come up to the booth. There were quite a few in San Francisco, but not like L.A. And, of course, St. Louis, it was like homecoming on a weekend anytime you were there.

They began to show up in New York pretty early during that rivalry between the Mets and the Cubs and there were always a lot of them that went to Pittsburgh. There were a lot of them that went over to Cincinnati to follow the ball club. I remember tours that were made to Montreal when we'd be there.

Do you have a game that sticks in your mind as the most exciting?

Opening day in '69. We had beautiful weather. We knew we had a good ball club. We thought we were going to win it that year. And we get into the bottom of the 11th inning and little Willie Smith comes off the bench. Willie didn't really have a lot of power, but he came off the bench in the bottom of the 11th inning and hit one far over right field onto Sheffield. Won the ball game. I don't think the crowd stopped screaming for 10 minutes. We win it —2-1, I think, or 3-2.

What do you remember about the Bleacher Bums?

Well, I always got a kick out of them. And I think one of the things that always tickled me was Dick Selma doing his act of being a cheerleader for them from the bullpen.

He'd get up in the bullpen when things were getting a little tight and he'd wave a towel, get the attention of the Bleacher Bums, and get them going in cheering. Get the ball club going.

He figured in one of the most bizarre incidents I've ever seen in a ball game. We were in Philadelphia at the old ballpark. It was toward the end of the season. And at the very critical time in the ball game, they had the bases loaded. Santo is our third baseman, of course, and he's playing about even with the bag. He wants to shut that run off and Selma goes into his motion and all of a sudden fires over towards third and the ball is over Santo's head and behind him. Hits off the wall and ricochets down into right field and the ball game is over.

The thing had been set up in spring training, that in a certain situation, if the third baseman wanted to try to catch that runner at third, with a throw from the pitcher, that he would shout this phrase, a very common one, "Throw it to me big boy," something like that. And the pitcher would then wheel and throw it to third. But they had never, ever used it. And of course now, you're towards the end of the season and this is not the situation where you would use it anyway. But Santo, completely unmindful of this little thing they had practiced for five minutes back sometime in March, pounds the glove and happened to hit on that one phrase and—boom—here comes the baseball over his head, off the wall, two runs score and the ball game's over.

I'll never forget Bill Hands, who was a super pitcher. In '69, we're battling to hang on to that lead, but you know it's going to be dissolved. We open a three-game series against the Mets in New York and if we don't win that series—you know it's all over.

Tommy Agee is leading off the bottom of the first inning. We go down 1-2-3 against Jerry Koosman, pitching for them. And Agee steps in, and the first pitch...if he didn't have great reflexes, would have taken his head off. I mean, he was out to get him. And Agee got up, doubled that time at bat, and he wound up that night having one of the greatest games of his career; he had three big key hits. And, in my mind, I blamed Durocher for Hands doing that and igniting that whole Mets ball club.

I found out a few years ago that Durocher had nothing to do with it. It was Bill Hands' own idea. He said, "I got to thinking about it on the flight in there. I know I'm going to be the pitcher. I made up my mind I was going to put Agee down with the first pitch. Really shake him up." And he laughed and he says, "Wasn't that a brilliant idea?" We got swept in the series, by the way.

Hank Sauer was always one of my favorite ballplayers. In Ernie

Banks' first year in the majors...Sauer that year was off to a terrible start. I think he had just been the MVP the year before.

Well, we're about in the month of June and Ernie is off to a great start. And we're playing Pittsburgh. Vern Law is pitching for the Pirates. He uncorks a fastball that caught Ernie along side the nose and right under the eye and down he went. And they carried him off the field on a stretcher. Well, we got a report a little later that it wasn't critical. I came out to the ballpark the next morning and Banks is sitting in the dugout and Sauer is right along side of him. And you know that big nose that Hank has...this is the part of the story. Ernie has this big bandage around his head and over his nose. And just the three of us were there. And Hank says, "Ernie, how can a guy be so dumb, so stupid, as to stand in the batting box and let a guy throw a baseball and hit him right in the nose?" Ernie said, "Henry, if that ball hit you in the nose, you'd get your first home run of the year." That's a true story.

When did you leave the Cubs?

The last year with the ball club was '84, on the air. I was doing mostly color that year because Jack Rosenberg and I had started a radio network for the Cubs at the insistence of management. And we ran that thing until I retired in '87—summer of '87.

I think I was lucky to work with the bunch of guys that I did. With Jack Brickhouse, Lou, and Quinlan.

Well, it was a super...super time to be there and just a wonderful bunch of guys...and Boudreau...you know, he was a lot of fun. We got to leave a little contribution with every racetrack in the country.

═══ JACK ROSENBERG ═══

Veteran Chicago broadcaster with WGN, who worked for over 30 years with the same group of seven people to bring Cub baseball to millions of fans. Speaking of the closeness of these seven, he became misty-eyed.

I started with WGN Television in 1954 and came up having been a newspaper man in Peoria to write news and sports shows, work the ball games, provide Jack and other announcers with the anecdotes that we believed added to the game.

We all had a thing about statistics. They were necessary, but in many cases, the human errors part of the game transcended anything statistical. So, my primary duties, with regards to Cubs baseball, were to spend a few hours in front of each game hanging around the dugouts, the clubhouses, the manager's office, wherever, to pick up maybe that one little line that would add to the broadcast. Once the game started and I'd lined up the pre-game guests and that sort of thing, I would keep my typewriter in the booth right next to Jack and make my items extremely short. Maybe a sentence or two. And Jack, being the professional that he was and that he is, would just weave it into the telecast. He was expert at that and you talk about team work on the field, we had team work in the booth. Surrounded by people who knew what to do, wanted to do it, and enjoyed what they did.

You had quite a family at WGN.

Well, the family actually started with Jack, who came here in 1940. He brought Vince Lloyd here in '47 and that was the beginning of the influx of the Peoria group. I came in '54. Arne Harris came in the mid-'50s. Boudreau in the late '50s. And on and on. We had a group of seven. In particular, that would be Brickhouse; Vince; Boudreau; myself; Arne; Bill Lotzer, who was the production manager; and Jack Minovich, who was a radio producer; who stuck together through thick and thin for 30-plus years at one station. A mark of which we are extremely proud. We not only accomplished a lot professionally, but personally as well. We had the great, great personal friendships that the public—the listening public and the viewing public—was aware of. I mean, it came through. We were fortunate, those of us who were not on the air, to have Jack and Vince and the rest continually mentioning our presence and our duties and giving us credit where they felt it was due. It was an era almost unto itself. Whether this type of relationship ever would be duplicated again by this many people at one single station, I have to wonder.

What are some of the high points?

Well, I think, probably Ernie Banks made one of the major impacts on all of us because Ernie not only was a tremendous baseball player, but a tremendous human being. He came up in an era where the players were very, very close to the fans. If you go back over his era, and that includes a number of great ballplayers, Santo and Beckert and Kessinger and Hickman—types like that. Fergie Jenkins, Kenny Holtzman. These people were never found wanting. The fans were never found wanting. When they wanted an autograph or to say "hello" or lean over that brick wall out there, that railing, and get some response—I mean this was an amazing era in Cubs baseball. I think it's proved by the fact that all these years later, those players are still part of this city, whether they live here or not.

What about the Harry Caray situation, when Harry got very ill and you guys executed quite a coup?

Harry suffered a stroke, a serious stroke, in, as I recall, February of '87 or '88. Obviously, he could not come back for opening day. Our program manager then, now the general manager, Dan Fabian, WGN Radio, came up with what turned out to be a brilliant idea. We can't really replace Harry, let's do the best we can. Let's have a fill-in schedule of great announcing talent and let them fill-in day by day until Harry returns. The station management called me to implement the program. And being a baseball purist, I said I will go after the top sports announcers who are available. Musberger, Enberg, Harry Kalas, on and on…Jack Buck, and they said, "That's great. That's what we want. But, what do you think of this idea? We have access to a handful of show biz people. How about blending in their talents with those sports announcers?" I said, "Give anything a try."

They then delivered the likes of Bill Murray, Jim Belushi, Dennis

Franz of "Hill Street Blues," Tom Bosley, on and on—and we tied the two in together. I would meet each guest and coordinate and line up all the fill-in replacements. As this project wore on, I was getting calls from all over the United States from people dying to get on. Because people were speculating on who the next person was going to be. As my boss, Jim Dowdle, the president of Tribune Broadcasting, was to say later, it probably was the biggest PR coup in the history of the station. A classic case of turning a minus into a plus. We went on for 32 games.

The Cubs' management was beautiful. They let these guys take batting practice and hang around the clubhouse. I always took them on the team bus on the road games. That type of deal. The players could hardly wait to see who was going to show up each day that they could visit with. At the end of 32 games, Harry came back and this had really snowballed.

I never will forget the day he came back, when he showed up to wave to the great fans at Wrigley Field and got perhaps the most heartwarming ovation for a non-player in the history of that ballpark. It was an incredible thing to see and to have President Reagan calling on the phone to welcome him back. And to see the tears flowing from Harry's eyes when he looked out and saw this great outpouring of the people that he had considered himself one of all these years, was a tremendous thing.

Whether anybody could make a deal like that fly again, I have no way of knowing. But the conditions were right. The fact that the Cubs generally were figured to do very poorly on the field that season, but during that period when the fill-ins were there, did extremely well and were fighting for first place early in the season, just made it ever more captivating and it was great. We really enjoyed that.

I would like in the fantasy of my dreams to think that Jack Brickhouse and Vince and Lou Boudreau and the rest would still be here as part of this great company for ever and ever. But, we all have to take a pragmatic view of things—life in general—the evolution goes on and even though I don't see them every day as I once did, and fly around with them, the trains and the buses and the cabs and the whole thing, we stay in touch a lot. They were at my children's weddings and those were great reunions and, as far as this company is concerned, as a media company, I defy anyone to show me a company which through the years has had a more consistent goodness about it than WGN Radio and Television.

——— ARNE HARRIS ———

*Considered one of the best producer/directors of baseball in the
country. A native Chicagoan, he has been with WGN-TV since
1964.*

I'm the producer-director of the Cubs' telecasts. I've been doing
the game since 1964. It's kind of a funny story. I went to Drake
University in Des Moines and played some basketball there, but
then realized that I'm about 5'9" and I figured at that point that I
wasn't going anywhere being 5'9" and playing basketball.

I went to Drake in the middle '50s and television was then comparatively new. They were opening up a TV station in Des Moines
and I was majoring in drama and journalism at Drake and they let
the people in the drama and journalism department work in the television station. After going to school for a couple of years and working part-time at the TV station, I knew more about production than
probably a lot of people did in Chicago or around the country.

My mother passed away so I came back to Chicago. I had a
younger sister and my dad worked horrible hours. Went to WGN.
What had happened, I had met Jack Brickhouse in Des Moines doing a wrestling tour and Jack said if you ever come back to Chicago,
give me a call if you need a job. Well, in Des Moines I was doing
both production work, directing stuff and also doing some announcing. I did a man-on-the-street show, I did a disc jockey show, and,
in my mind, I really wasn't sure which part of the business I wanted
to go into.

I stopped by GN and Brickhouse remembered me and got me
an interview and I got hired as an assistant director at GN and while
there used to work shows with Vince Lloyd and Brickhouse and,
you know, all the sports guys around then. Harry Creighton—remember Harry? And while there, Abe Saperstein, the owner of the
Globetrotters, used to appear once in a while. Abe and I got to be
pretty good buddies. He was looking for a PA announcer to travel
around the world with the Globetrotters. He said, "You interested?"
And I said, "Yeah." I'm...you know, young—19-20 at the time—
and I said, "I'm still looking around."

So, I left GN and Abe hired me as the PA announcer/publicity guy and I traveled with the Harlem Globetrotters for three years around the world. Which was great. My first year was Meadowlark Lemon's first year, both a couple of kids sitting in the back of the bus. Looking at the world for the first time. Bob Gibson, the pitcher with the Cardinals, was with us. He was then making his mind up whether to pitch or play basketball. And he was very unhappy with the Cardinals because he felt they weren't giving him a chance to pitch and Abe offered him a year-round job with the Trotters both in the states and when they went to Europe in the summertime, and Gibby just about took it. At the last minute decided to play baseball. He ended up being a pretty good pitcher.

After three years, I met my wife-to-be, Arlene, and she wasn't too thrilled about me traveling around the world every day. So I went back to GN. They were doing the Cubs then, obviously, and the guy directing the games for them I knew was about ready to move up or move out or do something.

I went to GN and I said, "Look it, I'd like to come back here if I can, but I'd like to get a guarantee from you guys that I get a chance to do the Cub games." And they said, "Sure." So I went back to GN and in '64 I started doing the Cub games and I've been doing them ever since.

You guys have a great reputation—probably the best for baseball coverage.

Yeah. Probably. I think the fact that we were the only team to do all the games helped. They keep saying that we're the best; it's great to know and certainly it's appreciated. But you've got to remember that we did more than anybody else, too.

And, the thing that I ran into all the time is that, "Boy, your home stuff looks so great, but on the road it doesn't look as good." Well, that used to be the case 'cause when we first started doing games on the road, like anybody else, we tried to save money. So, instead of using five or six cameras that we used at home, we used three on the road. One of the cameras we didn't have on the road for a long time was the center-field shots and most of our pitcher-batter shots were from high home, which is horrible. First of all, more of the high-home camera shots are too high. Just pitcher-batter and second, a lot of them are shooting right through the screen. So, you get bug-eyed after a while. Now once we went to our center-field camera on the road, then our home coverage and road coverage began to look alike.

When I first started with GN, we only had four cameras at Wrigley Field. Now I've got nine. Eight or nine depending. Eight normally and then, if it's a night game or weekend game, I have nine.

When on the road, do you ever use the cameras of the home team?

No, because the telecasts are so complicated and there's so much money involved, we always want to do our own telecasts. There was a time in the early '70s when we did. In other words, teams came to Chicago they took our picture and when I went on the road, we took their picture. And that was fine sometimes, sometimes it was lousy. 'Cause, you know, depending on who was doing the game. But as soon as we could develop people on the road who could do games, 'cause in the '60s when I first started doing television, there weren't many people televising baseball. In fact, many of the crews on the road really learned baseball from me because we were the only station that really televised three-game series. They might do one game. You know, somebody in the National League might do one road game. But nobody did all the road games like we did. So basically, good or bad, the people who engineered and ran cameras on the road in the National League really learned baseball from us.

What were some of the more innovative shots that you guys invented?

Well, I think the center-field shot was a great shot. It's a great story how that thing was developed. We never had a center-field shot at Wrigley for a long time. That was before I came there. It was always a high-home camera. And what had happened is we booked ourselves a little league baseball game to do in the Chicago area. And the field was so small that we couldn't put a camera behind home plate, we had to find another position to use to get the pitcher-batter shot. And they finally decided on putting a camera in centerfield and that was our first center-field shot—a little league baseball game.

Was that Thillins?

Thillins, right. And from that point on it looked so good that we ended up using it at Wrigley Field.

Nobody had cameras in the dugouts for a long time. That's comparatively new in the last maybe 15-20 years. At Wrigley Field we have used cameras on top of the scoreboard, which certainly is an unusual shot, because at Wrigley Field, being by the lake you get a clear view of downtown Chicago—it's a great shot to sell the City of Chicago. There are times we have cameras on both foul lines looking in from the left-field corner, looking in from the right-field corner, trying to get the foul line angle and balls that are hit to either corner. Wrigley's a unique ballpark to direct baseball in because the corners are indented, so you can't stay with the high-home camera once the ball is hit because, if the ball goes in either corner, you're blocked off—you don't see it. So you have to cut off the coverage camera to another camera covering one corner or the other corner to be able to see the ball rolling in the corner.

I can tell you after doing games all these years that the two telecasts that stand out in my mind are the two pennant clinchers. The one in '84 and the one in '89.

Rick Sutcliffe is a real good pal of mine and Jody Davis, before he left the Cubs—they both are good pals of mine—and I remember in '84 that we were kidding around before the game. We were at Pittsburgh and a very small crowd. I'm guessing maybe 4-5,000 people and they were all Cub fans. I don't think there was one Pittsburgh fan in the Pittsburgh ballpark that night. And, we were kidding around in the dugout before the game if they were going to clinch it that night would the Cub fans run on the field in Pittsburgh. Rick and Jody were trying to figure out what can we do if we win it to celebrate on the field—make ourselves noteworthy in the history of baseball. And, I remember both of them saying that the ideal situation would be for Rick to strike out the last guy and for both these guys to jump on each other on the mound. And as it turned out, Rick did strike out the last guy and Jody and Rick both jumped on each other, as Jody came running out to the mound.

In '89, it was at Montreal. Mitch Williams struck out a Montreal catcher to win the game. And that was a little unique because a lot of the guys in Montreal had never seen a pennant-clinching celebration before. And, most of them spoke French. A lot of them did and it was kind of funny in the dressing room, with these guys not being used to what the heck was going on. They'd never seen it before. I got to the point where I thought, "I'm never going to see a pennant-winning celebration."

The most disappointing time of all, obviously, was in '69 when we thought we had it. I always thought the Cubs had the best team in baseball in the late '60s and early '70s.

They were the all-star team. Santo, Kessinger, Becker, Ernie, Billy Williams, Randy Hundley, Bill Hands, Kenny Holtzman, Fergie. I mean, they were the National League All-Star team. Some people bum rapped the Cub front office for years saying, "Well, they couldn't develop a winner." Well, you certainly can't bum rap John Holland, because I thought he had the best team and things just didn't work out. It's wild. I mean, it's almost like somebody up there is saying, "Have a good time but you aren't going to win it all."

Why do people love the Cubs so much? It's like a cult.

I'm not sure what the reason is, but I'll give you a couple of prime examples. I think our television, our telecasts, are better if they're on a winning streak than on a losing streak. Not that the coverage is any different, but reaction is different. Even the crews juiced up more when they're winning, rather than when they're losing. The crowd is more alive, so if the crowd is more alive, there are more reaction shots if they're winning than when they're losing. So, I mean, winning is certainly better for television than losing. I'm not talking just about ratings—I'm talking about the game itself.

But you also forget sometimes that people literally spent most of their winter planning to come out there for one game. Now, certainly they want to see the Cubs win. But, to them, it's a day out. It's a big deal. I mean, I walk out of that truck sometimes—I'll give you an example: when Ernie Banks would play for the Cubs, I've walked out of that truck among the people when the Cubs have lost a doubleheader, I'm talking like, you know, 8-4 and 9-1. But Ernie hit a home run in both games. And those people left that ballpark happy. I mean, they want to see the Cubs win but they saw Ernie hit a home run. I mean, how do you disappoint people like that? It's an amazing thing. I marvel at it every day.

The last couple of days they've had a horrible home stand. They lost a series to the Dodgers. They lost a series to the Padres. In three or four of those games, they've lost the game in the eighth or ninth inning because of passed balls or mistakes that you hope won't happen this late in the season and, yet yesterday, they played the Giants and they scored a couple of runs with two out at the end of the game—there are 35,000 people standing up. It's just an amazing thing.

When I first started the games in the early '60s, and then after '69, '70, '71, '72, they weren't always filling the ballpark. People forget that. They had some lean years. I think the guy that really turned that franchise around is Leo Durocher. Now, they didn't win with Leo. But Leo kept their name in the paper every day. 'Cause he always did something.

From that point on, as you say, "cult" is probably the right kind of word. I go on the road. I mean, it's the damndest thing you ever saw in your life. We go to Houston and there are 12,000 people there—11,000 are wearing Cub shirts.

The cable thing really—aside from Leo—the thing that really made the Cubs an American team is obviously the cable thing. And the thing that's surprising about the cable thing is that they are popular in towns—I mean, if there was no team in town, you'd say, great, people could see them play every day so that's why they're popular. But they're popular in a lot of towns where there are teams, which is kind of strange.

I remember one time in San Francisco we were panning the crowd and the phone rang in the truck. It was the FBI. They spotted some guy they wanted for questioning for pick-pocketing and they spotted him in the crowd. They wanted to know if I still had the tape of the crowd shot I took the inning before. We gave it to them. I think they caught the guy, too.

I'll tell you, of all the shots I've taken, it's hard to pinpoint one —but, I do remember in '89, you may have seen or heard of it. One of the shots that probably was seen more than any other. Ryno hit a home run and a postman was on duty over the left-field wall. I guess he had the radio on and heard somebody, Harry or somebody, who's ever doing radio at the time, yelling there it goes, he jumped out of his car and caught the ball—leaping catch. We got a great shot of it. And the poor guy, they wanted to fire him for leaving his job. They got so much heat, that I think they gave him a raise.

I'm lucky. I really am. It was a question when I was a kid whether I wanted to be in front of the mike or behind the mike. But I always wanted to do sports. I'm lucky there.

I don't have many autographs. I mean I've got a lot of pictures, 'cause I've taken pictures with a lot of guys that have played. But the only autograph we have in the house, really, I mean, there may be one or two laying around somewhere, but the only one we show is—we've had Ronald Reagan out at the ballpark a couple of times. And, he wrote a little note to me. He's got very scribbly handwriting and all he said was, he was on a couple of times, "Hi, Arnie. Thanks for everything. Ronald Reagan." Which I thought was kind of a kick. But I mean, where else do you get a chance to work with presidents? When Harry got sick, we worked with every big name movie star in the country.

It's a fun job. The only thing you hope for sometimes is—you know, I'd love to see them win the whole darn thing one time.

Any difference in directing Brickhouse as opposed to Caray?

Ah...there's always a difference. I marvel at Jack Brickhouse for a couple of reasons. One, many of the games that I worked with Jack, he worked by himself. He didn't have a color man. And rain delays and three-and-a-half hour ball games he did by himself. Jack was a unique personality. And you have to marvel at him more because here's a guy that did games through all those years and never had a winner. I mean, that's tough. The average guy goes to work and you have a good day now and then, right? Or a good year, now and then. Poor Jack never had a winner. I mean, the guy was amazing to have all that enthusiasm and never have a winner.

Harry, on the other hand, is a different kind of guy. Harry's unique broadcasting style where he talks to me on the air, asks questions—people love that. I thought to myself when Harry came over, boy...and he started doing that—I said, "Are people going to go for stuff like that?" They love it. His use of his color man, Steve Stone, I think is tremendous. I mean, he knows just when to bring Steve in and when to use him to the best of Steve's knowledge and get the most out of him. He's got a unique way of being able to deal with people whereas Jack didn't really have to do that, 'cause Jack worked by himself most of the time.

Many people still think that Harry Creighton used to get "bombed" doing his Hamm's Beer commercials.

No...no...no. You know, I don't think I've ever seen Harry take a drink in the booth. What happened was—we used to do the Hamm's commercials live. And what would happen is he'd hold the glass up to his lip and we'd cut away. Your imagination would —they'd swear they saw Harry guzzle down beer, but he never did.

Harry was a good guy. Harry was unique 'cause Harry really wasn't a sportscaster as such. They made him one. He was a staff announcer at GN for a long time. And, he was like Lloyd Pettit. When they hired Lloyd, he was really more of a staff announcer than anything else. He had never seen a hockey game, 'til he did a Blackhawk game.

But, no, Harry, he was a good guy. It was funny, I'd bump into him all the time saying, "Boy, that's all that guy does is drink." And he never drank. All he did was hold the glass up to his mouth and then we cut away back to the ballpark.

The Wrigley Field booth we used to have was at the corner of the press box. Right at the end. The camera was on the ramp and Harry would be sitting doing the commercials looking out so people underneath him and people walking up and down the ramps would just stand in line—six deep—watching him do a Hamm's commercial. But he never drank. When it was over he probably had a few and the way some of those games went, he probably wanted a drink. But on the air—no.

As usual, he speaks his mind.

In the mid-'50s you teamed with Jack Buck and Joe Garagiola on KMOX-St. Louis covering the Cardinals. Some consider this the best team ever.

When I was with the White Sox, everybody raved about the team between myself and Jimmy Piersall, because it was strictly uninhibited. None of the usual school of announcers...don't say anything critical about the home team or you get fired. I thought that was an outstanding team from the standpoint of fan enjoyment and I think Steve Stone and I right now are a pretty good team.

So, it's hard to compare things. Jack Buck, of course, an outstanding announcer and Garagiola was one of the early color men and was very good.

He was one of the first jocks, wasn't he?

Well, no, the guy I broke in with was long before him. Gabby Street. Gabby and I started in St. Louis and then we worked together a long time until he passed away. You see, the difference between Gabby—all of his humor came from things that actually happened. It wasn't a joke book routine like you cut out funny quips out of a newspaper and use them whenever you can. Here, everything he talked about he had lived.

When did you start on the air?

1945. The last year the Cubs won a pennant. Yeah, they beat out the Cardinals that year. And I was, of course, doing it for the Cardinals.

Do you see a difference in attitude in players when you started in '45 and now?

You definitely do. And all for the better because they make a lot of money now. Instead of reading *The Sporting News*, they're reading the *Wall Street Journal*.

So you think you have a higher caliber of ballplayer?

Well, certainly more people have graduated from high school and perhaps even from college today than did 25 years ago. It's just the natural development of our society.

Not too long ago individuals owned ball clubs. Now it's corporations.

Well, it's a bottom-line operation. I think the old time rich sportsman is no longer involved. If you have a corporate ownership, it's owned by the corporation.

I don't think baseball is really owned for the enjoyment of the fans. Now that Bill Veeck is gone, he was the last owner who really cared about the people. And now it's bottom line. How much money can you make. You know, they talk about the fact that the baseball ticket hasn't risen as much as a Broadway show ticket has risen or a movie ticket. They don't tell you about the hidden increases. The hot dog costs four or five times more. A bottle of beer costs you four or five times more. When you take a family to the ballpark, the admission ticket may be relatively reasonable, but by the time you finish getting the kid out of the ballpark, it's cost you a pretty penny.

How do you describe Cub fans?

Fans are fans everywhere. As soon as your team has a chance to win, they come out of the woodwork. The only difference for the Cub fan is they never won. And yet they keep turning out. They keep turning out in goodly numbers for a reason that nobody seems to understand and they should. And that's because the Cubs play day baseball. And they've been making fans out of youngsters forever. A kid goes to the ballpark. He's home by 5:30. The mother and the father don't have to worry about where he is. He gets on the "L," he rides to the ballpark, gets back on the "L," rides home and from that day on he's a Cub fan. And he later grows up, has children...the same thing goes on.

And—the Cubs now have lights. They didn't want lights. They were forced by baseball to put in lights so that they could live up to the contract with the networks in the event they had a playoff or a World Series. But we still draw more people in the daytime than we do at night. They average about 31,000 per game in a stadium that only seats 36,000. And play more than 80% of their games in the daytime.

Would you go with another team?

Oh, I doubt it seriously, but you never say "never." I can't conceive my being happy anywhere but in Chicago with the abundance of day games.

Do you see any difference between Sox and Cubs fans?

No, that's an old wives' tale about if you're a Cub fan you hate the White Sox. If you're a Sox fan you hate the Cubs. It sounds good and reads good, but I used to broadcast the games at night for the White Sox and quite often, as frequently happens, both are at home at the same time. I'd go out and sit in the sunshine at Wrigley Field during the day game and then head right for Comiskey Park. I'd give autographs at Wrigley Field and see the same people at Comiskey Park that I had earlier in the day at Wrigley Field. So I know that fans are watching both games. It's the ideal setup. The White Sox play most of their games at night. The Cubs play about 82% of their games in the daytime. So, the baseball fan in Chicago can see...has the best of two worlds. Moreover, the Cubs by playing in the daytime, keep up their mystique for the young fans.

Now ball clubs are hiring high-priced marketing and merchandising people, trying to emulate the Cubs. And the Cubs, because of the foresight of a guy named Phil Wrigley, who when it all started, turned over all his baseball radio broadcasts to whoever wanted to carry it. They didn't have to pay a dollar. At that time, the old-fashioned owners thought if they listened to the games they wouldn't come out and watch them. Mr. Wrigley proved how wrong it was and then when television came in, the same thing happened.

And now, of course, the Cubs by virtue of the day games...out here—I'm in Los Angeles—you'd be surprised when you get to the ballpark tonight to get the reaction of the fans. They may still be Dodger fans, but through watching the Cubs—you know, Cub games come here about 11:00 in the morning. And so by watching the Cubs, they have kind of a curiosity about the players. They may still want the Dodgers, or the Angels, or whoever it might be to win, but they're more interested in coming when they play the Chicago Cubs because they know the players from watching them on TV all the time.

What has been your biggest thrill covering the Cubs?

Oh, well, you know, the Cubs—they're perennial losers. And

when they won in '84 that was a tremendous thrill. They had a 2-0 lead going out to San Diego, needing only one victory because of the five-game playoff in those days, and they couldn't win another game. That was a big thrill—winning the first two and realizing that for the first time they had a chance to go to the World Series since I started broadcasting with the Cardinals in 1945—that's the last time they were in the World Series. And then in '89 the same thing happened. They won their division. That, too, was a thrill.

How do you describe Chicago?

Well, Chicago is the most dynamic—let me think of the word—let me see...No.1—it's the greatest city in the country. Forget about New York. People are afraid to go to New York. Chicago—it's a young, dynamic mixture of sports-minded, fun-minded people. That's about the best way I can describe it. You go to Chicago as a stranger, but you find you make friends right away if you want to. Because people will draw you into their conversations, they're nice to you, they'll have a drink, they'll chew the fat—it isn't the suspicion and the awareness of other people being around you find in other cities. It's really a tremendous city.

THE FOURTH ESTATE

Author of several bestselling books and the number one columnist in Chicago. For years an astute observer of the Chicago scene. He is not happy with the state of present-day baseball nor the Cubs. He definitely knows his baseball.

What do you believe the average Cub player is thinking today? What's on his mind?

Since you asked me this question at a time when a team that was picked not only to win the division, but probably win the National League title and maybe win the World Series, just lost their ninth straight, I don't think there's anything going on in their minds. This is the year they go down as one of the...not one of the major disappointments in Cub history, but in the last 10-20 years. This is a very disappointing team. I don't know what's going on in their minds. Obviously, it's not baseball. They run the bases like clowns. They represent to me the deterioration of baseball—the quality of baseball—this Cub team does.

People talk about how—it's become a cliché—your modern athlete is better than your old time athlete. Bull shit! They may eat a better balanced diet. They may not go out after a game and drink beer the way Mantle and Ford did...the way Hack Wilson did. But are they better baseball players? There may be more outfielders who are fleet of foot. But does that mean they're better outfielders. The modern ballplayer doesn't play fundamental baseball as well as players did during what I consider the golden age of baseball, which was from about 1947, when Jackie Robinson broke the color barrier, and sometime into the 1970s. I think that's when the greatest baseball was played.

Expansion diluted the quality of players. Professional football wasn't that big until they started the Super Bowl hype. So, a lot of guys who would have become baseball players were able to go into football and make pretty big money. Professional basketball is a recent success. We've only had a franchise in this town—a successful franchise—for 25 years in Chicago. So, it might be that a John Paxton might be an outfielder. Or Michael Jordan might be a slugging first baseman or pitcher, or damn near anything he wanted. All these other sports—hockey has drained off ballplayers. Tennis—there are some fine athletes who are playing tennis who might have been playing baseball. Remember, at the end of World War II there were only really two major professional sports. Boxing and baseball. Pro football was still a struggling thing. Pro basketball really didn't exist. There was boxing and there was baseball. And college football. Those were the big sports in America.

Who are the heroes they talk about in the golden age of sports? Jack Dempsey, Babe Ruth, Red Grange. They're not talking about any basketball players. They're not talking about any pro football players. So, the sport gets diluted. You got guys playing baseball today who are no better than Double-A or Triple-A players in those days. In those days, you had Class D, Class C, Class B, Class A, Double-A, Triple-A. You had professional baseball all over the country and to make it to the big leagues, you had to really be a well-rounded baseball player. Somebody like "Neon," "Dion," Leon," whatever they call this guy, who—my God—he would have been offered a Class C contract. They'd say, "Go down there, kid, and learn how to play the game." He wouldn't have made it to the major leagues. He would have been a Class B minor league ballplayer. There were guys who would hit .370 in the minors, but they had a qualm. Maybe the guy was an infielder and he had a really poor arm. Sorry—you know. Sure you can hit .280 up here, but you don't have a position.

So, you've got guys who are playing major league baseball who really shouldn't be playing major league baseball. There's an enormous shortage of pitching. When was the last time—except for Tony Gwynn—that you saw somebody shorten swing with two strikes on him, then just make contact? Today you've got .245 hitters. They have two strikes on them—they swing out of their heels instead of just trying to do what Nellie Fox did. Get the bat on it and do what many fine hitters—many power hitters used to do. I saw Johnny Mize. My God, Johnny Mize hit 51 home runs one year. I saw Johnny Mize shorten up on his bat with two strikes and go with the pitch. Knock a single. Drive in a run. You don't see that today.

The management of baseball teams has lost control of the players. They have no control over the players. I think a manager, at best, his only job is to try to keep them alert and hope that they'll listen to what he and the coaches say. I don't think managers can say, "Look, you boob, here's what I'm going to do to you. If you don't straighten out your act, I'm going to trade you to the St. Louis Browns. You can go down there and you're going to make less money, you'll never get a chance at a World Series check and you will be obscure the rest of your life." You can't do that to the guy. "You can't do that to me. I've got so many years in. I can veto a trade. I'll be a free agent next year. Screw you."

The power has now shifted to the players. A guy only needs— if he's good —or if he's better than mediocre and he's not a fool with his money—if a guy can get in eight or 10 years in the major leagues, there's really no reason why he has to work again. Give somebody who's 25 years old, 10 years at an average of $1 million a year and, even after he pays his agent and his taxes, he should wind up with a few annuities, plus he's going to get a major league pension eventually. He's going to wind up with $2-3 million bucks stashed. Put that in tax-free municipals, you know—my God. I'm 35. I'm assured of having $150-175,000 a year the rest of my life.

When Moose Skowron was a rookie...Moose lives in Chicago. Moose said that he made the team in spring training. Some of the veterans took him to dinner. They said, "You're on the team now. You don't screw up. If you screw up that can cost us money. We rely on World Series money. We budget for World Series money." Do you think that anybody—Jose Canseco—really cares about World Series money? How many guys—even on the Cubs—okay, they don't make it this year. Is Andre Dawson going to have to go out and take out a loan? Ryne Sandberg—any of them? World Series money—that's kind of cute. It's like Michael Jordan picked up an extra $60,000 'cause the Bulls won the championship. That won't even buy him a car—the kind of cars he likes to drive.

So the big money's a big factor. If a guy is good—not great— just good, he's going to make a vast amount of money. If he doesn't get injured, he's going to have a long career because today they're so desperate for ballplayers. If a guy stays in good shape, which these guys do because they understand the economics of it, they're working out all winter, they're pumping iron, they're getting strong, they're doing all the exercises so they can play 'til they're 36-38-40 years old. And so you would think that since the money is assured, your wealth is assured. You're not thinking, "Geez, when I hang up my uniform, what am I going to do, open a bar, maybe get a guy and go in partnership in a bowling alley, the way Gabby Hartnett did?" Andy Pafko, in the Chicago area, he was working some golf club. In those days, they had to worry, you know. Stan Hack, I think he had a restaurant. Or maybe I can be a coach. Maybe a minor league manager, you know. Why are all minor league managers former second-rate ballplayers? Because they didn't make the big bucks.

That was one of the unfair raps against that poor goof Campanis, who got in all the trouble for his remark. Maybe what Campanis may have been saying is that, are you going to ask a Willie Mays to go manage in the minor leagues? Are you going to ask a great star to go be a minor league manager? No. The guys that go down there are second-rate ballplayers. And, that may have been what he was trying to say, that the great black stars are now making a lot of money. They don't want to stick around and go down to some hick town.

So you've got baseball diluted. There's the big money. Probably less peer pressure. Skowron said that a few years later he was sitting down with rookies warning them—"You don't goof off on this team. You play solid, fundamental baseball. You'll get into the World Series."

You don't see solid, fundamental baseball being played today. My God, they talk about some of these guys being able to hit behind the runner as if this is something like they reinvented the wheel. It used to be everybody knew how to hit behind the runner. People knew how to bunt. There were guys that played for the Cubs back in the '40s and the '50s who would be 12-year veterans making big money today. Ransom Jackson—he was a good solid .275 hitter at third base. He hit 15 home runs. And he knew how to play third base.

So, I don't think the ballplayers today are as good—individual ballplayers, obviously are as good—but in general, no. There are just too many other sports that have competed. There are too many teams and not enough good ballplayers. They don't spend the time in the minors. I remember when guys came up; my God, Hank Sauer was almost 30 years old before he got up. And that was only because some manager in the minors insisted he swing a heavy bat which turned him into a home run slugger. That's right out of pulp —these old pulp stories. And he was a good minor league player. But until he shifted to the heavy bat, he was just a minor league—

a Triple-A, .330 hitter who couldn't make it in the majors. And even Sauer was a flawed player because he was a slow outfielder. So he wound up with the Cubs. He was a big slugger with the Cubs, but the Yankees wouldn't have wanted him. Are they going to put him in that big left field? Even with hitting his home runs, he couldn't have played with the Yankees. He couldn't have played with the Cardinals. With the quality teams. He fit in fine on a team that needed the box office guy who could hit 30-35 home runs and the team would finish in fifth place. Because he was a flawed ballplayer.

The best teams didn't have flawed ballplayers. And today—every team has flawed ballplayers. Guys who don't know fundamentals. Cubs have got a center fielder, for Pete's sake. He's supposed to be a fast runner, which he is. The natural place in the batting order for him is lead-off man. He doesn't want to take a base-on balls. Now in 1952 or '53 on a good team, the manager would say, "You will swing at those 2-0 pitches, huh? You will swing at 'em down in the minor leagues. Goodbye. Here's your ticket. We'll see you someday, when you learn the strike zone."

How would Durocher do today?

They would drive Durocher crazy. Durocher couldn't handle it. The last guy of the Durocher type who was able to handle it—and he couldn't handle it—was Billy Martin. I think Billy Martin managed partly through intimidation, partly by drinking with his guys, partly by being such an emotional person. Billy Martin was able to motivate these guys. He was ready to duke it out with Reggie Jackson right in the dugout. I think it almost takes that today.

If I was running the Tribune, I'd find myself a manager about 6'8," about 250 lbs. with scars on his face, some guy who had been in Vietnam or somewhere and have him scare them. Threaten to beat the hell out of them. That might work. I don't know what can work with these people. They just...they're going to play at their own pace. Guy makes a baserunning blunder—what do you do? Sit him down? Well, maybe you might shift him to the minors if he's basically a borderline player. But if he's a fairly good player, what can you do with him. You gotta play him. Can you cut his salary the next year? They used to do that.

I think managers are very limited in their impact on a team. I think that probably the coaches he picks are important. I mean, having good pitching coaches is very important. But, I think baseball has become essentially front office—it starts in the front office— if you've got somebody up there who knows how to find young talent, young pitchers. It's pitching, pitching, pitching. That's all the game is about now. Teams of pitching are good teams and it's always been that way. But today, it's even more important because there aren't enough pitchers to go around.

But I find baseball today, and it's not just nostalgia, I find the level of play to be not as good as it used to be. There's great athleticism. You've got good athletes out there. But when I see guys who don't know how to bunt. I see guys who don't know how to run the bases. I see outfielders who don't know how to throw to a cut-off man. Compare that to a guy like Jimmy Piersall, who, by the time he made it to the major leagues, knew exactly how to throw—knew how to play the outfield; it was an art. There are so many blunders. So many blunders. And then when you see teams with a lot of talent and they look half asleep, such as the present Cub team.

What bugs me though, overall, is the hitters who don't know how to take a walk. Refuse to take a walk. Guys who, if they swing out of their heels all year, they're going to have 15 home runs. What's 15 home runs? What's that? That's one home run every 10 games? I'd rather have a few singles thrown in, in a key situation. Selfish players. Players don't want to listen. Aren't coachable. A Cub center fielder is Rookie of the Year. Fine. He goes out and does a book on himself. My God, I'm 58. I haven't done a book on myself. And I've done a hell of a lot more than be Rookie of the Year.

The kids today—you and I didn't have as many leisure time options as kids have today. We got our baseball off the radio. If we wanted to see a game, we went out to the ballpark. And we could get into the ballpark. Today, even if a kid wants to go to the ballpark, can he get in? In most cities, the ballparks are located in places that you have to drive to. At least in Chicago a kid is fortunate enough, a city kid, he can go by public transportation. Christ, when I was in Kansas City, I went out and looked at their ballparks. Lovely, lovely ballparks. Football and baseball. How in the hell do you get there. If you're a kid, your mommy or daddy's gotta drive you.

The modern young fan today in a city like Chicago might be a Cub fan when they're going okay. There are those who will go out there just because it's a social thing. They go out there because they want to sit and drink beer in the bleachers and it's a fun thing to do, but they're not really baseball fans. Most of them just don't pay attention. I quizzed some of the yuppies who claim to be Cub fans. And I asked them things that—when I was a kid, if you would have asked me these questions 20 years earlier...30 years—I would have known. They don't know about five years ago. They don't know about 10 years ago. They jump aboard.

That's the danger in owning a franchise. If a team slips, look what happened in Pittsburgh. When they got bad, everyone disappeared. You had mentioned to me that you thought this was a Cub town. Won't necessarily remain a Cub town. If they don't come up with a winner, I'm not saying it will happen in one year, but if there should be several years, as take Atlanta, they weren't filling the seats in Atlanta. And today with these salaries. Used to be if you drew a million fans, you had a good year. Today, a million fans, hell, you're going to go bust. They're not going to get the big TV contracts.

So, it's a Cub town right now for a lot of historic factors. Marketing is the big thing. The Sox were foolish—they pulled themselves off commercial television where they could be seen. An entire generation of fans grew up in this town not knowing what a good hitter Harold Baines was. They never got to see him. They had Ron Kittle—one of the most personable, appealing sluggers in modern times in Chicago. People didn't see Ron Kittle. If Kittle had been a Cub, my God, he would have been a hero. It's a Cub town because the Cubs are there. If you're home for whatever reason, if you're a shut-in, if you're retired, if you work nights, you got the Cubs on television. So, a lot of it has been merchandising. Marketing. The Cubs have been visible. If the Cubs had been buried off on cable and the Sox were the big team, a lot of young people who say they're Cub fans today would be Sox fans.

So you think it could turn. It could go to the Sox.

Oh, sure. They've got this new ballpark and, I'll tell you, the Tribune Company is very lucky this year. Sox come up with a new ballpark. Terrific year which is why, I think, one of the reasons the Cubs went out and signed these free agents. They realize the potential for competition was there. This isn't a dumb corporation. They better beef things up. They've got the edge, they want to keep the edge. They were lucky; the Sox have floundered almost as bad as the Cubs. Right now, people in this town don't care about either team.

Well-known writer and television commentator, who grew up in Champaign, Illinois, listening to Bert Wilson on the radio doing the Cub games.

"Part of the cult of the Cubs is unhealthy. It's the cult of failure and mediocrity and isn't this cute—all this suffering. I don't think it's cute at all. I think the Cubs have been badly run more often than not for as long as I have been following them. All teams go through ups and downs, but this is ridiculous."

It was my birthday present each year to be taken by my parents to a Cubs game. Usually, a Sunday doubleheader when those were quite common. I also would sell subscriptions to the local newspaper, the *Champaign-Urbana Courier*, now defunct, and often either by selling newspapers or selling magazines in connection with the newspaper. If you passed a certain quota, they'd take a bus load of you up to the Cubs game.

Aside from that it was radio. Back in those days, radio was everything. There was no television in my house, until I came back from Oxford in 1964. So I had no television upbringing at all.

What was your reaction when you went to Wrigley Field?

Well, to me it looked enormous. I mean, today when you go into one of those ballparks, the giant concrete donuts they've built in places like St. Louis, Cincinnati, Philadelphia, and Pittsburgh, Wrigley Field looks quaint and cute. It didn't look cute then. It looked like a big deal to me. But anything remotely touching major league baseball was developed in a great aura of mystery and grandeur at that point. As was Chicago. Chicago had a tremendous hold on the imagination of someone growing up downstate.

In those days, to live in Champaign, Illinois, was to be midway between two major league cities with four major league teams. You'd hear Harry Caray and Gabby Street on the Griesedieck Brothers' baseball network for the Cardinals and you had Buddy Blattner, I think sponsored by Falstaff, doing the Browns. You had

Bob Elson doing the White Sox and Bert Wilson doing the Cubs.

All my friends became Cardinal fans and grew up happy and I picked the Cubs. I don't know why. I think the pull of Chicago. And no doubt I was probably fumbling down the radio one day and found Bert Wilson.

Chicago is in some ways the capitol of the United States. It's radio power beamed out all over the Middle West. Remember, back when I was growing up, they had a "Game of the Day" on the radio. And quite often that was the Cubs 'cause they were playing more day games than anyone else.

Do you believe baseball fans are disillusioned to some degree to-day?

I don't believe that. I mean, I hear people saying it's out there, but I don't get it. I think what people are loyal to is not particular players. I mean there is somewhat more mobility among players now, which I think is an altogether good thing. But I don't think people, it turns out, are loyal to particular players. I mean, they like them and they like to see them in their team year after year, but if they're not there, the uniform is still there. They're loyal to the logo, the team, the pennant, the ballpark, the radio network. It's a whole experience that is not, I think, in any way significantly weakened by the mobility of the modern player.

Do you think there are too many teams and not enough talent?

I think it's false. One of the themes of *Men at Work* was to say why baseball today is better than ever, which I profoundly believe. Sure, there are 26 teams, soon to be 28 teams, there were only 16 when I was growing up. The population of the country is vastly larger. Black players are not shut out as they used to be. Latin American players are now a source of great talent. I think the pool of available talent has expanded much more rapidly than the major leagues' ranks have expanded.

I'm still a Cub fan, but I'm on the board of directors of the Orioles. You know, you tend to follow and become attached to the team you can hear on the radio and it's a little hard to hear the Cubs out here.

Part of the cult of the Cubs is unhealthy. It's the cult of failure and mediocrity and isn't this cute—all this suffering. I don't think it's cute at all. I think the Cubs have been badly run more often than not for as long as I have been following them. All teams go through ups and downs, but this is ridiculous.

I wrote a column a few years ago about putting lights in Wrigley Field. I was ardently in favor of putting lights in Wrigley Field because the tendency to treat the Cubs as a little baseball Williamsburg, a little artifact to be preserved, is unhealthy. I believe what makes baseball not only charming and amusing but important, is that it's a severe meritocracy. Over 162-game season. Excellence tells and mediocrity shows. It is not funny for a franchise to go as long between successes as the Cubs have gone...with all the advantages the Cubs have.

DICK DOZER

Veteran Tribune *beat reporter who covered the Cubs from 1958 to 1981.*

My first full-time year was 1958. First game I covered was 1955, when I filled in for the late Irving Vaughn late in the season in a Cub game that didn't amount to a whole lot because there were only about 1,000 people out there I think.

When did you retire?
I retired in 1981 at the end of the baseball season.

In that period of time, what was the reputation of the Chicago franchise?
Well, I think for a time there, it was sort of a joke. Because of the time in the early '60s when they added what was called an athletic director and a College of Coaches where...Mr. Wrigley's idea was to rotate the coaches as manager so that he didn't have to fire anybody. And as you probably know, there were six people involved in that. I can list them. Elvin Tappe, Harry Craft, Charlie Metro, Lou Klein, Vedie Himzl, and one who never actually served as manager, Goldie Holt. And there was Bob Kennedy, who's also included in that, but he later became a full-time manager, so he was a little of both.

Did the stature of the Cub organization rise when Durocher was hired in 1966?
Well, yeah. We were at Long Beach. I remember we were greeting him and I was sort of in awe of the man because of his reputation. I think, from the start, it wasn't that much change. But as he progressed and as the team progressed through 1969, when they had a pretty good season, and even '70 when they had a good season and finished even closer to Pittsburgh, I think Pittsburgh beat them out by five games, whereas '69, the season everybody remembers, the Mets beat the Cubs out by eight games. So, I think as Durocher stuck around, the reputation of the Cubs grew and

maybe he kind of wore out his welcome toward the end, but most managers do after seven years, don't they?

Would you say that, in your tenure covering the Cubs, he was the best manager the Cubs had?

I think he probably was. Maybe, only because of his longevity. There were other short-term managers that you couldn't really judge how well they had done because, first of all, the talent wasn't there. He did have himself surrounded with a pretty good ball club at a couple of stages. And, of course, the fact that some of them have gone on to the Hall of Fame—Williams, Banks, and Ferguson Jenkins—is an indication that he had good talent.

Was he difficult for reporters to deal with on a day-to-day basis?

Yeah, he was in a large sense, but the one thing I would have to say about Durocher was that he didn't carry a grudge against any reporter. In other words, you might think that when you went home one night that he was furious with you for asking a question that he didn't like, but the next day you come out and he'll say, "Hi, buddy, how you doin?" and you're starting over, more or less.

I probably should relate the one incident that I had with Durocher, because I received some rather unwanted publicity when, late in the 1969 season, I can't give you the date, but it was certainly in September, I had gone into his little cubicle like all the reporters did when we were surrounding him and he was shaving. And I said, "Leo, is your team tired?" Which I thought was a pretty logical question, because that had been circulating that the Cubs looked tired and they were losing and weren't winning like they were earlier in that season.

He said, "Well, I'll tell you what, let's go find out." So he's got shaving soap all over his face and he takes the reporters that are standing around him and he goes out into the main body of the clubhouse and he says, "Everybody out of the shower." Well, you could have heard a money clip drop in there that day. They all came out of the shower or in the various stages of dressing in front of their lockers and he says, "Mr. Dozer here wants to ask a question. So I'll have him ask the same question to you that he asked me." So, now, I don't know what to do. I've gotta do it of course. So I said, "Well, what I had asked Leo was, are you fellas tired?" And, of course, not a soul said a word. Nothing. And then he turns around and he says, "Well, I guess that's your answer." And he goes back about his business.

And, of course, that made the papers, the fact that I had asked that question. It even got on the wire service, I later found out. But, then I talked to some of the players privately after that, and one in particular I had an awfully good rapport with was Don Kessinger, and he said, "You bet we were tired. No question about it. But nobody wanted to say anything that day in front of everybody else."

I think probably the thing with Durocher, he did have a fault, he played his regulars too much. He had a little bench depth there with Popovich and Willie Smith and I think Al Spangler, but it seems that even in a game where you'd be leading by seven or eight runs or trailing by the same amount, he'd stay right with the regulars all the way through and didn't rest some players when he might have. I think in retrospect he thought that maybe that was a mistake also. That he should have rested players. I'd heard him say that off the record a time or two after the season, or in subsequent seasons, that maybe he should have rested some players a little more than he did.

What was Phil Wrigley like as an owner?

Well, I thought Wrigley was doing it the right way. I think you see too much meddling by owners these days. I think there's some pretty good examples of that in, well, maybe the Yankees where Steinbrenner tried to meddle too much. I think when you surround yourself with the right people, you should stay a little bit aloof.

But Wrigley was not that bad a person to get ahold of. He was always accessible. I called him a number of times on his private number in the Wrigley Building and he would answer it. Not even a secretary. And, so he was quite accessible, but I don't think he wanted to be accessible. I think he wanted to surround himself with the right people and that's why he tried all these innovations with the athletic director, several different general managers along the way. At one point, he even had a newspaperman as a general manager, Jimmy Gallagher; goes way back. He was kind of an innovator, and wanted somebody else to run the club and wanted them to run it successfully, but recognized the fact that he was there to be talked to if he had to be.

Was there one reporter that was particularly hard on the Cubs?

I don't think we had that in Chicago. Not among the beat writers. We did, occasionally, by a columnist. Columnists, of course, are famous for that the world over because they don't have to live day-in and day-out with the ball club. They can make their little observation on a hit-and-run basis and sometimes the ownership or the management would be a little disturbed by what they had written because the guys at the racetrack one day and he's talking to football players another day and now he drops in and talks about baseball. He really doesn't know what you know because you're with the team every day. I don't know if there was any resentment among the writers. I think we chuckled once in a while when one of these guys would write something, as a columnist, that was kind of vitriolic about the team.

Who do you remember doing that?

Rick Talley was one that occasionally wrote some things that aggravated—he didn't aggravate me, don't get me wrong, I enjoyed reading it sometimes—and, in a way, I guess we were glad we didn't have to say it. But the columnists on the *Tribune* were not that way. David Condon was our No.1 columnist and in later years Bob Verdi. They didn't write things that would, to me, sound mean or harsh. Once in a while a little sarcastic and that's about as far as they went.

Was it hard to be objective as a reporter?

Not at all. I don't think I had that problem at all. People used to ask me because I spent half the season with the Cubs and half the season with the White Sox, "Well, which team do you like?" And I said, "I like them both." That was my answer. My stock answer to everybody. And the players, they were great to get along with...most of them, we had a few over the years that give you a little hard time, but I was not a fan. I did want to see them succeed, but I don't think I was a fan to the extent that I was a "homer" or anything of that sort.

Who was the most cooperative Cub you dealt with?

Over the years? Oh, golly, I could name an awful lot of them. Banks, Williams, Kessinger, Beckert, that takes us to another era, of course. Joe Pepitone, I got along fine with him. He was kind of a character at times. Then there were some pitchers—Fergie Jenkins was excellent. Bill Hands—they called him "Froggie"—he was a great guy to talk to. Phil Regan, the relief pitcher that we had for a couple of good seasons. You know, I could name virtually all the Cubs. I didn't have any problem with any of them, really.

Was there one, or a couple that were tough to deal with?

Well, Dave Kingman I think is going to be one that anyone you talk to will mention as...he ran hot and cold. Sometimes, he was all sweetness and light and other times, for no good reason, he'd be quite aggravated. He might have read something that one reporter had written and so he's mad at all the reporters. That kind of a thing. Thinking that maybe they'd all written the same thing, whether he'd read it or not. I thought that was kind of unfair.

The only toughness involved with any ballplayer is when they don't say much. When they're a "yes" and "no" interview, that's tough. Rick Reuschel was a fine guy, but all he ever said was "yes" and "no." He was always nice to talk to, but then when you got done with your interview after the game, you'd say, "Well, what have I got here? Not much."

In talking to people, Yosh Kawano comes up all the time. Do you have any stories of Yosh?

Actually, he stowed away on one of those ship-to-shore boats that used to take the players to Catalina Island and this, to the best of my knowledge, is the year 1938, 'cause he himself said, "I think it was 1938." I would say he'd be a teenager at that time. Probably 13 years old, 12-13-14 in there somewhere. He stowed away and got friendly with some people after they landed over there. He was from the Los Angeles area. He got a job immediately as a bat boy. And then, of course, they got him to cleanin' uniforms and spikes and everything else. He did all the dirty work around there. Then Frankie Frisch took a liking to him and kind of took him under his wing and, according to Yosh, was kind of responsible for him getting his feet on the ground with the Cubs.

Then, of course, Yosh grew up through the organization and stayed with them and has now the title of Equipment Manager and they've even named the clubhouse after him. So, he is really the only survivor of many, many decades. He has survived, by my count, 22 managers, plus the College of Coaches, which would make 28.

When the Tribune purchased the Cubs from the Wrigley family, there was a stipulation that Yosh Kawano must never be fired. Not that they'd ever want to fire him, but they put it in there because they wanted to protect him and he'd become a Wrigley favorite over the years. And, of course, he also has established friendships of the rich and famous the world over. Raymond Floyd is one of his very best friends, the golfer. And, he's been invited more than one time to functions at which Frank Sinatra presided— that was back in the days when Durocher was around. But, Yosh doesn't talk a whole lot. I think probably that's the measure of his success.

What was your biggest thrill?

Well, some of these no-hitters really stick out in my mind. I covered four Cub no-hitters that I can recall and each one of these no-hitters had something unusual about it.

The first was by Don Cardwell—1960. He had just been traded from the Phillies. He makes his start on May 15 and he pitched a no-hitter over the St. Louis Cardinals. I can still remember the last out was a sinking line drive going to left field and the left fielder was Walt Moryn, who was not known for his defensive prowess, and he came charging in and everybody almost gasped in the press box. 'Cause here's two outs in the ninth inning and Moryn is going to be called upon and he caught the ball right off his shoe tops—didn't even break stride and ran right into the infield. That to me was quite a thrill. A story developed that next day that he had been experimenting with a new windup and the headline, I remember on my story, was "Cardwell came empty-handed for his no-hitter"—something like that. He wound up without the ball in his hand and it's been done quite a bit subsequently, but then as he delivered the ball, he'd take it out of the glove and pitch. So that was a little unusual.

Then I saw another no-hitter in 1965—this was a perfect game. Sandy Koufax. That was quite a thrill, although we were on the losing end of that one and it was in Los Angeles, September 9, 1965. The run actually scored without the benefit of a hit. Lou Johnson walked and was sacrificed to second. He stole third and came in on a wild throw to third base by a catcher, whose name was Chris Krug and that was the only run of that ball game. But the unusual part of it was, there was a hit later, and that also was by Lou Johnson, who ironically was a former Cub. He was nurtured in the Cub system. But the ironic part of that game was the opposing pitcher, Bob Hendley, pitched a one-hitter. The only hit of that game was by Lou Johnson, did not figure in the run, and so a Cub pitcher lost the one-hitter when Sandy Koufax pitched a perfect game.

Then there was another no-hitter in that same season by Jim Maloney of the Reds against the Cubs and it was a 10-inning job. This could be a record if they kept such things. He walked 10 in that game and still pitched a no-hitter. He beat Larry Jackson.

The other no-hitter that I covered was August 19, 1969, and I think this is noteworthy because it was by Ken Holtzman. He fanned no one in that game. Not that he was a big strike-out pitcher. He only averaged about six a game, anyway. But that was unusual that he fanned nobody. It was August 19, 1969 and when that game was over, the Cubs led by seven and a half games. Now, with a seven-and-a-half-game lead over the Mets on August 19th, you'd think they'd breeze in and yet they lost 25 of the last 41 games after that. So, here they were at their high point on August 19th with a no-hitter, and everything was downhill after that.

I saw Ernie Banks' first game. I wasn't covering at the time. It was September 17, 1953, and the Cubs started four rookies in that particular game. One of whom was a pitcher, Don Elston, who later became a fairly decent relief pitcher. The other three were Ernie Banks and Gene Baker, who had started at second base and shortstop together—vica versa. And the fourth rookie was Bob Talbot, a center fielder, who really was only up for a cup of coffee and didn't play much after that.

Anyway, that was an unusual game and the reason I had gone to that game is I had worked in Sioux Falls, South Dakota, as a sports editor of the paper and we had a Class C Cub franchise and two years prior to this, Don Elston had pitched for us. I went to that game to accompany his wife because she was real nervous and we sat back of the dugout and I know he got knocked out early, I think about the second inning. I also remember that it was against the Phillies and the winning pitcher against them that day, in other words, the first major league pitcher that Ernie Banks faced was Curt Simmons.

Did you look on your job as hard work, glamorous, or somewhere in between?

Well, parts of it are glamorous, but I think it's a young man's job. There's an awful lot of travel. A lot of temptation and you don't have much to do. Didn't have a whole lot to do with your days because you played so many night games. And, if you didn't have something to occupy yourself with in the daytime, you'd go stir crazy. But we did have to write a couple of stories, usually, so there's quite a bit of pressure. You'd write an early story for the early editions of the paper. Us being a morning paper. And then at the game, you'd write another story. That was the actual game story and that would sub-out the early story you had written unless that one was worthy of keeping also. So, there was a lot of work and a lot of pressure and you always needed to be at the right spot, at the right time, or you could easily get scooped by somebody else. And not for lack of diligence, but only for the fact that you couldn't be everywhere. There was a lot of pressure, I think, as years went on.

And I think that's indicated now. You don't see writers stick around as a beat writer. It's very rare that a beat writer would have as many years as I did, or some of my predecessors. I had 25 years full-time on the beat. And nowadays, I think they'll write five or six years and then they'll become a columnist or they'll get into some other line of work or something.

IT CAN DRIVE YOU CRAZY

HERMAN FRANKS

One of the underrated managers. Got the most out of his material. This is evidenced by the performance of the 1977 Cubs, who made a run for the pennant with mediocre talent. One man, though, got to him and helped to drive him out of baseball.

I played under some great managers and they all had an impact on me, but Leo, you know, was a feisty guy and he loved to win about as much as any guy that I ever played for. And there was always a fight going with Leo around. I think I picked up a little from all those fellows...Connie Mack, Charlie Dressen, Leo Durocher. I was very fortunate that I played for those kind of guys and I incorporated all of that into my managing.

What is the biggest difference in ballplayers today as opposed to when you were playing in the big leagues in the late '30s and '40s?
Well, I would have to say the money that's involved today. It's pretty tough managing some of these guys that are making $2-3 million a year, every year. In those days, in '41 Whitlow Wyatt and Higbe, they won 22 games a piece that year. They were making about $20,000. So, it's a little tougher handling all these players today. I think what's happened today is that they sign these four or five-year contracts and, if you'll look up the statistics, I think you'll find that they're on the disabled list more today. However, in the last year of their contract you'll see where they're playing more.

In your last year in Chicago, in 1979, you had a problem, and re-signed, with seven games to go.
My biggest problem was with Buckner at that time. I thought he was a selfish ballplayer. Played for himself. And he had two or three more years to run in his contract and I just elected not to be around him. So that's when I resigned. That's the only fellow I really had a problem with.

The thing with Buckner is you couldn't discuss anything with him. He was just all for himself. I had a little bit of a problem with Kingman, but nothing that I couldn't get over with him. But the rest of the ball club was great. I just can't go for a guy when you win a ball game, he doesn't get any hits, that he's discontent.

109

I enjoyed Chicago very much. There's something about those ball clubs there I enjoyed even more than San Francisco, because they played more than up to their potential. As strange as it seems, in '77 we were in first place around August or so. And we got those injuries...oh, we lost Sutter and we lost Reuschel. We lost two or three guys in one week and we couldn't replace them. When you lose Sutter and Reuschel, you've lost the better part of your pitching staff.

Strange as it seems, I was really, really happy with that ball club. They played more than their potential.

I loved it out in San Francisco—Willie Mays and that group, but the thing that I enjoyed most about Chicago was, you know, mediocre ballplayers playing like they played. Kelleher—he was great. I mean he was always ready to play.

I think Chicago has the greatest fans anywhere in the United States. They have the greatest fans around.

San Francisco's a little tough. When we first went out there in '58, they didn't accept Willie Mays, you know. DiMaggio was their man and later Cepeda. They liked Cepeda more than they did Mays at the time. It took Mays quite a few years to be accepted there.

We've always felt as though Chicago...of all the major league cities, we enjoyed Chicago the best of all.

Hall of Fame shortstop who unfortunately did not play for the Cubs. He did, though, manage them for part of the 1960 season and spent many years in the broadcast booth doing Cub baseball on WGN Radio.

The Cubs were having a very poor season in 1960. They had no youngsters in the farm system to bring up to try to have new blood in the organization. And Grimm was the type of manager who just tossed out the baseball to the fellows in spring training and said, "Let's have a game." He enjoyed that. Stayed away from a lot of fundamentals and hard work. He did some—but not enough in my opinion at that time.

When you took over, then, the team was lacking in fundamentals?
Yes, definitely. In fact, I worked on fundamentals in the morning prior to games. But, how I got the job is a very interesting story.
We just came off of a 10-day road trip where the Cubs won only two games. And, to open up our home stand, I went to the ballpark around 9:30 or 10:00, which I do every morning that I was working, and I was met by Clarence Rowland, who was then the vice president of the Cubs, and he said, "Mr. Holland wants to see you." Well, immediately, after only two years in the radio booth I thought perhaps I said something that upset the Cubs, Mr. Wrigley, or Mr. Holland. I went up to the office and John Holland was behind the desk and he told me to sit down. He said, "How would you like to manage this ball club?" And the first thought that came to my mind—something dreadful has happened to Charlie Grimm. And I immediately said, "Is Charlie alright?" And Holland said, "Yes, only last night when he got to his hotel room and tried to go to sleep, he started to read *The Sporting News* at 3:00 in the morning and the lights were off. So after thinking about that he said he'd had enough of managing." So, he came in that morning and resigned. I said, well, of course, it would have to be up to Mr. Ward Quall, who was then the president of WGN, who hired me. And I called Mr. Quall and he said, "Certainly, you take that job. It's what you always wanted—to get back into baseball."

So, I accepted the job and that afternoon went down to the field and Grimm went up to the radio booth. And then I talked it over with Mr. Holland after a week or 10 days and we decided to bring up Ron Santo, who was in the minor leagues at that time. My third baseman at that time was Don Zimmer. I told Don that Santo was his protégé. To work with him, make a third baseman out of him. And that's exactly what happened. In 1960, we finished the season, didn't do well at all.

Then in 1961, Col. Whitlow, who was in the service, got to Mr. Wrigley and talked Mr. Wrigley into hiring coaches as they do in colleges and high school. Mr. Wrigley went for it and I did not agree to be one of the 10 coaches that would rotate every two or three weeks in managing the major league ball club and then go down to the minor leagues and manage for two weeks and make a complete circle and get back to the major leagues in about two months. I did not agree with that and told Mr. Wrigley that and then he and I both, on the telephone, asked Mr. Quall if he would take me back, which he did.

It did not work?

Well, no, because you have different managers every two weeks. Ten men with different thoughts on how to run a ball club. Ten men with different systems as to playing defense and how they want to play their offense. So, this is more confusing. And the disciplinary actions were different from each man. Some were a little loose. Others were very tough and consequently the ballplayers themselves were running in circles. They didn't know which way to go.

Did this have a debilitating effect on the Cub organization?

No doubt about it, plus the fact that we lost a lot of young ballplayers who graduated from colleges and from the sandlot teams that did not want to join the organization, looking forward to 10 or 12 managers at the top.

Charlie Grimm won a number of pennants for the Cubs. He always had the reputation of being lackadaisical—have a lot of fun.

Well, he himself could play that way and play the best. And he was a great man. He didn't want to hurt anybody's feelings and he managed that way, too.

Why did that work in the '30s and '40s and it didn't work later?

Well, because the manager was making more money at that time than the ballplayers. It's changed very much right now and consequently different attitudes in ballplayers. They always had a man looking over your shoulder that would say, "Don't you make a mistake or I'm going to take your place."

Getting back to the radio booth, you started with Jack Quinlan in 1958?

Yes, very fortunate to start with a man of that caliber. A great individual off the field as well as behind that mike. He taught me a lot about broadcasting and I was quite frightened when I first saw that mike in front of me.

How did you get your start in radio?

Well, Jack Brickhouse—I was managing Kansas City and then when I was released from Kansas City, Brickhouse interviewed me. And after the interview he said, "You're a great interview. I wonder how you would be on the other end of the job and you be the interviewer?" And he said, "Have you ever thought about getting behind the mike and analyzing baseball?" And I said, "No, not at all. I want to stay in baseball if I can in some capacity." And he said, "Well, why don't you come back to the WGN studios with me tomorrow and we'll get Jack Rosenberg to fix up a fake inning and you and I will discuss it over the mike." That's how I got started and I was horrible at the beginning, there's no doubt about it. The timing wasn't there and I would step on Quinlan's lines a lot and finally learned not to do that. But Brickhouse is the one that first brought in and thought about an ex-jock in baseball analyzing the game and he deserves all the credit in the world because look what happens now. Every station has an ex-jock doing the analyzing.

Quinlan died in 1964 at spring training. It was an automobile accident. I had played golf with him in the morning in Chandler, Arizona, and he decided to stay over with some friends and I had to get back to my family in Phoenix. I had promised them that I would take them to a carnival and I kept my promise and Jack drove to Chandler. Normally, when we would drive any place, I would drive. But this particular time in coming back from Chandler, he missed a turn where four other individuals had died from automobile accidents on the outskirts of Phoenix and he ran into a truck.

So, in '64 you were teamed with Vince Lloyd.

I was very fortunate to work with a man such as Vince Lloyd also.

What was it like going north with some of those clubs?

Well, I had to bite my tongue on a lot of occasions because of the type of ball that I witnessed and the individuals that I witnessed. You can see the change of atmosphere and attitude of ballplayers coming along. Consequently, it affected their play and the Cubs did not have a good minor league organization at that time where you could look forward to next year or this year bringing up some young ballplayers. It was quite difficult.

What thoughts do you have of 1969?

It looked as if they were going to win the division championship very easily. And then I think overconfidence entered into the play very much. They were a little lackadaisical. Chicago itself and the suburbs went wild because they anticipated a championship. Consequently, a lot of ballplayers were going out on appearances when actually they should have been in the clubhouse, thinking about baseball and thinking about what they're going to do on that particular day and who they're going to face, how they're going to hit him. And the Mets got hot. And the team getting hot at that particular time could gain a lot of ground—which the Mets did.

Durocher had a reputation of being a disciplinarian. He was letting this occur?

Yes, definitely. I think Leo at that particular time weakened also and thought that the team was definitely a championship team. It was a championship team, but not champions at that particular time.

What would you have done in '69 that Leo didn't do?

Well, you'd have to make rules then. If you could see it coming—Leo did not see it coming, nor his coaching staff. And that's what helped me tremendously as young as I was in managing major league baseball teams and players—that I had coaches that would come to me and suggest things and then if I liked it I would make the decision to go ahead with it. If I didn't like it, I'd tell them I appreciate their thoughts, but I think it should be the way it is.

You were made the playing manager at Cleveland at 24 years of age in 1942. Did you apply or did they give it to you?

I applied for it. I was freshman basketball coach at the University of Illinois when Mr. Slapnika, who was general manager at that time, and who incidentally signed Bob Feller, had a heart attack and passed away and they moved Roger Peckinpaugh, who was then manager, up to general manager and left the manager's spot open.

And one afternoon after basketball practice at Champaign, I wrote a letter to Mr. Bradley explaining that I thought that I could handle the team. I was playing at that time also. I just joined Cleveland in '39. And I wrote the letter to him and then after I mailed it, I got nervous—frightened. And went to my baseball coach—at that time was Wally Roettger—the late Wally Roettger, an ex-major leaguer—and went to my basketball coach, Doug Mills, and told him about it and I'd like to get that letter back. And they said, "Well you can't get it back now," but they talked me into not worrying about it. "That Mr. Bradley will file it in what they call 'File 13' and throw it away," they said.

I forgot about it, but in two days I received a telephone call and they called me off of the basketball court and it was from Mr. Bradley asking me to come in for an interview. I agreed and then sort of chickened out after I agreed. Once again I talked with Mr. Roettger and Mr. Mills that I didn't want to go. And they insisted that I go and get the experience of an interview before a board of directors...in front of Mr. Bradley. But you'll never get it. They said just relax and come back and you've got your job back here. And after 45 minutes of questioning in front of the board of directors, which there were 12 with Mr. Bradley at the conference table—I was told to wait in the waiting room and would get a decision.

Well, after about an hour of discussion and shouting, they asked me to come back in and said that I was the manager of the Cleveland Indians at the age of 24, but suggested that I hire older coaches for added responsibilities. And after talking with Mr. Bradley, he told me the story of how Mr. Martin—George Martin—an 82-year-old gentleman on the board—changed 11 votes of no's to 11 votes of yes's with his for me to become manager of the Cleveland Indians. His story was that Cleveland in the last 10 years had eight managers and was known as the graveyard for major league managers. And he wanted to change that particular idea and said,

"Let's give the kid a chance." And that's how I became manager of the Cleveland Indians.

What's the difference from when you were playing to now?

Well, of course, the salaries is No. 1. And that salary, I think, shoots down arms and fingers to where the problem is on the ball club. Attitude-wise. I don't blame the owners for giving outstanding salaries. But I do blame them for extending contracts for two, three, four, and five years. To me that is not good business. Now, whether I hurt somebody's feelings or not, I don't know. But I can't see putting out that much money for a number of years. Anything can happen to that individual and you still have to pay on guaranteed contracts.

Now they have some incentive contracts, but if you walked into a president's or general manager's office during my time and asked for more than one year—they'd point to the door..."We just can't agree to that." It's your performance this year—you get paid next year. That's what they were working on in my time.

What about the Cubs now?

Well, it's a fine organization. There is no doubt in my mind it's one of the best organizations in the business. They've now worked on the minor leagues system in making it a little better where they can create a machine where at least one man can move up from their own organization into the major league franchise—into the major league roster. Which is very important.

There's no other city—and I've been in one that didn't have a championship for 28 years—in Cleveland—and those fans are very loyal and when you put out and win they're behind you, but the Cubs have not been winning over a number of years and they still have the great following of fans. They're the greatest fans in the world and I think that's due to the day baseball games that Mr. Wrigley played. Because you got the family to come out. You got youngsters to come out when school was out. And it started at the age of 12, 14 years of age and they stayed with the Cubs all during those years.

DALLAS GREEN

The general manager of the Cubs from 1982 to 1987. Very compe-
tent man who helped find, sign, and develop many of the Cubs on
the team today. You know where he stands at all times.

How did you become GM of the Cubs and was this your first job
as a general manager?

I was the manager of the Philadelphia Phillies. We won the
championship in 1980 and I came back in 1981—that was the
strike year, you'll remember. And that was also the year, if I'm not
mistaken, that the Tribune Company bought the Chicago Cubs.

During that year, Rollie Carpenter called me and said that the
Cubs had made a call to him and asked permission to discuss the
possibility of me becoming the general manager for the Chicago
Cubs. Andy McKenna was the first contact, if my recollection is
right, with Rollie. Rollie and I talked a little bit. He was in the process at that time of selling the Phillies. Had made the announcement that the Phillies were going to be sold and that he and his
family were no longer going to be owners of the Phillies. And, of
course, we had been together for 25 years at that particular time,
and it came as quite a shock and I discussed it with my wife and
family. Talked it over with Paul Owens, who was my mentor with
the Phillies, and also discussed it briefly with Giles because he
looked like he was putting the ownership group together that was
going to buy the Phillies. They all wanted me to stay. I considered
staying and, as a matter of fact, two different times I told the Cubs'
people that I really had no interest in moving. That I had been in
this part of the country all of my life and really had no interest in
leaving.

I felt that I could accomplish my goal of becoming a general
manager with Philadelphia and that because I had a farm at that
particular time that we had just purchased, my family was going
away to college, I just didn't feel that I could make the move. I did
that twice. Two different times. And finally to Mr. McKenna's
credit, he kept trying. He kept pestering me...not pestering
me...but he kept talking to me about what Chicago was all about
and what the Tribune was willing to do and what they were hop-

ing to do in the future with the new ownership. The more I discussed it, the more I became interested in taking something like the Chicago franchise, which, at that point in time, was not very well respected in baseball, and hiring people that wanted to work hard and had the same kind of philosophy about the baseball business that I did and putting together a team that could make something happen in Chicago. And the more I thought about it, the closer I came.

The latter part of the year we played a series out in Chicago and Mr. McKenna and Mr. Cook and Mr. Madigan had me out to dinner with the family. They flew Sylvia, my wife, out to visit with them as well. We had a private meeting and just talked baseball. Talked philosophy. Talked about the franchises and the direction that I thought they should go, etc. And after the discussion, we got into some financial discussions and the more I talked and the more I thought about it, I talked it over with Sylvia and we decided that we'd like to take a shot at it.

After the season was over, I called Andrew McKenna back and said that I wanted to give it a try. We were in the playoffs in '81 and, after the playoffs, they made the announcement that I was going to Chicago.

You said that in 1981 the Cubs were not well respected as a franchise. Why is that?

Really, 1969 was the only time that they even made a spurt in terms of winning. I was Director of Minor Leagues and Scouting and very involved with a lot of the trade talks, etc., that had gone on in the past 10 or 12 years between the Phillies, Cubs, and other ball clubs. And we just come to find out that they really had not done a good job in terms of their scouting and development. They had no quality players coming up. They had no quality players at the major league level and, basically, they were somewhat stagnant. They just seemed to be very satisfied to open the doors and hope that Wrigley Field would bring the fans in and if they won—fine; if they didn't, that seemed to be fine, too. That's the way I saw them from the other side of the fence, so to speak. And I think most of the other people in baseball judged them to be the same. They weren't very aggressive. They weren't very progressive and they just played the game of baseball. And as I said, accepted losing with gusto it seemed.

But that had really been the case in Chicago for years, don't you think?

Well, I didn't know much about that until, truthfully, I got there. Then I found that losing really had permeated the entire organization. I mean, hell, when we got there, it was an accepted thing that the Chicago Cubs were going to lose. That was accepted by the fans. It was accepted by the personnel on the field. It was accepted by the minor league people and the scouting department. It was accepted by the ushers and the people that worked in the ballpark. It just was a very sad situation because I had never, as a baseball person, run into anything like that.

What did you do to turn that around?

Well, we worked very, very hard. The first thing I wanted to do was hire a guy that I felt could do, at the major league level, something that we felt was needed. We needed to get some disciplines going. We needed to get some work habits established. We needed to set some goals and some policies and some ideas and the guy that pushed that for me was Lee Elia.

Lee's taken an awful beatin' at times and I fired Lee Elia, but Lee was the guy that established an awful lot of things that Dallas Green believes in, because he was brought up in the Phillies' organization like I was and we were taught that winning was important. That developing a winning atmosphere was important. Accepting losing wasn't part of it and that you had to try to win every single baseball game you possibly could to change that. And you had to set policies and establish work habits that would start to build up the pride from the very bottom so that everybody would eventually become proud to be a Chicago Cub. There was really no pride in the organization when we got there. And we helped change that.

Lee is pretty volatile and I was volatile as well. And probably we were not as accepted as we thought we were going to be. I mean, we had just come off a world championship ball club. We had just backed that up with a playoff appearance for the second straight year. But when we got to Chicago, it was like, "Well, who are these two bums?" You know, "What have they got to offer?" And, Lee and I were ruffled at times with the resistance to change. There was so much resistance to change the old ways of doing things in the Chicago Cubs organization that we, at times, became very frustrated. I think the tirade he went through was a sign of that frustration.

That's when he went after the guys in the box seats and called them "unemployed bums."

Right. You know, Lee did something he shouldn't have done. But, that was borne out as a result of everybody's resistance to change and everybody's acceptance to losing. We weren't used to that and we didn't want the fans to start that. We didn't want the fans any longer to be a part of that. We wanted the fans to feel a pride about their baseball team that had never been there before. Or, at least had not been there since 1969, to the best of our knowledge. We were determined to change that. And, you know, in a fit of rage, he did something he shouldn't have done, but at the same time we all make those kind of mistakes. He should get a lot of credit for the beginning of the disciplines that we felt were necessary to begin the winning vein.

You were instrumental in getting lights in Wrigley Field.

Well, I pushed it because I really honestly, at the time I came to Chicago, felt that one of the reasons the Cubs were always battling uphill is that they didn't play baseball like the rest of the clubs. I felt that night baseball was the standard for the game. Obviously, everybody else but Chicago played that way. And the longer I was there, the more I understood what day baseball was all about. But when I first got there, I insisted that we needed the change and the change had to come with the establishment of lights. We just had to have the lights to play like everybody else.

We were coming into the airport at times at 2:00, 3:00 in the morning, many, many times after a road trip and had to be out at the ballpark at 8:00 or 9:00 in the morning to play the day game. And nobody else does that. Nobody else in the league does that. I really think that's the reason the Cubs faded in '69. I think that's the reason that many Cub teams are unable to maintain a September battle. You know, because eventually it wears you down. And I screamed and yelled that clear up until about 1985-86 when I stopped fighting because I finally came to realize that day baseball was very, very interesting. Day baseball, to me, is very misunderstood by the game. I don't think that ownership, television, and everybody else understands that day baseball is really the way it should be played. It's a great boon to the industry—greater than a lot of people realize, because it nurtures youth to come to the ballpark. Night baseball does not do that. It nurtures a family atmosphere at the ballpark. Night baseball does not do that.

That's why the Cubs have done well over the years.

That's exactly right. They keep building up that fandom—grandfathers take their kids and the fathers take their kids and pretty soon you've got a new generation of fans.

And truthfully, what a lot of people have failed to talk about is that 1984, we sacrificed the home-field advantage because we didn't have lights. That's not talked about very much. That's not discussed an awful lot. But we won two ball games in our ballpark and lost three in San Diego. At that time we were supposed to get the three home games in Wrigley Field. But because of television and because of the night baseball situation, we had to change. And that was the compromise. The compromise was that we start in our ballpark and play two day games and then play the rest of the time in the other ballpark.

Not many people even discuss it. But that was the compromise that we had to make and, of course, we threatened after that to move to St. Louis, move the playoffs to St. Louis should we get into the playoffs in '85 and '86.

You're credited to a large degree for putting that '84 team together. What trades did you implement that you think were the most important?

It goes right back to what we started to talk about. I had to change the atmosphere on that ball club. I had to obtain guys that I knew, knew how to win.

My first trade was probably the most important. And that was the Larry Bowa trade that also brought Ryne Sandberg here to Chicago. I came from Philadelphia and I knew darn well that I had the only shortstop available to give back to the Phillies. They had to trade Bowa because Bill Giles had made it public that he was not going to sign Bowa and they were feuding in the paper. I knew that I had the upper hand and we pushed for Sandberg and were able to get him.

But what that accomplished, you see, was to get a guy like Larry Bowa, who had come off a championship ball club, who had great, great work habits, and who taught Ryne Sandberg what those work habits could achieve. And he helped Sandberg as much as anybody, set the tone for his future because of the work habits that Larry Bowa had.

What other trades helped that team?

I think Keith Moreland was a key guy. Certainly the Dernier-Matthews trade for Bill Campbell right at the end of spring training in '84 was a key trade because it gave us a lead-off hitter and it gave us a leader down at the clubhouse, like Sarge. They were very key. Then, when I traded Mel Hall and Joe Carter and got Sutcliffe, Frazier, and Hassey, it filled the gaps that we had in middle relief in the bullpen and left-hand-hitting backup catcher, as well as a starting pitcher. So that was, obviously, a key trade.

Speaking of '84—would you do anything differently in that series with San Diego?

Well, not really. You know, Jim is a low-key guy as opposed to me, who at times is a screamer and yeller. And I just felt that...I just felt after getting waxed a couple of ball games by the Padres that we needed to turn the momentum and the only way you're going to turn the momentum at that particular time is a little bit of screamin' and yellin'; saying, "Hey, let's get our act together." I don't think Jimmy did that for us. But personally, as far as running the game, you know, you can look back and second-guess anything that happened. But there's really not much we could have done differently.

You come very highly recommended by your contemporaries. You're considered one of the most competent guys in baseball today. You did great things in Chicago. What the hell happened? Why were you let go?

Well, I'm not sure I'm the guy to answer that. They never did tell me other than this...what the hell did they use?... I can't think of the term that they used, but anyway... we had reached the point in our growth. What happened to the Chicago Cubs is that we were not prepared to win in 1984. We were building a foundation. We were building a nucleus at the scouting and development level and, of course, you know '82 was our first year. So '82, '83, '84— the third year we were there we win the championship. Well, we were not prepared to back that up with quality youngsters at the minor league level because there wasn't anybody ready. We had scouted well, we had signed very well...but those kids that came on in '86 and '87 were not ready in '85 when we had the injuries. '85 we fell apart because we had physical problems. As a matter of fact, we actually had the entire starting rotation go down on the disabled list at one time or another. Because of that, and because we had no quality players ready at that particular time, we were trying to fill gaps with second-line and third-line guys that we could steal in trades, or waivers, or what have you. And it didn't work. We failed in '85 and we failed in '86 again.

'87 it was obvious that I had not made some good choices as manager. I fired Frey and brought Michael in and Michael didn't have a feel for the Cubs, or for the National League, and finally let him go.

I was prepared at that particular time to get down on the field. I mean, I had done pretty much what I wanted to do. I had the people in place at the key levels and scouting and development and I felt that I could leave the general manager's position and go down on the field and take over and I was willing to do that. But, when I was willing to do that, I also wanted to make sure that the key people that I trusted and that knew me, and knew my work habits, and knew what I expected of everybody, were going to be in place.

And I wasn't able to convince apparently the Tribune Company that those were the quality people that we were talking about. They wanted to bring in a couple of people from the Tribune and involve them very heavily in the decision making process. I told them at that time it would be very difficult for me, as a manager, or as a general manager, to get down there and put somebody up here making decisions that had really no baseball background. And, the more we discussed it, I finally said, "Well, fine. I'll train the guy that you want and I'll stay right where I am and train him and do whatever I have to do to get this guy into a quality situation where he can make decisions based on his background in baseball and the experience and teaching that I can give him. And I'll name the manager."

They were prepared I think at that particular time to become more and more involved in the every day baseball decision making and that was totally against my grain, as you well know. John

Madigan was the one that told me that apparently we have philo-
sophical differences...that's the words that he used... and whatever
they are or whatever they were —that's why I got fired. But I still
am not sure of the real reason. In firings, as you well know, there's
the real reason and then there's the reason that they give the press
and give everybody else.

That was in...'87. That was right at the time where all those
kids—Maddux and Grace and Dunston and Walton and Dwight
Smith, Berryhill—all those kids were starting to come along. And
we knew—Gordon Goldsberry and I knew—very well that this was
about to happen. As a matter of fact, if you could get ahold of
those five-year plans that the Tribune Company made me submit
every year since I started, you'll find that it's pretty well docu-
mented for them that that was going to happen. And we were really excited about the future because we knew we had signed quality kids and they were about ready to become major league baseball players. And that's really what it's all about. That growth of
the development group is very, very important to the stability of a
franchise and we knew that.

What are you doing now?

I have two farms. I have a farm here in Pennsylvania—in
Westgrove, Pennsylvania, and I have another farm in Cottawingo,
Maryland, about 20 miles away from there. Sylvia and I like to gar-
den and plant shrubs and trees and flowers and what have you. I
do some hay business because I also have some beef cattle. I'm
interested in the game preserve idea and the shooting preserve. So,
I've got a lot of things going. A friend of mind, Frank Cashan,
called and said, "It's time you get back to work," and asked me to
do some scouting for the Mets—that's what I've been doing.

THE BIG EXPERIMENT

According to Elvin, it was his idea to start the College of Coaches. His plan was to rotate only the coaches and not the manager. Phil Wrigley had another idea.

When did you first get involved with the College of Coaches?

That was in '61. Mr. Wrigley called me in 'cause I was the only coach that was retained all those years, under Scheffing and under Boudreau, then under Charlie Grimm. We kept making changes and he called me in at the end of the season and he says, "What is the matter?" And I says, "Well, you're making too many changes. Every time you make a managerial change, you make a pitching coach change and all coaching staff changes. You've got some real great arms on Drabowsky and Hobbie and Drott and Anderson and Fodge, Ellsworth. Even if you bring in a new pitching coach, they're going to make changes. We've gotta systemize this thing. You've got too much talent there to be changing all the time. That's like going into the school and changing the teacher half way through the school year." So, he says, "Well, what would you recommend?" I says, "I recommend, if you want to change the manager, you have your own coaches and let him take the coaches that you have." You know, like Jim Essian, now. He's made manager of the Cubs. But, hell, he's got the same coaches as he had when Zimmer was there. You know, you don't change everything. You just upset everything.

What was his reaction to that?

He bought it. Hook, line, and sinker. And I told him that we had to get a system to play. And he says, "Will you write the book?" So I did. I wrote the book. That no matter whether you're playing in A ball, Double-A ball, Triple-A ball or the major leagues. You play the game the same way. Everybody bought the coaches plan but the press. They didn't like it 'cause they didn't have anybody to blame.

But didn't Wrigley turn that around and he rotated the managers rather than the coaches?

Well, yeah, it was his idea to rotate the head coaches. My idea

125

was to hire eight guys. Four of them would be coaches in the major leagues. Four of them would be in the minor leagues. We had a hitting coach, pitching coach, catching coach, infield-outfield coach. We had them all different ages. We had old ones, we had young ones, we had intermediate ones, and everything like that. I went out and hired all of them. And all of them were organizational people. They were not buddy-buddy to the manager. They were organizational people. They paid them all the same salary. Everybody on the coaching staff, whether in the minor leagues, or in the major leagues, made the same. Everybody was the same salary. So, if we rotated a manager, we just rotated the manager. We didn't rotate the whole school system. We just fired the superintendent.

But that was Wrigley's idea to rotate the head coach?

The head coach, yeah. He didn't want to hire one man. He says, "Well, could one of the rotating coaches be a manager?" I said, "Well, yeah." Like Harry Craft—he managed all over. Lou Klein managed all over. You know, we had guys that had managerial experience. So, he says, "Well, let's do it that way, then." I says, "Well, whatever you want to do."

I was not in favor of rotating the manager because I thought it presented an alibi to the players—which it did. And it would present an alibi to the press—which it did. What I started in baseball was kind of revolutionary but now everybody's doing it. You look around. Everybody's got a minor league hitting instructor. They've got a minor league pitching instructor. They've got a minor league catching instructor. They've got a minor league infield instructor. What we did back in the '60s everybody's doing now.

The only thing bad about it, we should have hired a manager. And then he had to accept the concept of the system of play. He had to take the concept of the rotating coaches. You know, like, you'd be with your kids every day and you don't see them grow. Now, if you're out instructing the minor league player and you get away from it a while and go back to him, you can see everything he's doing wrong and everything he's improved on. Now you can instruct. You can't teach a kid every day. So my idea was to rotate the coaches in the major leagues and let the manager have it. But if he doesn't do the job—don't fire all the coaches and get a whole new system in there.

When I started with the Cubs in A ball, they played relays and cut-off one way. The Double-A ball played it the other way. Triple-A played it another way. And the big leagues played it another way. So what you end up doing with young kids that you sign—hell, they were all confused. You've moved them from A to Double-A. Hell, they had to learn a whole new system.

I said, "Let's systemize that whole thing." Let's do everything the same way all through the organization. This is the Cubs way of playing. And everybody else went for it. Hell, the Dodgers use our system of play. They even use our outfield cut-off. So, everybody's gone to it. It's just the fact that we got chastised 'cause we managed to rotate the manager. Which wasn't my intent. My intent was to rotate the coaches, not the manager.

So it was your idea.

I was the guy that started it all, right. I was the guy that hired everybody.

You go out and play and do your job, you know when to hit and run. You know when to do this and do that. If you're a good player, you don't care who's the boss. You just do your job.

That was complicated by the fact the Cubs had pretty bad personnel back then.

Yeah. We didn't have anybody. And we knew whoever we had as manager—we could have had Jesus Christ as our manager and he'd end up getting fired.

When did the College of Coaches end?

I think it ended in '63 when they hired Bob Kennedy. See Kennedy and I changed places. He came from Salt Lake City and I went out to Salt Lake City. Everything that Mr. Wrigley did, he did with good intent. And we had so many great young players back then with Williams and Hubbs and Banks and Santo and Brock and all those pitchers I was talking about. We had babies. They weren't big league players yet. So no matter who managed them, you were going to end up getting beat. But we had to teach at the major league level. Hell, half of them became Hall of Famers. So it wasn't all bad.

I had Brock in center field. Brock couldn't play center field. But Billy Williams couldn't play anything but left field. And Brock had to play left field. So there you've got a situation where great players had to play the same position. And Banks, his legs were getting so bad, you know, I had to move him to first base. All I did was prolong his career about 10 years.

We traded for Zimmer. We traded Ron Perranoski, a great young pitcher, for Zimmer and Zimmer became our third baseman. But you knew it was just going to be a matter of time and Santo was going to take his place. So we bring Santo up and we put Zimmer on the bench. And so when expansion came along, Zimmer was in expansion, Ashburn was in expansion. You know, we got rid of....Bobby Buhl in expansion. So we got rid of a lot of that old talent and kept the young talent.

Actually, that was the beginning of the '69 team.

Hell, yes. I mean, it started in '61, all those young kids. But we had to suffer with them because we had to teach them to play in the major leagues, which really, probably, they should have been Double-A or Triple-A.

The whole nucleus of the ball club was developed back then.

Mr. Wrigley—they always call him Mr. Wrigley.

Well, he was class. Yeah. I mean, you don't find people like that in baseball anymore. You've got your Grenesko and all those ding-a-lings, you know, that don't know shit from shinola, but you don't have the Crosleys there anymore. You don't have the Comiskeys. You don't have the Rickeys. You don't have the Stonehams. You don't have the real great people in baseball. It's corporate-owned now. And it has to be. For the money they're paying. You know, an individual can't afford that. It's got to be a corporation.

One of the three rotating managers for the Cubs' College of Coaches in 1962. When they told him it was his turn to be rotated, he told them he did not want to go.

Charlie, were you working for the Cubs when you were first contacted regarding the College of Coaches?

No, I wasn't. I was the manager of the Denver Bears in the American Association. Rube Wilson contacted me. He was a special scout for the Cubs.

I had managed five years in Triple-A. I managed three years in the Coast League. Had a third and second-place club and then I won a pennant the first year at Denver for the Tiger organization and the second year we won the championship playoffs. I wanted a shot at the major leagues. So when he approached me, I was receptive to it. They explained the concept to me and I didn't disagree with anything at the time. So, I signed with them.

Elvin Tappe said the College of Coaches was his idea, but that Phil Wrigley wanted to rotate the managers.

Well, I don't know. I was under the impression it was Mr. Wrigley's idea. In fact, it was relayed to me that it was Mr. Wrigley's idea. I didn't find a heck of a lot wrong with it at the time. In fact, I asked who the other guys were that were going to manage and none of them had any kind of a record near what I had. I felt this was going to be an opportunity for me to find out if I could manage on the major league level.

You were at the helm longer than anybody. You managed for 112 ball games in the '62 season.

Yeah. From June 6th to the end of the year. I refused to be rotated. I said publicly that if they wanted to send me to Duluth, or whatever that club was, their Class C club, I would go but I wouldn't like it. I wouldn't like it worth a damn. So, they never approached me again to get down.

What did the players think?

Well, they didn't like being laughed at. You know, it was a little bit of a laughing matter. When I took over, I had had five successful years in Triple-A. I ran things with a firm hand. I don't believe I was ever called unfair by any ballplayer and I've had an awful lot of ballplayers play for me that eventually have gone on to the Hall of Fame.

My approach to managing was entirely different than the other guys. What I felt they were doing was just keeping a job open for themselves. They were promoting a job. I was interested in managing a good ball club and winning.

Who do you think of those rotating managers was the least effective?

Well, I managed against Elvin Tappe in the Coast League and he wasn't much of a player. No knockin' Elvin Tappe. He's a fine guy. But he didn't know how to manage and he wasn't much of a player. Hell, we never even spent time on him in the meetings when we went over the ballplayers.

There was just the three of us. Elvin Tappe, Lou Klein, and myself that year. So I couldn't say too much about anybody else. Both Elvin and Lou Klein were kind of easy going and didn't take a firm stand and there were things that I didn't like. When I took over, I decided I would put my knowledge and my abilities into the thing. And I can relate some pretty interesting incidents.

For instance, as a manager I was a great fundamentalist. I figured you played like you practiced and I wanted all 25 men to participate in practicing prior to the game—the 15-minute infield and outfield. All except the starting pitcher. I would hit the infield. I hit the infield pretty much all year. I also coached third base both when the others managed and when I was the manager.

I was very unhappy with the effort and the drive and the tenacity. So, one day I'd just about had enough. The outfielders being lackadaisical. Missing the infield , missing second base, missing home plate. The catcher was just waving at a short hop. Infielders the same way. Outfielders not being accurate. So, we had an off day and I called a workout in the morning. I don't know if they ever call workouts on the major level, but I called many a workout on a Triple-A level.

So, I called a workout. I got everybody out there. In fact, I made the statement that anybody that didn't show up, it would be a $250 fine, cash, on my desk the next day. So everybody showed up and I said, "Men, this is all we're going to do. We're going to take infield. We get a perfect infield—no boots, no errors, no bad throws, no bad hops, no nothing, no ball laying on the ground—we're going in. So let's go." I had the pitchers as baserunners. I'd hit a ball to left field, the pitcher would run down to first base, make the turn, left fielder would throw the ball into second base. All routine fundamentals. And, I says, we'll make it perfect. Well, we went around and then they got a little careless and now we start all over again. They made, what I called, an error. Missed play. So we started all over again. Now we got all the way around to the infield and one of the infielders made a bad throw, so now we start all over again. We finally got as far as first base. Going all the way around. And then we made another bad throw so we start all over. Well, by this time, they went through all the emotions of anger, frustration, relaxation, don't-give-a-damn, and everything else that you could think of that a ballplayer would go through practicing. The longer we went, the worse we got. Finally, after an hour and 45 minutes, I threw my hands up, threw my fungo bat aside, and said, "That's it." We never did complete a perfect infield.

Now, I did that for these reasons. I wanted to get it over to them that you play like you practice. And the other thing, you can't turn the darn thing on and off like a water faucet. At one time I counted 21 boots during a 15-minute infield. I was furious about that.

Well, we got results. We got pride. We were improved. I don't recall whether we ever had a perfect infield, but we got down to where we were making one or two boots is all. So, I accomplished what I set out to do. Gave them pride in their practicing. Gave them pride in their abilities to throw a ball, catch a ball, field a ball, and everything else.

The other things was, and Elvin Tappe was the culprit...he was my bullpen catcher. He talked Mr. Wrigley and John Holland into staying on as a player/coach. And I told him, "If you're going to be a player/coach, you're going to follow the same rules as the players. I will not shade you in any manner whatsoever. You'll be just like any other player. But I'll treat you also as a coach."

So, he's down in the bullpen and I'm making a pitching change. I'm making a pinch hitter for the pitcher and I had 1-2-3 fingers signed that the first guy that we had agreed would be the first reliever, No. 2 would be the second, No. 3 the third reliever. So I turned around without even looking down there and I got my hand up and I got one finger raised and Tappe was in the bullpen and I don't pay any more attention, I'm paying attention to the hitter, the game and everything else. I turned around and nobody's warming up. He didn't even see it. If he saw it, he ignored it. Well, I brought in a guy that was cold and he pitched—I forget, I think it was Don Elston. And he wasn't warm and he did a pretty good job when he got warmed up. So I stormed down to the bullpen and I stormed into the clubhouse and there's the guy shavin' in the club house. My pitcher was shaving.

I was furious. There was nobody to warm up and I asked Elston, I says, "Go in and do the best you can. We'll get somebody warmed up and maybe you can come around." Well, he did a pretty good job, as I recall.

I stopped that damn shavin' in a minute. And I use that term just the way I said it. We went on the road and I said, "No shaving." And there was no shaving for five days. Incidentally, if my memory serves me right, we won five games in a row. And they were really mad. But they played baseball like I knew they could and would. And then they talked me into lifting the shavin' and then we continued to lose the way we had before. At least I found out they could play better.

We had Billy Williams, who was coming around real well. He was a sweetheart of a ballplayer. Lou Brock—I kept him there. I kept them from sending him on. I was responsible for him staying there all year and Buck O'Neil, one of the coaches, who was a fine coach and a tremendous asset to the club at the time, will tell you that. And then we had George Altman who played right field. At first base, of course, was Banks. Second base was Kenny Hubbs. Shortstop was Andre Rogers. Third base was Ron Santo. And incidentally, at about this time, I felt that Ron Santo was the toughest hitter that I'd ever seen and ever wanted at bat when I wanted something positive done with the bat. He was tremendous. I never saw a hitter in all my experience like he was. Our catching was slow. We had Bertell who was in and out of the service. Then there was kind of a make-shift and Barragan and, I can't quite recall the other guy.

Our pitching staff was Dick Ellsworth, who turned out to be a fine, fine pitcher. He was a professional all the way. Barney

Schultz was there and I loved Barney Schultz. Barney came up to me at one time and says, "Skip, I'm not getting enough work." And I said, "Alright, Barney, if the time comes, I'll work you." So, the situation did come around, because our club wasn't that good, really. We didn't have much pitching. So I started Barney in relief and then I used him the next day in relief and the next day in relief and the next day and finally the fifth day he says, "Hey, Skip. You know, I need rest." I said, "Go and sit down in the bullpen." If my memory serves me right, I used him nine straight times in relief. And I think that was the National League record for a while. He says that's the highlight of his career.

But we didn't have any pitching. We had young Calvin Koonce who was a rookie. Did a pretty good job for us.

I ran the club. I finally ran the club the way I wanted to run it. We were kind of...our ball club was kind of like a...I'd use this as an example. Like an automobile with three brand new tires and one bald tire. And that automobile's going to go safely as fast as that bald tire's going to take you. Not the three new tires. That's just the way I felt. I made the great mistake of not going up and talking to Mr. Wrigley. 'Cause I loved my experience. I loved Chicago. Good gosh, I still brag about it—being an old Cubbie.

The Cubs then started rotating coaches in the minor leagues, which is used now.

Absolutely. And that's one of the finest contributions to baseball that's come along in a long time. In fact, when I was the Director of Player Procurement and Instructions at Kansas City during the expansion, I implemented the two-coach system in the minor leagues. I copied it from Mr. Wrigley's idea.

They were the innovators as far as I can recall. The thing was great. The thing was great. A major league coach coming down was great. Teachin' the same manner that you taught on the major level. It was good. The thing that I disagreed on, and perhaps that's what caused me not to be returned, was I felt that a pitching coach should not be rotated. It's tough enough for a pitching coach to get everybody's confidence in his teaching. As soon as you rotated him—Bang—it went all to heck.

The other thing that I thought was really good was the fact that we could use anybody we wanted to out of the whole 12 as coaches. If you had an infielder who was having problems and you had an infield rotating coach in the minor leagues, you'd bring him up and he could help straighten your guy out. If you had a hitting coach, you could bring him up.

Possibly the biggest regret I had, and it's bugged me ever since, was I didn't put Buck O'Neil as my first base coach. Buck O'Neil had played in the Negro League for I don't know how many years and he was a first baseman and, if anybody would know when the pitcher was going to throw, Buck O'Neil would. And I've regretted that ever since. I wanted to do it, but when I mentioned it to one guy, he says, "My gosh, you can't do that," which I never did believe in anyhow. 'Cause I managed in Montgomery, Alabama, when Hank Aaron and Frank Robinson were all in the Sally League.

In other words, someone said you shouldn't have a black first base coach?

That's right. And I won't say who, but it was mentioned.

Why were you let go after the '62 season?

Well, I didn't pursue it. I didn't really go after it aggressively. When I left there I asked John Holland, "John, are you satisfied with the job I've done?" And he says, "Yes." I says, "Can I go and talk to Mr. Wrigley?" He says, "I'd much rather you wouldn't." I says, "Will you go with me?" And he says, "No." And that was the end of that.

So, I thought that they all got together and I wasn't to be returned.

A solid major leaguer who played 14 years in the bigs with a life-time batting average of .269. He is a firm believer in what the Cubs tried as the College of Coaches. He was one of the coaches, but never a rotating head coach.

1959 was my last season on the field—playing. In the winter of 1960 is when they come up with the idea of the College of Coaches and John Holland recruited me and wanted me to be the infield coach for the organization. He presented me with the idea from Mr. Wrigley. It was something that I believed in very strongly and as baseball was, at that time, I swore I'd never be a coach. But when they came up with this idea, I was very strong for it.

My duties were setting up the infield play for the organization. The whole organization. Not just for the big club, but for the whole organization. And that's what everybody in the College of Coaches were doing. It was something that everybody agreed on. They didn't just have your idea, and somebody else had another idea, and somebody else had another idea. Everybody had to agree on what plan of teaching we would give, not only to the big club, but to the whole organization.

Standardizing everything.
Cut-off plays, everything. The rundowns, just the whole principle of infield play.

Was that being done by any other major league team at that time?
Not at that time.

So this was very innovative?
Oh, yes. In fact, several years ago, every ball club was doing the same thing that we did at that time and it was just a great idea. They have now...all the ball clubs now have placed coaches in rookie ball all the way up to Triple-A. In those days, the only ones that worked with those ball clubs was the manager. He did it his way in the minor leagues and, if they advanced from rookie league

ball to A Ball to Double-A ball, the managers were the ones that taught the game. And there was no coordination in those days of what style of play you're going to have.

Why was the press so down on it?
I don't think they understood it. I just don't really believe they understood it. And they fought it and they presented it negatively to the fans. Then the fans were not going to accept it. It turned out to be the right thing and baseball has proven that now.

Were the players confused?
Yes, they were. They were confused mostly with the situation of the head coach. The head coach on the major league ball club. We didn't have a manager then. So, he was considered the head coach and he was going to coach for one month—be the main man for one month. And, there were five, I believe, at that time.

Did it confuse the players because there'd be a different personality with each head coach—was that the biggest problem?
I think that was it, yes. Even though their method of play and everything didn't change.

You stand by the head coach concept, too. You think that was a good idea?
Oh, it was great. It was great. It's the way it should be. They didn't receive the teaching and everything. When they came to the major leagues, a lot of those guys didn't even know how to play ball. As far as the principles of the game go.

The rotating of coaches in the minor league level—do you think that significantly strengthened the Cubs' minor league system?
I think it did because it brought the players closer to contact with the major leagues. Before, the players down in the minor leagues in Class A, Double-A and Triple-A—they had no contact whatsoever with the major leagues. So what we tried to do is to make that contact and coordinate. They actually felt like they were part of a major league ball club.

136

Exaltation, Despair, Bewilderment, & Other Assorted Fruit

DICK SELMA

Many people do not realize that Dick Selma was with the Cubs only part of the 1969 season. But he made a big impact both on the pitching staff and in leading the Bleacher Bums. Close your eyes and you can see him in the Cubs' bullpen leading the Bleacher Bums in cheering.

What do you remember of the 1969 season?

It was kind of a hectic year for me, because I had been with the Mets in '68 and that was the year of expansion and I had been told by Gil Hodges that I was going to be protected. And the next thing I know I pick up the paper and I find out I've gone on expansion in the second round to the San Diego Padres. Well, I was kind of happy with that because I live in California and I said, "Boy, I finally get to go home," instead of having to go 3,000 miles to work every year. And, from about day one that I was in camp in San Diego, I kept hearing rumors that I was getting traded to the Chicago Cubs. I kept going up to Preston Gomez, who was the manager at that time, and to the pitching coach, who is now the manager of the San Francisco Giants. That was Roger Craig. And I kept asking and they said, "No, you know, it's just flyers." So finally, I decided it's time that I go talk to the No. 1 man, who was Buzzy Bavasi. And I ask Buzzy Bavasi and he says, "Look, the only way we'd ever trade you is if we could get three or four ballplayers for you." Well, we went into Scottsdale in spring training and what happened was we were playing the Cubs and I heard rumors that we were going to change lockers that day. And it never came about so I figured, you know, it was just over with.

So then the season started and I did start out with San Diego and I was having a pretty good year right at the start, even though we were a real poor ball club. And the next thing I know I missed an airplane ride to Houston, Texas. Preston Gomez had a rule that if you missed the airplane, it's going to cost you $100 a minute for every minute that you're late on the field, but he'll fine you $500 for just missing the airplane. Well, what had happened was I had just moved into a new house and the alarm—I thought I'd set it for

137

6:00 A.M. and I set it for 6:00 P.M. So I missed the flight. So I scrambled around trying to catch a flight to Houston. I finally caught the flight. I got to the ballpark. I was 10 minutes late, which cost me $1,000. Plus my $500 for missing the airplane. So I'm in debt $1,500. That was a lot of money then. And, after the ball game, Preston Gomez calls me up to his room at the hotel and he says, "You've just been traded to the Chicago Cubs for four players." And all that time I thought, "All because I missed an airplane?"

It was that thing that was brewing in spring training and they finally worked a deal and the Cubs felt they had a legitimate shot at the pennant—which they did—and they were looking for a fourth starter. And Leo Durocher had always been high on me because I had always had good success against the Cubs. So, we were on a three-day road trip...they were starting a 15-day road trip and it just so happens that I had to join that ball club in New York.

So now I gotta join 'em...I gotta join the Cubs in Shea Stadium in New York the next day. I'm sittin' on the bench and I always got to the ballpark early and I was the first guy there and I was sittin' out there on the bench and I look across and there's Tom Seaver. Well, Tom Seaver and I grew up together in Fresno. I was kind of directly responsible for getting Tom Seaver signed with the Mets. And I just looked over at him and the Cubs had an eight-game lead and I just put a big old dollar sign up in the air to Seaver and he says, "Go for it."

And then, you know, after that I really felt comfortable with the Cubs. I mean, I'd never been traded before. I had been with the Mets all my life. I went to San Diego, but that was a brand new ball club—that wasn't a direct trade. But this was actually my first trade. The whole ball club—it was like I'd been there all my life. I mean, every guy was so warm. And it was like, "Hey, this guy's been here for 15 years." I just couldn't believe it. I mean, I was not an outsider or anything. And that's just the way the whole Cub organization was.

I remember when I signed my contract with the Padres. Buzzy Bavasi said, "We don't have any money. We spent it all on expansion. So we're going to have to ask you guys to sign for a lot less than what you're really worth." And I had had a pretty good year with the Mets the previous year and I was asking for...I think it was $25,000 was what I was asking for. And I ended up signing for about $18,000 with the Padres. We always called him "Mr. B"—

that was his nickname. Buzzy told me, he said, "Someway, somehow, I'll repay this to you." Well, the day that I got into Chicago, John Holland, the general manager, called me up to the office and he says, "Mr. Bavasi told me that he sold you a little short on your contract. We're going to give you $25,000 a year." So I knew darn good and well it came right from Mr. Bavasi. Anyway, I'm sure that was part of the deal. So, I felt like, "Gee whiz—I'll go out and buy me a new Cadillac." So anyway, that's the way it all started and, like I say, from day one I felt like I'd been there for a long, long time.

The decline started in a doubleheader against the San Francisco Giants. We were playing in August and the first...the first game, I can't remember what happened...but the second game, we were in extra innings and there was just a routine groundball hit to Beckert at second and it didn't touch his glove...I mean it went right through his legs. It wasn't hit hard or anything—just a two-hopper. He bent down, and I mean, he just didn't catch it. And nobody thought anything of it. I think we went on and we lost about eight or nine in a row after that. And we had to contribute to it but you have to give credit to the New York Mets. I mean, their win record from that point on was just unbelievable. It was like—they lost maybe 10-11 games the rest of the year and won like about 40.

When did that skid start against San Francisco?
It was about the 15th of August and then we went into New York the first of September. We had a three-game lead, they'd cut it from eight and a half to three. We went in there and we lost all three games. That was the time when in the newspaper they had a black cat that walked out in front of our dugout and, you know, there was big talk about that. That's when we had the big blowout with Donnie Young.

Pressure had started to build up a little bit. We've got a three-game lead and we walked in there with all the confidence in the world. We said, "Hey, they've still gotta come get us." I mean, if we just go out and do our job, even if we don't win every game, they're still not going to be in first place when we leave.

Donnie Young was a very, very quiet individual. Didn't say much at all. He was instructed in spring training, I'm just saying this from what other people have told me, 'cause I was not in spring training with the Cubs, I was with the Padres. That Leo

139

Durocher...they had traded Adolfo Phillips, who was their center fielder and Donnie Young was going to be their center fielder and they brought him up from Double-A ball...they told him, "We don't care if you hit .000. All we want you to do is catch the ball in center field. That's the only thing...we need a defensive gem out there. That's all we need. We don't need any offense at all." 'Cause we had the best offense in the league.

And what had taken place was he'd dropped the flyball...you know, crucial situation. I don't know how old he was at the time. He couldn't have been more than 21-22 years old, I imagine. Right out of Double-A. Now he's fighting for a National League pennant. I imagine some things were going through his mind, too. And he ended up dropping a ball that cost us the game. Ron Santo had said something to the effect that, "All you're here to do is catch the ball and you can't even do that anymore." You know, something to that effect. That's not a quote, of course. It was something to that effect. The sportswriters naturally got wind of that. I mean, the sportswriters from all over the country were following us and the Mets, because of all the things that were happening.

Well, when we left there, we were tied for first place. That's basically what took place with that Donnie Young and Santo thing. You know, in Ronnie's defense, Ronnie was the captain of the team. He kind of carried the Cubs on his shoulders for a long, long time. And he always felt like, as Ron Santo goes, the Cubs will go. So, here's a guy that had been with the Cubs for, geez, I don't know how many years he'd been there. It'd have to have been at least 10 or 11 years. He and Billy Williams, and all those guys altogether, with all those losing teams. Now they've got a chance to win it. Then it's starting to slip away. And the pressure started getting to Ron. As it would to anybody. And I think under normal conditions, Ron would have never said that to Donnie Young. He'd have gone over and said, "Hey, don't worry about it, kid." If we'd had an eight-game lead, I guarantee you, we'd have gone over and said, "Hey, don't worry about it, kid. We'll get 'em tomorrow."

Then you go to Philadelphia. Explain that pick-off with you and Santo.

Well, what had happened was, when I was with the San Diego Padres, Roger Craig told me about this pick-off thing that he had come up with but we'd never done it before. What it was, you have men on first and second with two outs and 3-2 on the hitter. As you take your stretch and you start to make your delivery to home plate. the runners are going to be running on the pitch, 'cause there's two outs. Well, Roger Craig decided why don't we just throw the ball to third base. We'd have the guy in a rundown automatically. He said it's gotta be the right situation. I mean, if you've got a .210 hitter up there, you don't want to show this play. Because this play's only going to work one time. And once they find out about it, then the word is going to get out and you're not going to be able to use it against them. You better use it in a crucial, crucial situation.

So, I had talked to Ron, oh, I would say a few months prior to that about this play, because there'd been a couple of times when I was in that situation and I'd thought about it and I says, "Nah, we've got an eight-game lead. There's no sense in showing it now." And so I sat down with him one night and I told him about it and he says, "Hey, that's a great play. How do you want to key it?" And I says, "Look, we'll just use a verbal sign. That way we don't have to worry because you're only going to do this one time and you don't have to worry about, 'oh, did he get the sign or not?' We'll just use a verbal sign and you answer me verbally and when you answer me I know that you've got it." Well, the verbal sign was his nickname "Dage." I'd say, "Hey, Dage, knock the ball down now. Keep it in the infield," which is a common thing that you say in that situation. And now, we're going back to that pressure that was buildin' up and everything... he feels like everything's on his shoulders and right away he says, "Yeah, I got you. Knock the ball down. OK." And that was the answer.

So, I've got Dick Allen hittin', OK? I've got a two-run lead and 3-2 on Dick Allen. And it's like the eighth inning. Now, here's a guy that in one pitch you could be behind. Okay...here we are. We're tied for first place now, so I give him the thing, he answers me—I take my stretch—I pick up my leg and as I start to throw it, I see him down on all fours—just really going to knock this ball down on the infield. And as I'm throwing the ball, as I'm throwing the ball—I'm yelling "Ronnie" and it goes right over his head and it goes all the way down in the corner at Connie Mack Stadium. Both runs score to tie the game. So we end up losing.

Now, we're a game out of first place. After that game, all the writers came to me and they...well they came to me first. And I'd made up my mind that I was going to take the blame for everything because I didn't want any more pressure put on Santo. I mean, I can still see him in the locker room. I don't know if you've ever been in Connie Mack Stadium or not. The locker room is about— oh, 15 feet wide and 100 feet long. And just a long narrow hallway is all it is. And I can remember him sitting inside—inside his locker—just with his head buried up against the screen. And when I saw that, I said, "Hey, I gotta get some pressure off of him." So the sportswriters they went over to talk to him first, 'cause he's the captain and he just told them, "Hey, I don't want to talk right now." So they came over to me and I said, "It was my fault." Then they said, "Well, what do you mean it was your fault?" And I said, "Well, I gave Ronnie the sign but I didn't get the answer. And why I did it I don't know, I just threw the ball. I threw the ball to third base and..." And they said, "Here you are in the heat of a pennant, isn't it kind of foolish to do a play like that?" And I just...you know, I just acknowledged with, "Yeah, it probably was." Which, to this day, if that play would have worked—I've used that play in college, coaching college. And I'll tell you what—it's never failed yet. And it would have worked because Gonzalez was on second base and I just saw—as a matter of fact I just ran into Tony Gonzalez in St. Petersburg, Florida, at the Alumni Association meeting and Tony to this day even told me, he says, "You know what—I was nailed. I was half way to third base and that ball went over Santo. I couldn't believe where the ball was coming from."

I went and told Ron. I says, "Hey, don't say nothing. I just took the blame for it. We'll just leave it at that and we won't worry about it. We've got some things that are more important than having some sportswriter come up and try to build a big thing out of this."

We just kept losing and they just kept winning.

I think the guys that had been around a long time with that ball club, they will never, ever get over it. I mean, it was like something that was just taken away from their life. Something they'd fought for. See, something that people don't understand about that team is —that team was together longer than probably any other team in the history of baseball. I mean, from the time that I was in the big leagues, which was 1965—that was my first year—it was Hundley, Banks, Beckert, Kessinger, Santo, Williams. And they didn't add anybody. And it was Ferguson Jenkins and it was Bill Hands and it was Kenny Holtzman.

How did Durocher handle it?

Well, I think Leo is just a very, very typical manager. I mean when things like that went wrong and when things were happening —boy, I tell you, you talking about ass-chewings in the clubhouse, he could flat chew ass. But when you left that clubhouse, I mean, it was a completely different story and like the next day you'd go in there—he'd be right in the middle sittin' down there playing cards with the guys. He did exactly what a manager is supposed to do. I mean you're supposed to chew ass and jump on some people, but there's no sense carrying it over to the next day and say, "Well, I ain't goin' to play you today because you messed up yesterday."

We have a coach here at Fresno State, Bob Bennett. Very, very successful coach. And Durocher and Bennett are almost out of the same mold. It's very, very hard for a rookie to break into his line-up. They're all on this veteran stuff all the time. I remember Rich Nye—he was a rookie that year. Archie Reynolds was a rookie that year. Those guys didn't get any pitching time in. Even when you look back and you take our utility players—we had guys like Nate Oliver, who'd been around for years. We had guys like Gene Oliver, who'd been around for years. We had a catcher—Bill Heath. Bill Heath had been around for years. Al Spangler—he just didn't go for the young people. He knew how to manage seasoned players. But when it came down to having a bunch of young pups —I think he would have gotten frustrated. I don't think he would have quit on them, but I don't—you know, when you're a professional, part of becoming a professional is learning how to accept criticism and stuff. Well, when you're a young professional, a lot of times you don't want to even hear criticism much less try to accept it. He's going to criticize you when you've got it comin' to you and he's also going to pat you on the back when you got it comin' to you—but, you know, he's got that real rough voice and he's just...he comes across as a tough guy and you have to be a veteran to understand where he's comin' from.

How did the writers handle the stretch?

Well, they were on Leo more than anybody else. I don't know if you remember or not, but for a while there, I think Hank Aguirre had to be doing Leo Durocher's interviews. Most sportswriters, and I shouldn't say most, I should say 99% of all sportswriters do not print the truth. They turn a word around. When you get all these

143

quotes in the paper from these athletes, I don't even pay attention to 'em. You know, when it says, "Well, I told this sucker to do this or that." I don't believe it. I don't believe it one bit because I've been there and I've...you know, I sat right next to Steve Carlton with Philadelphia the year he won 27. I listened to Steve make his statement, read it in the paper the next day, and it is not the thing that he said.

There wasn't any real bad guys, you know. They were just—I think all writers are just—they're just basically the same. I mean, it's very hard to have any trust in them because you never know when they're not going to—you know, some days you read a quote and, boy, it's quoted exactly as you said it. And other days you'll read a quote and, I mean, it's...you know, half the time when they write down a quote, they've already made up their mind what they want to hear from you. They have. They know the answer, see, but they want to hear the quote so what happens is with them knowing the answer and what you quoted, they put the two together and they fit it into their story.

When people think of Dick Selma, they think of a good pitcher, who really helped the '69 team, and they also think of the Bleacher Bums. How did all that start?

The Bleacher Bums...well, it went back to...we were playing the San Francisco Giants again. And it was like the 11th inning and at that time the clubhouse was way down in the left-field corner. It wasn't underneath the stands like it is now. And I had to go to the bathroom and so you gotta walk...I always sat in the dugout and the reason I always sat in the dugout was because I wanted to sit around the guy who was pitchin' that day and the catcher. And if there was a hitter that I was having trouble with, I could talk to them between innings. "Hey, how you getting this guy out? I can't get him out," or whatever. So, like the 10th or 11th inning, I had to walk down to the bathroom and I came out and, you know, Wrigley Field has got a distinct noise to it. It's got a little kids' noise. There's always kids at that ballpark. I mean, you could blindfold me and put me in Wrigley Field and I'd tell you I was in Wrigley Field as soon as I heard the noise. And I walked out and you could hear a pin drop. I mean, it was just complete silence. And when you walk out of that clubhouse, you're not more than 25-30 feet from the bleachers. So, I yelled up to them, "Hey, for crying out loud, make some noise. We haven't lost this game yet." And so, they started singing "Please don't kick my dog around," which was a big song that they used to have. They used to go "ala-be-well, ala-bi-well, beeble, bible, bum" and stuff like that. Well, when they started singing that, I jumped out and I threw my hand down and, boy, they just went bananas. The next pitch Ernie Banks hit out of the ballpark to win the game.

So, the next day, I went back down in the dugout. Durocher grabbed me and says, "You get down there in that bullpen and you get those Bleacher Bums goin'." I said, "Leo, I want to sit up here on the bench." He says, "No, I want you down there in the bullpen getting the Bleacher Bums goin'." Leo Durocher was probably the most superstitious man I've ever seen in my life. I mean all baseball players are superstitious. All athletes are superstitious. I mean, they'll put their socks on the same way every day. They'll have game socks. They'll have whatever it may be. They all have superstitions and Durocher—I mean anything that happened that was good, boy, he just kept milkin' it.

One thing that always stayed in my mind was, one day our regular bat boy...I don't know what happened, he was sick or something, and so Yosh Kawano, who was the equipment manager —still is the equipment manager and I'll tell you a little story about him—he went out and got this young kid. So, down at the end of the old dugout—the way they used to have the bat racks in Wrigley Field, all it was was a 2 x 4 and it was laying right in front of the dugout—the whole length of the dugout and then they had holes drilled in the 2 x 4 where you'd slip your bats in there. Well, at the end of infield, the bat boy would always take the four fungos and stick them down at the very, very end of the rack and that's where they stayed. That was Durocher's superstition. Those fungos stayed in those last four holes in the dugout. Well, this kid didn't know any better and he took the fungos and he took them out of those four slots and slid them underneath the bench. And Durocher fired him on the spot. I mean, Yosh Kawano had to go get him and just get the kid out—the kid didn't know what he did wrong, but I mean, that's the way Leo was.

That's basically how those Bleacher Bums got started because Ernie hit that home run and all I said was—"For crying out loud, we haven't lost yet." Make some noise—it was like, I'm the one that did it. And I didn't do anything. Ernie's the one that did it. And that's how it started and then from there it was just...it became national TV and everything.

I think Yosh probably had the greatest statement I ever heard from a clubhouse man. He used to walk around with... shoot, he must have had 30-40 pieces of paper in his back pocket all the time. And I always used to ask him, "What are those things in your back pocket for?" He says, "They're just blank pieces of paper. When I need something, I got some paper, I write it down." And I said, "Oh, that's not a bad idea." So, anyway, one day—I can't remember who it was—somebody got on Yosh about something, you know. He asked for a new jock or something and it wasn't in his locker. I don't remember who it was. And I mean it doesn't matter if it was Ernie Banks or who it was, but Yosh walked up to him and he says, "Let me tell you something. I was here before you were here and I'll be here when you're gone. And don't you forget that." And you know what—he still tells those guys that today.

Did you ever get involved with the Bleacher Bums after hours?

Every once in a while, Hank Aguirre and myself—mostly the guys in the bullpen, you know, Don Nottebart and Ted Abernathy —the four of us, what we would do is, when we were out running wind sprints—they weren't wind sprints, they were quarterbacks; Joe Becker used to hit them with a fungo, 'cause he was too old to throw the darn thing, but he could dial in on that fungo. We'd run from foul line to foul line with these quarterbacks. Well, all the bleacher people would throw money out there all the time to us. They would throw us, you know, nickels, dimes, quarters. So we'd pick 'em up and we'd always put them in a sanitary sock in our locker. And when that sanitary sock was almost full, then after a ball game one day we'd all go over to Ray's Bleacher Bums' Bar in center field and we'd take that sanitary sock and we'd dump all the money out on the counter and we'd make poor old Ray count the money and then we'd say, "You just buy drinks until this money's gone."

They had gone to Cincinnati. Hank Aguirre kept bugging me about—hey listen, they're down here at this tavern down here. You oughta go down there and at least say hello to them or something. And have a beer with them. And I said, "Nah, I'd rather not, Hank." And he said, "Come on, I'll go with you." And I says, "Well, alright." Well, I didn't know that they were settin' me up. And I got down there and I mean, it was—I can't even remember where it was in Cincinnati—but I mean it was a little teeny hole in the wall. So we were sittin' around and we were having a couple of beers and I was gettin' ready to leave and this one good lookin' girl comes up and she says, "I'd like to dance with you before you leave." I said, "Alright." So, I dance with her and they were all laughin' and I couldn't figure out what was goin' on. It was a guy! It was a guy! I mean, I got set up bigger than heck.

Was 1969 one of your better years in baseball?

It started out that way. I was 10-3 at the All-Star break and then what happened was Durocher—like I say, he's real superstitious—and after the All-Star break, we had a schedule that was just unbelievable. We'd play three days, we'd be off a day. We'd play three days, we'd be off a day. So Durocher didn't want to change his rotation, so I was the fourth starter. So what he did was he went with a three-man rotation and the only time he'd use me is when we played four days in a row. Well, what happened was I just got flat. I remember after the All-Star break, I didn't pitch for like 15-20 days. And then all of a sudden we play four days and I go out there and, hell, by the fourth inning I'm taking a shower. And, it just turned my whole season around because I had a chance...I think without a doubt, if we'd have stayed with the rotation, I probably would have won 15 ball games that year.

Now, I don't know what would have happened to the other three—Ferguson Jenkins and Holtzman and Hands—I don't know, maybe they would have decreased, because they're used to working on every fourth day. I'm sure he made the move that he thought was best for the club. We'll never know if it would have worked out better the other way.

Hall of Fame pitcher—winner of 284 games and one of the all-time Cub greats. Looking back at the 1969 season he said, "...the only factor that hurt is we didn't have much of a bench." He is convinced you will never again see ball clubs with all-star lineups as in the past.

You were traded to the Cubs in April of 1966 from the Phillies. What was that 1966 Cub team like?

Well, we had a lot of unproven rookies and about four veterans —Ernie Banks, Santo, Williams, and I think we had Dick Bertell. And Dick Ellsworth. We weren't a team of solid ballplayers that were gonna, you know, lead our division. I came over from the Phillies, and my idea of staying in the big leagues was to pitch pretty good relief—which I did. I got into about 50 games out of the bullpen and I started probably about 10.

They always say the first appearance can be lasting. I pitched against the Dodgers about five and two-thirds innings and I hit a home run against Don Sutton. And also a single to drive in both runs. We ended up winning, 2-0, and Ted Abernathy relieved me, I think in the eighth inning.

But my outlook on the game was to try to win possibly 50 games as a relief pitcher. But that didn't hold up too long because in 1967, when I went to spring training, Leo had been talking to some of the front office people and they said if Jenkins can win himself a spot as a starter, he'd be one of the young starters along with Holtzman and Hands and possibly Nye and Joe Niekro. And, we still were an unproven team. But, we turned it around and in part of '68 and then in '69 we led the division most of the year and then the Mets caught us in September.

I learned how to throw an offbeat change-up and an offbeat slider from some of the pitching coaches in the Phillies organization. Plus, the fact that Joe Becker was avid that if you didn't run to keep your legs and body strong, you couldn't pitch for the Cubs.

I was a hard worker when I was younger and I put some games together. A string of 20 wins for like six years in a row. Only because of the credit I give guys like Joe Becker and Leo, who left me out there, and players like Santo, Williams, Kessinger, Beckert, Hundley...these fellows scored me the runs and played good defense behind me.

The '69 team played together for a number of years—really started in '65. You had three Hall of Famers—Banks, Williams, and you.

Yeah, that's something that a lot of times you might not see. We had some solid athletes in certain positions, but we were a little short still in the bullpen and in the infield, like for the extra players. Because teams that win nowadays have a strong bench and a very, very strong bullpen. And the bullpen in the '80s and '90s has changed drastically. They've got the middle relievers, the set-up men, and then the closers, which these three individuals do most of the work to win ball games. And if your starter is really washed out bad, then they've got the extra guys in the bullpen to come through and, basically, they're mop-up artists. But the set-up and the closers—they become such a tradition in pitching nowadays that they get "X" amount of dollars and they are just as important as the starters.

What happened in '69?

Leo was playing most of the veterans because he had more confidence in them. I think that we didn't have a strong bench but if you look back at the Mets...they started a string of games—they won like 30 of 37. Had a phenomenal record. And they were the only team in baseball that had a five-man rotation. And if you look back now, they're the team that basically started this with Koosman and Seaver, Nolan Ryan, Gentry, and another pitcher named McAndrews. So, they were really a young pitching staff that really came on. They had good young hitters that played well. They had Grote behind the plate...and they had a pretty solid ball club that played well through the stretch. We faltered I think the second week of September. We started losing bad on the road trips...Phillies, Cincinnati, St. Louis and then we had to face the Mets, I think eight times and they swept us in, I think, a four-game series in New York and then they came back and beat us two out of three at home. So, we just couldn't catch 'em. We had a six-and-a-half to eight-game lead. They caught us and went by us and we ended up in second place.

It wasn't a case so much of the Cubs losing it, it was more that the Mets just played better baseball the last six, seven weeks of the season.

Oh, definitely. I think they played well over .800 ball. And in that stretch—as I said—they won so many ball games 1-0, 2-1—they were winning the important games. They played phenomenal baseball and credit to them. They were called "the Miracle Mets." They ended up winning, then went on to beat Baltimore in the World Series.

Did Leo handle the '69 team well?

I think we had an outstanding ballclub. Leo could only do so much. You know, Leo couldn't play for us. He put the right fellows out there, I thought, at the right positions. But at times the guys were tired. They wanted to continue to play. If you look at some of the records, Billy Williams played 160 games, Randy caught 150, Santo played 155. Ernie at the age of 38 played about 140. So, I think the only factor that hurt is we didn't have much of a bench. We had Gene Oliver, Nate Oliver, Willie Smith, and, I think, Paul Popovich, and we really didn't have guys that we could throw in, that could step in and do a real good job to overcome a lot of the veterans that were playing. They're playing so good.

It was one of the better teams I played for. Unfortunately, we didn't win it. We had almost the same team next year in '70. We added Joe Pepitone. We had Hickman in the outfield. And we got overtaken by Pittsburgh. And I think if we had won it that one year, and shored up a little better bullpen, we might have put a couple of World Series together, but it just didn't happen.

Does '69 bother you?

It doesn't bother me. I played one year at a time. I was trying to pitch as well as I could each year to win. I know that we had some things happen that year. But, there has been like a phobia about the '69 Cubs not winning and they should have won. You take the '84 Cubs. They should have won—they didn't win. It's really unfortunate that the Cubs really haven't put a championship ball club together 'cause they have a championship city.

What was your biggest thrill as a Cub?

Well...ah, geez, I've had a ton of them. That winning 20

games, six years in a row. Winning the first time 20 games and the last game of the season Al Spangler hitting a home run against St. Louis. 1967 All-Star Game. Striking out six men in three innings, Mickey Mantle included. There's been so many. Getting voted to the Cub Hall of Fame along with Santo, Beckert, Kessinger, a bunch of guys that were all All-Stars. Knowing guys like Ernie Banks. Roomed with him for two years. Playing with Santo and Williams and Kenny Holtzman...these type of individuals.

And you know, there's no teams that play now in the '80s or the '90s that have the type of personnel that you'd seen in the '60s. You take a team like the Giants—you got McCovey, Mays, Perry, Marichal, Bolin, Davenport. You don't see teams like that. Or Pittsburgh had Sanguillen, Clemente, Stargell, Clendenon, Alley, Mazeroski - you know, you won't see teams like that anymore in baseball only because they're not as good.

They're just not as good. You won't see the name players ever again, I don't think that will ever happen.

You feel when you played in the '60s and '70s, the quality was better than it is now?

Oh, definitely. Definitely. You just won't see that caliber of individual come along. You'll never see another Marichal or another Gibson...another Carlton...another Seaver. You just won't see these people anymore. They won't want to win 300 games because they make too much money. There is no incentive. You won't see another Pete Rose who plays 22 years. Or Jim Kaat that played 23 years. Or Tommy John that pitched 25 years and Niekro. These guys are forgotten individuals. You just won't see it again.

What was your top salary?

Oh, probably about $375,000 to $400,000, I think, was my top salary with the Cubs. Mr. Wrigley, I think, was fair, but he could have probably done better. There were teams that were paid a little higher. But, you know, I was happy with the money I got. And when I came back to the Cubs and the Tribune Company, I got paid handsomely for what I did.

You just missed that '84 season. You retired in 1983 with the Cubs.

Yeah, well I went to spring training in '84, but being the older pitcher, they were going to go to a youth movement. I thought I could have still pitched, but when I got released in the spring, there were some teams that wanted me. But, I didn't want to play with anybody but the Cubs.

You said you roomed with Ernie. What kind of guy was Ernie?

I call him "AM" and "FM." Just like a radio. You can't turn it off. A bubbly individual. A guy that loved to play the game. Wanted to win. And wanted to just prove that he was capable of doing a job day-in and day-out. They gave his job away four or five different times. Lee Thomas. To I think, Boccabella. Shoot, who else—Dick Nen. I'm trying to think of who else—George Altman and Ernie just kept winning it back. Ernie was that type of player. He didn't say too much. Just went out and done the job and hit some home runs and that's why he's a 500 home run hitter.

Would you want to get back in baseball?

On the coaching aspect, sure. I had an offer with the Giants. But unfortunately, you know, with my wife passing and the Hall of Fame, I'm trying to stick close to home as much as possible. I have a sitter that comes in on the weekends and, you know, she's helping me with the kids, but handling two very young children, you have to be home.

One of the best shortstops in Cub history. His regret is that the 1969 team did not bring a pennant to Chicago. He often thinks about it—he believes they were the best team in baseball that year.

Were you signed by the Cubs?

Yes, I was. I was very fortunate. I went to college here at "Ole Miss" and signed with them in 1964. And that was really before the college draft, to date myself a little bit. I was sent to Double-A baseball in the Texas League. I played the rest of that year, starting in late June '64, in Double-A and then played about six weeks of 1965 in Double-A ball and then went straight to the Cubs. And so I was very fortunate to have spent probably less than a full season in the minor leagues. I went up around the first of June in '65 and played the rest of that year.

They put you in and you stayed in.

Yes, I did. I'm not sure if all of that was on merit, but I did stay in the rest of that year, yeah.

What shortstop did you replace?

Well, you know, Ernie Banks had been the shortstop a couple of years previous to that and then they had a guy named Andre Rodgers, who was a very fine player who had played a couple of years there. And then the year that I came up, they had had a guy start that season named Roberto Peña and Roberto and I just kinda switched places in June. He went down to the Texas League and I came up to the big leagues. I was fortunate to have stayed quite a few years after that.

I came up in '65—you know there was two 10-team leagues at that time. We finished eighth that year and then at the end of the year, they made a managerial change, if you remember, and Leo Durocher came in and took over the Cubs. In fact, Leo made his famous statement, he said, "I'll guarantee you one thing. This is no eighth-place ball club." He was dead right. 'Cause we went out and finished 10th. When we finished 10th in '66, he played an awful lot of young guys and took his lumps.

But you were really building a nucleus.

Absolutely—positively. I can't tell you that in '66 I felt real good about it. We lost a hundred and some games, but we kept the same nucleus of players. The infield was Banks-Beckert-Santo and me and Hundley behind the plate and Billy Williams in the outfield and Ken Holtzman and Hands and Jenkins—so, you know, the nucleus was there. And they kept that and then they would add to it each year with some players and guys like Jim Hickman and some of them that came in and just did fabulous jobs. But you really felt it in 1967. I'll never forget about half way through the year in 1967. We went into first place. And you know, the city just went nuts and the ballpark did as well. I vividly remember that Sunday when we went into first place and, although we didn't stay there, our ball club realized that we could contend. We could compete and ended up finishing third that year.

When you went to spring training in '69, did you feel that you could do it that year?

We felt we were the best team in baseball. And we came out of the gate as if...and I still believe we were the best team in baseball, but we didn't win.

When did the Cubs begin the slide in 1969?

You know, I don't know...I can't pick a day. I can't tell you it was against the Pirates, or against the Mets, or against the Phillies. I can't pick a day and tell you that's the day it went south. I can tell you that starting in mid to late August, we were up by eight and a half games, but I know that our ball club was tired. I know that I was tired. And you don't consciously say that. I mean, I certainly felt like we were strong enough to finish the thing out and win it. But, we were a tired ball club and people forget how well the Mets really did play. I mean, their record down the stretch in the last month and a half was absolutely phenomenal. And, you know, every night we would go out there, they had won. Or every day you go out—you know. It's just one of those deals that the harder you try sometimes, the worse you do. I think that's what happened with us.

Did Durocher do a good job in '69?

Yeah, I think...you know what Leo did that I particularly liked is that Leo had a lineup and he played that lineup and I know he's gotten a lot of criticism for it. But, you know, you have to put yourself in his shoes in the sense that if you're going down the stretch and you're trying to win a pennant—the first one for the Cubs in many, many years—and you're the guy who has to make that lineup out every day, are you going to write the guys in there, the eight guys down that you think are your best eight guys for that day or, you know...and that's what he did. We had a set lineup and we played it. Now, sure, there's been a lot of arguments that Paul Popovich, who was a great utility player, could have spelled some of us and, in hindsight, that's probably true. But, you know, I didn't ever go to Leo and say, "Skip, I need a day off." So, maybe we're as much to blame as anybody else.

I have to tell you that in all candor it was the best of times and the worst of times. It was the greatest experience I've ever had in baseball. And playing in 1969, in Chicago, the fans were phenomenal. In fact, probably so good that that's another thing that probably helped to make us more tired. Because they came to the park at 9:00 in the morning. They opened the gates early that year 'cause there was such a big crowd outside the park. And they opened the gates like at 9:00 or 9:30 or something that year. You know, normally a lot of times you come on the field and you take batting practice and the gates aren't open and you relax. Well, you know, that year, man, our stands were full. We would have big crowds when we were hitting. So, it was an unbelievable time.

You drive down expressways and people standing on over-ramps recognize your cars and wave at you. It was an unbelievable time in our lives. It's unfortunate that we couldn't do the one thing that we wanted to do more than anything else and that's win a pennant for those people. And we didn't do that. So it ended up being a very unhappy ending for us, but an unhappy ending to an overall great summer.

I don't think we'll ever forget it. I don't think it's accurate to say we'll never get over it. I think we got over it the end of the year. But, you know, I don't think we'll ever forget it. But you know, I have to tell you the truth. I went to spring training in 1970 and 1971 and thought going into spring training those years that we were the best team. I felt like those years we were every bit as good or better than the '69 team. Perhaps had we won in '69, maybe we would have won in '71 or '72 or '70...who knows?

Everybody focuses on the '69 season. But if you go back and look, we were an exceptionally good ball club in 1970, in 1971 and, you know, we went into spring training totally believing we were going to win the pennant in those years and they were very exciting years. It's just that we didn't lead from the starting gate, but as far as the ball club, I thought it was every bit as good a club. It was the same people. You know, the same people. We talk about the '69 team—but it was really the same team basically.

What about the salaries today?
I have absolutely zero bad feelings. You know the game is as popular today as it's ever been at any time in the past. The ballparks are full. Everybody's building new ballparks. Apparently the game is very healthy. Why can I complain because I didn't happen to be born at the right time?

What was your highest salary in the big leagues?
Well, the year I was player-manager with the White Sox. Totally, I was probably $250,000. That may be a little high, maybe it was $225,000.

What was the most you made playing for the Cubs?
Oh, gosh. I'd have to go back and look, but somewhere—$80,000 to $90,000. I don't complain. I'm not complaining. Sure, I wish I was playing today. I could adjust to $2-1/2 million a year. I wish I were playing today. You know, when I was a rookie in 1965 for the Cubs, Robin Roberts was on the Cub ball club. We had a lot of older pitchers that year that had played for a long time and I have great respect for Robin Roberts and Larry Jackson and Bob Buhl. They had a veteran pitching staff and I remember that year, Robin Roberts when I came in made a statement to me, I think it was Robin, said to me, "You're very lucky to be coming into a game at a time when they're paying such good salaries."
So everything in perspective. I mean I don't understand it...No. I don't understand how 30 something guys can be making over $3 million. But obviously, I have to believe the owners are intelligent men and they know what they can and cannot do.

You are coaching at "Ole Miss" in the Southeastern Conference. What is the caliber of ball?
I would have to tell you that this league that we're in now,

when we play inside our league and we have 27 conference games —it is an exceptionally good brand of baseball and the last five or six years, college baseball has come light years in my opinion. And it's really a good caliber ball. If a guy can come out of this league, if he can excel in this league, he can go into pro baseball and do very, very well. In fact, I truthfully, and I'm prejudice because I'm in the college game now, but I really don't think that the scouting directors in a lot of ball clubs today realize what a benefit it is to draft these kids that are coming out of these good conferences.

I think a guy that excels in this league can certainly come out of here and pull his own in high A or Double-A baseball. I'm not saying the league as a whole is Double-A baseball. But I think that a guy that excels in this league and comes out of here can certainly hold his own at the higher A, possible Double-A level.

Any regrets?

Yes. I have the regret that we didn't win. And I really mean that. Personally, I mean it and even more than that, you know, I truly feel that we let the people of Chicago down because we weren't able to do it. And, sure, I believe that I would be lying to tell you that I don't think about that often and don't regret that. I'm sitting here in my office and on a wall there's a picture of Beckert and Banks and Santo and Jim Hickman and Williams and Jenkins and Hundley, Holtzman and Young where we went back and did a benefit deal one time. You know, you look at that and you think...gosh, why couldn't we have done it, you know. So yeah, there are some regrets. But I don't know that I would do anything different if we had to go back and try it again, 'cause it was a wonderful experience.

Excellent second baseman who played for the Cubs from 1965 through 1973. He is not too happy with the game today.

Where is baseball today as opposed to when you were playing in the '60s and '70s?

Oh, it's big business. Back then it was a game. It's like you talking to your father and it was a lot meaner back when your father grew up. But now baseball is—don't pitch inside, don't throw at somebody, be nice, pick up your 60 grand a week, and go about business. Go back to our hotel rooms and play Nintendo and we'll bet some money.

You feel it was a tougher game when you played.

I don't feel it—facts will prove that. The fact that you can't throw inside. If you get hit, you charge the mound. You don't get in front of a groundball anymore. You backhand the ball now, so the scorer up in the booth, you put a question in his mind whether it's a hit or should have been fielded.

Everything now is stats. You go into a major league clubhouse now, they pick up stat sheets. And, of course, they call their agent —"Well, I went two for four. I had three assists."

We never thought of it (stats) back in those days. It was winning-losing. It's where the kids were brought up at my time. You either won or you lost. You won as a team or you lost as a team.

You think team spirit is out?

Oh, it is out. It's totally gone. You're talking about 25 guys that are individual corporations. Oh...it's a business now. It's not baseball. I mean it's a business.

Jerry Kindall thinks the kids coming out of school now are stronger, have better programs, nutrition is better and so forth.

Well, let me put it this way. They're bigger. They're stronger and an old friend of mine, Bill George that was killed about 10 or nine years ago—he says, "You know, in football, it's happening just the way it is in baseball. Guys look like Tarzan, play like Jane."

Isn't that simple enough? I mean, all you have to do now in today's game, with the benefits and all this stuff with the money involved, all you have to do is have one good year.

You realize the salaries are going to go much higher than they are now. Without a doubt. I mean, if you're a business agent, you've got to understand that. They're going much higher. Because the fact is, baseball within five to 10 years will be international. You have a society—Japan—that's crazy for baseball. Now, with the cable—can you imagine having maybe a million people in Japan at a dollar a piece for every game...162? It's a business now. Now, it's a total business.

The ballparks are all going to be standardized. And once Wrigley's gone—in maybe five or 10 years, whatever it is—you're going to see all standard parks. You're going to see astro-turf. You're going to see the roof. And that's tough.

The thing is you're getting not the hungry people anymore. You're getting kids out of college, right? And they play with...the big thing is aluminum bats. You play in college—nobody gets stung. They don't know how to play baseball. I mean, aluminum bats—there's a guy—Hank Aaron—would probably hit 2,000 home runs with an aluminum bat.

Why do they allow that in college?

I don't know, because it's cheap. Everything involved with sports today is financial.

I'll really be honest—I kind of put baseball behind me. I'm trying to master the game of golf—which I'm horse shit. I love fishing—but I can't believe some of the new players. I mean it's totally different.

They've never heard of you guys, have they?

No. I mean, here's the thing that I was shocked with. Ryne Sandberg, who I consider one of the best baseball players of today, didn't know Ernie Banks' name. Well, if you come from Seattle, you understand that. Isn't that amazing? But that's the way the kids are now. Now it's—how much money do I put in the bank? Who was the kid from the White Sox got hit in the head? The guy says, "Well, my this is shocking." And I think I remember Drysdale says, what is the use for helmets? Doesn't everybody look better on TV without the helmets? Wouldn't the player look better without a helmet on?

I mean, you know now—man, a guy comes in two inches inside you're out on the mound fighting.

If somebody hit a home run or you were whipping the team, you got hit.

In fact, I was hitting, like close to .200. First time in L.A., man, I'm a hillbilly. Billy Williams behind me says, "Glenn, Drysdale is going to hit you." I said, "If he's that dumb to hit me, I'm not even hitting .200." Drilled me in the side. Put down the bat and walked to first base.

Why did Williams know you were going to get hit?

Because he hit everybody. Any rookie. He just did it. I mean, you know, what is he—6'6"? Oh, he was fun...oh! He's a nice man though.

How would a new kid—24 year old guy, a year or two in the bigs —how would he handle Leo Durocher?

No chance! You know, Leo was something. We got him in the end of his career. They'd have no chance. He'd be too tough. He was tough on pitchers and extra men. The guys that played every day, he wouldn't be watchin' them. Just wrote the lineup every day.

It takes a psychologist out of the Harvard School of Medicine to handle a major league club. I mean, what do you know. How would you deal with a Canseco?

Any regrets?

No, no, no. I'm so happy. I'm still living at 51. You know, rooming with Santo was no pleasure. Jesus.

One of the all-time Cubs. Always in the game, tough competitor, Hall of Fame material. Did not like ending his career with the White Sox.

I was invited to spring training as a non-roster player in 1960. I was going to break camp with the club but they made a trade for Don Zimmer. They decided to send me to Triple-A ball and so I went down to Triple-A for two months, then I was back in June.

Lou Boudreau was up in the broadcast booth and he switched seats with Charlie Grimm, who was the manager at the time, and when he took over, he recalled me from the minor leagues.

I signed as a catcher. I didn't do any catching in the minor leagues. I came to spring training and they had a lot of catchers...young catchers in their organization. Bob Scheffing was my first manager. Bob Scheffing at that time said, "You know, the way you can hit, we'd like to find a position for you." And I said, "Well, I play third base." I played in high school and semi-pro and American Legion so that's how I got to third base.

Your career began with the College of Coaches. What do you re-member of it?

Well, it was kind of ridiculous. I was very young. I was more concerned about just staying in the big leagues. They had 12 rov-ing coaches, which came up from the minor leagues to the big leagues, and they would rove every two weeks. Every two weeks you were having a new head coach and they all had different thoughts and different ways they wanted you to play that position and the way they wanted you to hit. So, it was very confusing as a young player. But, thank God, it only lasted one year and I was fortunate that I was so young that it didn't really bother me.

Didn't that go into '62?

Part of '62. Then Bob Kennedy took over as the head coach.

What about your "beef" with Adolpho Phillips?

It wasn't a beef. There was a ball hit over his head and we

were really struggling. I mean this ball club was losing and the ball went over his head and he kind of walked towards the ball rather than hustle after it. And when he came into the dugout, I just took him underneath my...I was captain of the ball club at that time and I just said to him that you can't be showin' up this club by not giving 100% out there. That was pretty much it.

He had a lot of talent. He could run. He could hit. He could hit with power. He had a good arm, but evidently he just lacked that little motivation and he just didn't go full throttle.

Have you gotten over that '69 season?

Oh, very definitely. First of all, I never thought it was a bad season, when you say getting over it. In my mind, personally, that was probably the best year that I enjoyed because it was a ball club. You could see that we were starting to develop a good ball club in '67. In '66, when Durocher came, I think we ended up last but then in '67 we ended up third and we were just starting to come into our own. When '69 started, on paper I felt we were the best ball club in the National League. Of course, Baltimore was the best ball club in baseball, but it was an exciting year.

What about the death threats relative to the Don Young incident?

Well, that was just part of what went on after that incident. The Don Young incident was really blown out of proportion. After that, like a lot of players, there's people out there that send you death threats. And I just happened to have a person that was always sending a letter every Tuesday and letting me know where we were, my kids and everything. Went through that for about one year and then it stopped.

If you had won it in '69, do you think you would have won it the next few years?

Yeah, I think that's right as far as I'm concerned. I think if we had won in '69, we probably would have won in '70 for sure. And we came very close in '70 and '71. But, it didn't happen. It was a good ball club, but I think when we went to spring training in 1970, I think everybody went down there saying, "Look, we were close, but we can win it this year." We got close again, but we never won it.

What was Durocher like as a manager? Should he have rested the regulars more often in '69?

Well, I thought he was a very good manager and, in fact, when Leo Durocher came with this ball club in 1966 is when the Chicago Cubs started to get some respect from the opposing teams. He was the players' manager. He protected his players. He knew the game very well. As far as 1969 and saying that he should have rested a few of us, I didn't look at it that way only because it's pretty hard to change that lineup. It was very easy to walk in that clubhouse and put up that lineup, because there was eight solid ballplayers and they say that if he would have rested us occasionally, that we would have been a lot stronger at the end of the year. I know Kessinger felt that way and I know a few other players felt that way. But, when you're in the heat of things, the adrenalin's flowing and the last thing in the world you want is to sit down under those conditions. So, I never felt that way.

What was your greatest thrill as a Cub?

Coming up to the big leagues at 20 and opening up in Forbes Field in a doubleheader June 26th and going five for seven with five RBIs, was probably my biggest thrill.

What is the difference between when you were playing and the ballplayer of today?

When I was playing, there was only 16 major league teams in the big leagues. Eight in the National League. Eight in the American League. Each major league team probably had 20 minor league teams, so the teaching and the fundamentals were really taught well in those minor leagues. I only had one year in the minor leagues, but when I came up to the big leagues, that's where I got my experience and the coaching was outstanding.

Today, there's 26 teams. Every team has five or six minor league teams and kids are coming up very early. They're coming right out of college, right into the big leagues, and they don't have that fundamental teaching. And what I'm seeing is that it's not the same fundamental baseball that is being played. They're not thinking baseball as much as we were. And not everybody goes out there full throttle. I think the big reason for that is, is when you're guaranteed contracts—guaranteed the same amount no matter if you're going to hit .300 one year and .200 the next year. That incentive can't be there. You see a lot of that. There's still players out there that are giving you 100%, but I don't care who you are, when you're guaranteed so many million dollars for three years, that incentive...that little bit of incentive's gotta be gone.

Wish you had been born later?

Not at all. Not at all, because I recall when I was in spring training and I was sitting next to Walt Moryn and Dale Long, and they knew that I had an opportunity to make the big leagues as young as I was. They said, "Boy, I'd like to be making your money, you know what I mean, as young as you are and the kind of money you're going to make in the big leagues." In those days, maybe the highest player was less than $100,000. So, it's a matter of the era.

How do you like it in the radio booth?

I like it very much. I'm enjoying it. One thing that I've done here is I've taken this job mainly because I still have a few years left to get in the Hall of Fame. I felt this kind of hurt me, leaving the game and going into business and not keeping my face in the media. So I took this, plus the fact that we never did win—I never did win as a player and I feel like the Cubs, even though they're not playing that well, was going to be the team of the '90s and I felt this would give me an opportunity to be part of a winner.

His first at bat in the majors was against Lew Burdette of the Milwaukee Braves. His knees were knocking so he couldn't swing at the first pitch as he had planned. Along the way he got better...all the way to the Hall of Fame.

Has the theory of hitting changed since your playing days with the Cubs?

I think along with the pitching that's coming in the league and the relief pitching, I think hitting had to change because when I came up to the big leagues in 1959, the pitching at that time—it was like a 3-1 fastball, a 3-2 fastball, a 2-0 fastball. You faced the same pitcher throughout nine innings. But now, because so many pitchers are coming from the American League into the National League, you can't sit on a 2-0 fastball, they throw a lot of breaking balls and what have you.

The relief pitcher came into being about 10 years ago. Rolly Fingers dominated the league in 1972, '73, and '74 with the Oakland A's. Goose Gossage did with the New York Yankees. So, I think insofar as the hitter going up to the plate and really concentrating, sitting on the one ball, one particular pitch, I think he had to change his way of hitting, because if you hadn't, you'd be still standing at the plate waiting on that fastball that you didn't get many, many times.

This is primarily because of the emphasis on relief pitching now?

I think so. I got an article today and it was saying that Fergie Jenkins' father a long time ago talked to him about what you start, you finish. I guess Bob Gibson's father must have told him the same thing. So has Drysdale. So has Koufax. And these pitchers— they normally pitched 250 innings, 270 innings per year. You saw the same pitcher, maybe four times a game. And if you saw those Hall of Famers, quite naturally you see the ball but a lot of times they had so much stuff on the ball. If you see a mediocre pitcher for four times, the chances are each time you go up to the plate to face him, the percentage of getting a hit should be greater and greater.

The best pitcher I ever faced from the first inning to the last inning, having the same stuff, the fastball, the curve—the only two pitches he had, and he didn't throw a change up, but he had overpowering fastball, a breaking ball—and that was Sandy Koufax. It was a long time before he got the control. He always threw his ball hard. He knew what he was doing on the mound, but he just couldn't make the pitches. But his last years in the big leagues, I think he was one of the greatest pitchers I ever seen.

That came with maturity. You look at Sandy Koufax, you think about Bob Gibson—he was the guy that threw hard and was wild and Nolan Ryan, when he first came up with the New York Mets. These pitchers they threw hard. They didn't know where it was going and they had good stuff. They had a good slider and Koufax, of course, had the breaking ball and Nolan Ryan had the good curveball. But staying in the league, maturing, getting really comfortable on the mound and that comes with pitching and somebody had the nerve and the confidence to stay with them and let them get on the mound and just pitch. And what happens, they pay dividends at the end.

Who was the best Cub hitter you ever saw?

The two guys that was here, that won batting titles. I think Bill Buckner was a good hitter. He stayed here a little while. And, of course, Bill Madlock.

I know when I was coaching at the time, I was coaching hitting for the Cubs and Bill Buckner won the batting title. And I thought that year he put up some great numbers. He was a great hitter in the clutch. He was just an outstanding hitter.

And, of course, when I was with the ball club in 1972 as a player—Bill (Madlock) first came with the ball club, I could see the quickness he had at the plate. He had a quick bat, enabled him to wait a long time to see the breaking ball and adjust. I could see right away that he was going to put up some good numbers on the board, 'cause he won two batting titles here; he went to the Pirates and won a batting title. So I think, other than myself, the guys I've seen, I think Bill Buckner and Bill Madlock was two of the good hitters that performed for the Cubs.

When I first went to spring training with the Cubs in 1957, I had an opportunity at that time to meet Rogers Hornsby. Rogers Hornsby started working for the Cubs organization and I was out one day hitting and Rogers took a liking to me. I didn't know anything about hitting, the mechanics of hitting and stuff like that. Through working with him and he talking about the strike zone, making a ball be over home plate—which is 17 inches wide from the armpit to your knee—I began to look for certain pitches. I began to wait for the ball to come in the strike zone. And then I began to be a pretty decent hitter.

He was a guy who really knew something about hitting. He had performed so well in the major league and he is considered one of the greatest right-hand hitters that ever played the game. So, when he spoke, people listened to him. And I listened to him. He told me some good things about what to do and how to react to certain pitches.

Do you remember your first hit in the big leagues?

As a matter of fact, I don't. I remember my first time going up to the plate facing Lew Burdette. I remember striking out. When I called my father and told him that I was in the big leagues and I said, "We're going to face the Braves, the Milwaukee Braves." He said, "Well, if you face Lew Burdette, the first pitch he always threw is right down the middle. So you be ready to hit." I took the first pitch because my knees was knocking so much.

The first game of any season, you're nervous. When do you lose that nervousness?

You're not nervous through the whole game. It's just after you get back from spring training, you take six weeks out there. You've been off for about five months. You go through spring training. Your opening day of the season and you look forward to it. As a matter of fact, you look forward to the whole season. But it's just the excitement of opening day, all the fanfare and all the emphasis the people put on you having a good year, the ball club having a good year. But I think after you make an out or after you get a base hit I think for the next at-bats of the first game you're alright. It's just opening day jitters the first time at the plate.

You don't get nervous. Because you've geared your body to that. You build up your body to that—to concentrate when 40,000-50,000 people are out there looking at you up at the plate. That's baseball, so you've been groomed for that.

What was your biggest hit?

1970, I believe it was. Opening day of the season. We were

playing an extra-inning ball game and I'm facing Bob Gibson;
Fergie Jenkins and Bob Gibson on the mound. About the 13th inning I hit a ball out and we win. We go home winners. Anytime
you hit a game-winning home run it's a big thrill.

What do you do for the Cubs?
I go around and visit each team once. I go around and talk to
some of the players, just work with their hitting. Outfield play. And
just tell them some of the things that made me a good ballplayer.
It's going around spreading goodwill for the ball club and I do some
stuff here. I wear about five or six hats for the ball club, so it's enjoyable. I get a chance to do something for them and I get a chance
to do something for myself.

I think a lot of players, if they were left in the minor leagues
maybe another couple of years, they would be better. I think a lot
of players now have to come to the big leagues to learn how to play
baseball. And that's what we didn't do, because there was only 16
teams. When you came to the big leagues, you was ready to play
ball. You knew where the cutoff man was going to be standing.
You know how to hit him. You knew how to bunt for a base hit.
Hit the ball for a sacrifice fly. You knew how to slide both sides, a
hook slide. But because of the expansion, because of the players
needed in the major leagues, I think a lot of players are called to the
big leagues before they're major league baseball players.

What is the poorest executed element in hitting today?
I think bunting. I think bunting is a lost art now. You do little
things to win. I saw it the other night. I'm looking at Pittsburgh,
supposed to be a winning ball team. I looked at Pittsburgh, got a
runner on second base, I think it was, and Van Slyke probably only
bunted two times in his life. So he was put in a situation that he
couldn't do, which is not saying too much if a manager do this.
You gotta let him be himself as a baseball player. So, they gave him
the bunt sign and he popped the ball up. It's just a lost art for baseball players. They don't really focus on the little things that win ball
games.

You know, I saw my dad as a ballplayer. He played a little bit.
He played against some of the old guys—Josh Gibson and he knew
Satchel Paige. You look at that and you say, well, if those guys
could have got a chance to come in the major leagues, they could
have been good ballplayers, but they didn't.

MARK GRACE

The standout first baseman of the Cubs. Very solid performer who is always in the game. He doesn't agree with some of the current thinking on big league players.

Some fans and retired players think the current ballplayer is selfish, doesn't give 100%, and plays only for money.

I think that's a very ludicrous statement. Anybody that knows myself or my teammates, everybody I've ever seen, plays the game hard. I think it might be a situation where maybe a bad apple will spoil the bunch. There might be a guy that may be considered a dog, or a guy that doesn't play unless he feels like it, or something to that effect. Usually, that is the superstar-type player that does things like that, but those guys are very few and far between and I think in that situation, he may be the bad apple that gives us all the bad rap.

But I go out there and I play the game as hard as I can and I play for the love of the game. I also play because I'm not very good at anything else. It's my God-given talent and I'm going to play it as long as I can and I'm going to enjoy it as long as I can.

Yeah, there's a lot of money in major league baseball, but that's not why I play the game. I play the game because I love it and I will continue to love it when I'm done playing.

Do you think multi-year contracts take incentive away?

No, I don't think so. First of all, I'm signed to a one-year contract. And probably will be for the next few years. There's advantages and disadvantages to multi-year contracts. A lot of guys sign multi-year contracts for however many millions of dollars and then they find the market goes up, then they've missed out on some money. For instance, I know Ricky Henderson wanted his contract renegotiated because he thought he was getting under his market value. Well, he signed a four-year contract and he's going to have to live with it, unfortunately for him. So, maybe if he had signed one year at a time he would be making more money had he not signed the multi-year. So there are advantages and disadvantages.

How many years did you spend in the minors?
   I spent two years.

Some believe that players are not spending enough time in the minors and therefore lack the fundamentals when they make the majors.
   No, I don't think that's true, because I don't think they'd be in the big leagues if they didn't have the fundamentals and the know-how to play the game. I think there may be some guys—these No. 1 picks—you know, they sign these million dollar contracts, but other than that, I was a No. 24-round pick and I had to earn my way into the big leagues. I led the league in hitting in A ball and I was the MVP in Double-A and that's how I got to the big leagues. I think in our system you pretty much still have to earn your way to the big leagues. They're not going to silver platter anything for you. You're going to have to prove that you're better than the player that's the incumbent.

Were you signed by the Cubs?
   Yes.

There is a school of thought that a major league club would rather sign an 18 year old than a 22 year old from a good college baseball program.
   Oh, I think there's some truth to that. If a guy that's 18 years old is equally as talented as a guy that's 22 in college, of course you want the 18 year old. But, I think when you're dealing with 17 and 18 year olds, you're dealing with raw talent. And it takes a few years for him to develop, whereas a guy in Double-A may be close to ready to play in the big leagues because the college level is such a higher level of competition than high school.
   I came from a four year college, San Diego State, and I think that was the best move I ever made in my career. I would suggest to any player—go get your education because the chances of you making it to the big leagues, even if you sign a professional contract —I think 4% of the guys make it. So, I would say education is very important.

OVERACHIEVERS

GARY WOODS

During his playing days he was an anachronism. He did anything he was told, played hard and sacrificed himself—something out of the old days. He understood the work ethic of baseball. He was never a star, never a regular, but he had what every team needs, a great positive attitude.

1981 was a funny year. It was a strike year and I was with Houston all of that year. I spent that year in Houston and we lost to the Dodgers three straight games out in L.A. after winning the first two in Houston, and that was my last year at Houston. That following winter, my wife and I took our first vacation and really our first honeymoon 'cause we never had one.

We went to Puerto Vallarta, Mexico, around Christmas and it was around the winter meetings. I remember sitting on the balcony of a hotel in Puerto Vallarta, and picking up a three-day-old *L. A. Times* and having a cold beer...picking it up and looking at the transaction section and finding out that Gary Woods had been traded to the Chicago Cubs and assigned to Des Moines, Iowa. If you've ever tried to get a phone call out of Mexico—especially around that time of the year—you can't do it. So basically my vacation was ruined.

We got on a plane and came home and found out after a phone call to Dallas Green—he'd just taken over the ball club as general manager—that I was the first player he had acquired. His plans for me were not in Des Moines, Iowa. It was an option that they had administratively to take advantage of and if I performed like he thought I could perform, that I would be on the ball club in Chicago the following spring.

Chicago was a team that finished last I think for the last four or five years in a row, so going into the '82 season, it was quite a chore for us to be a winning ball club. Well, subsequent transactions that winter ended up with Ryne Sandberg and Larry Bowa coming to the Chicago Cubs. Keith Moreland—he was involved in a deal—and Jody Davis was already there with the Cubs. Leon Durham was already there in a previous deal and so the nucleus of the ball club was just now starting to be built by Dallas Green.

And, lo and behold that spring, mid-way through spring, Lee Elia, the manager of the ball club, called me in. I was having a good spring but numbers-wise, it was going to be tough for me to make the club. He asked me, he said, "Gary, have you ever caught —have you ever been a catcher?" And, taking advantage of the opportunity, and knowing that there was only so many spots on the roster, I told him sure, I'd caught. Actually, I'd never caught a damn game in my life. But, he said, "Good, because we like what you do and the spot that we have available is for somebody who can be a third catcher in an emergency." So, I spent the next two weeks in the minor league level getting some catching experience. Broke with the club and went north in the spring of '82 and spent '82, '83, '84, and '85 with the Cubs. My career ended in 1986 when I was released by the Cubs in spring training. I spent the remainder of the year with the San Diego farm team in Las Vegas and at the end of the year I retired from baseball.

1984 was the highlight of my life, and certainly my playing career in that we had an opportunity to experience in Chicago something that hadn't been experienced in that town very often. The 1984 Chicago Cubs, of which I was a member, won the National League East Division. It was the first time that the Cubs had won anything in a long time. And, to explain what happens in that town with the Chicago Cubs, and the relationship that we had with the fans and the city is just almost indescribable. It was an unbelievable spring and summer in 1984. It culminated with us winning the division in September and ended on a very sad note when we lost the National League playoffs by losing three straight in San Diego. But, the excitement and the pressure and all of the things that go into being in a pennant race, being part of a winning team, a winning Cub team in Chicago, will stay with me forever. I mean from the ivy, to Harry Caray, to brawls we had on the field, to clutch home runs, to plane flights, to particular fans. Memories of the city, the restaurants, the people that we met in the community and the reaction that they had to us as people, as people who were bringing some joy to the city... something I'll never forget.

We finally put everything together in 1984 and we'd been together almost as a family for two and a half years. We came together...as a family...as a team...and won the division.

I tell my sales people, "Think about some of the best experiences you've had in your life and look back at some of the greatest memories and joy that you've had and I'll guarantee you that a big part of those memories is something that you've done or accomplished as a team." And, that was the epitome of us accomplishing a goal. I don't care who you are, you have to have goals and objectives in what you're trying to achieve. You want to buy a new bike if you're a kid, or you want to be president of a company—you have to have a goal. And we had a goal to shoot for.

I've got to tell you, we grabbed the brass ring that year. It's something that I feel very, very proud of and I wasn't one of the nine that played every day. I was a guy who was there because I could do a couple of things. One, I could go get the ball in the outfield and I could play defense as good as anybody in the game. Secondly, I could hit tough lefthanders and, fortunately for me, we had a whole pot full of tough lefthanders in our league and I was fortunate enough to be able to hit the good ones.

I had good success against Steve Carlton. Steve Carlton tipped his pitches and I knew what Steve Carlton was throwing me every time he threw a pitch to home plate. Let me tell you, that makes a difference...if you know what's coming. But I was fortunate. I was able to hit Steve Carlton and I think I hit a lifetime of close to .500 off him and that was one of the things that kept me in the big leagues.

I was a team player. I was a guy that was good for the chemistry on the club. I knew my role. Role players were just coming into vogue and just like the reliever had been 10 years earlier. Utility outfielders were specialty players, role players. Platoon players were now really being utilized in the game of baseball. So that's why I was there.

Gary, you played in the American and the National League. How would you rate the Chicago fans?

The Chicago fans are like no other fans in the world. That's been said a lot and it's kind of a trite comment. I'm sure part of it is that everybody loves to hug the teddy bear and loves to feel for the perennial loser. I think that's part of it.

Every ballpark that we went to on the road, there would be Chicago fans. I don't know whether it was because of the super station WGN or because there always have been Chicago fans everywhere. When you look across the country you don't find Yankee fans like that in every city. You don't find Dodger fans like that in every city. But you do find Chicago Cub fans in every city. I can't explain it, and I don't think anybody could really put a finger on it, but it's a phenomena. These people are loyal through thick and thin. And they'll fight—they'll scratch—they'll bite—they'll do anything for the Chicago Cubs.

In 1982, about seven games into the season, the center fielder was not doing a good job. And, I was fortunate to be called upon to play center field in 1982 early in the year. I immediately had some success and next thing I know I am the center fielder and one week passes and two weeks pass and I'm still hitting—three weeks pass and I'm still hitting. A month passes and—how the hell it happened, but, you know, at the end of May I picked up the Sunday paper and Garry Woods was leading the league in hitting. So I thought I was going pretty good. I finally had a shot to play in the big leagues and I was making the most of it. We weren't doing real well, but I was playing and had a starting job.

And I'll never forget we came back from a road trip and about 11:00 A.M. the fans get let in the ballpark. And they're filling the stands in the bleachers. It's generally right when we're finishing batting practice and, as a starter, I had had my turn in the outfield shaggin' balls. I was just getting ready to go in to hit. And a little kid in the stands was yelling and I'll never forget...he says, "Hey, Woods." "Hey, Woods," he says. I turned around thinking that—the little guy was gonna—say, "Hey, Woods, hit the ball and keep it up." But this little guy says to me, says, "Hey, Woods, if you don't start swinging the bat a little bit better and hittin' for the long ball, I'm going to tear your fuckin' arm off and shove it up your ass." And, he looked at me—dead in the eye—and picked up a soda cup, fired it at me, turned around and grabbed his hot dog and started yelling at the next guy. I said to myself, "Boy, if these guys are giving me trouble now and I'm leading the league in hitting, I'd hate to see what happens if I go bad."

Were they fairly supportive in the left-field bleachers?

Absolutely. The bleacher people in Chicago, the Bums in Chicago, are all for Chicago players. This was an isolated incident. But they're tough people. They know their baseball. They're very, very knowledgeable. And, they're all for Chicago Cub players and against any opposing player and some get more of the raff than others. But there's a direct relationship between how controversial you are and how much grief the Chicago Cub fans give you in the bleachers. But, yeah, they're nothing but supportive of the Chicago players.

The same ones are there day-in and day-out. I don't know if they went to school. I mean it was like a sickness to these people. I mean we have our homeless here and they have their people who lived at the ballpark. I mean there were kids, 16 or 17 years old, kids 14 years old. They were at the ballpark every day. I'll never forget the wave was done in all the other ballparks, but the Chicago fans, they didn't want anything to do with the wave. And they're just real, real solid fans. They're amazing.

The '84 playoffs broke a lot of hearts. You won the first two games in Chicago and lost the next three in San Diego. The big game was obviously the fifth game. What do you remember of that game?

When I know that I'm going to beat that other guy, that things are going my way, and the other guy knows that I know that, it becomes...it becomes a tangible, a physical advantage. And that's exactly what happened. The momentum turned around. We won the first two and we went out to San Diego with all the momentum behind us. We lost the third game. The fourth game resulted in a Garvey home run to win the game. We knew we had a problem. The momentum had gone the other way. And we knew it somewhere in the third game. We came into the last day knowing that we had to turn the momentum around immediately. We had to stop the physical thing that they had going for 'em.

We had Sutcliffe throwing. We had an opportunity to throw Sutcliffe the fourth game, and we held him back to the last game. Looking at that again, if I'm the manager, I'm going to go for the jugular. Knowing what I know about momentum today, I'm going for that...nail that thing to the wall. And hell with the fifth game, let's get it done now. Let's worry about the fifth game later. All that does is prolong a situation. So, we let that fester.

We went into the fifth game with Sutcliffe and we got off to a 3-0 lead. And were able to turn the momentum around and then we got into the fifth inning and you could tell Sutcliffe was getting tired. There was a lot of adrenaline going on with the game. There was just so much emotion and so much going on that the guy started to lose it. It was obvious. It was something you could see plain as day. And Rick knew it. He tried to let us know on the bench. He walked around the mound. He tied his shoe laces. He did every-thing he could do...you know, Rick's the kind of guy...he didn't want to come out of the game. But, I think he wanted to be fair in saying, "Listen, I owe more to this club and this city than for me to stand up here and try to be a martyr. You know, we've got a whole bunch of guys out there who can come in and get the job done." I think he knew that he was going south quick and he just ran out of steam. Jim Frey had watched Rick get out of those jams all year long. But, Jim didn't do anything. He left Rick in there to win it or lose it. I think Frey's thinking was, "Hey, this guy is my ace. He was 16 and 1. He's been out of these jams before and I'm going to live and die with this guy." 'Cause we didn't have anybody warming up. It wasn't that Jim Frey had plans on taking him out of the ball game...until it got to the point where we were out of it.

A funny story that happened that not too many people know about. I remember that I used to sit by Don Zimmer and I'll never forget I sat on one side of the water cooler and Don sat on the other side of the water cooler and in the fourth inning before the players went back on the field, Don Zimmer and I were sitting there talking and most of the players put their gloves in a pile and leave it there so in case they're stranded on base the other player can pick it up and take it to him. The inning ended and Leon Durham was going to get his glove, it was laying on the ground in front of us and Zim popped up and somehow caught his pants, or something, or what-ever on the water cooler. I'm pretty sure it was Zim, in any case, the water cooler was knocked over and it was knocked over onto Durham's glove. We all sat there, and oh shit, you know, we've got to get Durham's glove wiped off. There was water on the glove and he patted it dry and went out to his position. Well, an inning later, Tim Flannery's groundball went through Leon Durham's legs to tie the game, or it was the game-winning run. But in retrospect, when we think back on it and think about some of the omens or the bad signs that the Chicago Cubs have had in their past and I'm referring to the black cat that streaked across the field in late '69, you think about the water cooler being knocked onto his glove and the irony of the ball going through his legs.

The biggest disappointment I had was that it was probably the last opportunity I would have to go to the World Series. I had two instances where I was nine outs away, with the lead, from going to the World Series and didn't do it.

Every kid's dream is to go to the World Series and that was...and I knew it, my last opportunity. So it was especially disappointing to me and as a team who had worked so hard to get to that point. It was devastating. And, it...you know, you just... it's something you can't explain...it wasn't the Chicago Cubs were losers or...I mean, we had a better ball club than the San Diego Padres, and would have represented ourselves better in the World Series. It wasn't the bad luck of the Chicago Cubs. I'm not buying that. It's just that we went out there and lost three games. And you can lose three games any year in a heart beat, on any given day. Any team, I don't care if it's a team who loses 120 games a year, can beat the best team in baseball on three given days. That was the case then. And, it was disappointing. I mean, to say that it wasn't a major disappointment would not be telling the truth. That was my major disappointment in baseball.

Reflecting back on your years with the Chicago Cubs, what are some stories that stick in your mind?

Well, a couple...a couple of stories do stick out. One has to do with my family and my wife. That 1982 year I'd come over from Houston. I'll never forget a national-televised game on Saturday, we happened to be playing the Houston Astros and my wife was about eight-months pregnant with my second son, Randy. It must have been April or May. She happened to be at the game, and it was a Saturday NBC "Game of the Week," and I was in the Chicago dugout. I can't remember who was hitting, but in any case, there was a pop-up that went down the first baseline and went over and behind the Houston bullpen... which was right against the brick wall there against the fans, and the next thing you know, boy oh boy, the players are reaching for it and the next thing you know here comes this pregnant lady rolling out on the field like a beached whale. And she gets up and dusts herself off and all the fans are applauding. The players in the dugout say, "Jesus Christ, look at that. Look at that lady. That poor lady, she's laying there like some beached whale." And I look over and I said, "That's my wife." She happened to be over there visiting with the Houston wives, who were sitting right behind the bullpen on the Houston side. The pop-up went up and she went flying out the gate as she was trying to get out of the way and rolled around the field a little bit and made national TV. And we have to laugh about that every now and then, but the Houston players who she knew, helped her up and dusted her off, and God she was embarrassed. So we tell my youngest son that he was on the playing field before he was ever born.

One instance that was funny, was about one of our teammates, Jerry Morales. He played with the Cubs in the '70s and '80s. He was a center fielder. He played with Cardenal and that bunch, but came back with us in '81 as a pinch hitter. He was a pinch hitter like I was and in those days the clubhouse was down in left field. The dugout was just a little space underneath the stadium where the umpires dressed and you could go back and get warm, or stretch if you had to pinch hit in the cold weather. Well, late in the year we were in a game with Philadelphia that Steve Carlton was pitching, it was a real blow-out and Jerry and I were back in the back room and Jerry wasn't feeling well this day. Jerry had, as he would say, sunk the Cutty Sark boat the night before. He was taking a siesta on the couch, his hat pulled down. He had his pants unbuttoned, his shoe laces undone, and he was taking a siesta, thinking that there was no way he was getting in the game. Well, the next thing you know, somebody runs in and says, "Morales, you're on deck." So Julie kind of tips his head up, and says, "Um," walks out, buttons his pants, gets one of his shoes tied and the other one he doesn't. He puts on a helmet, grabs a bat from the bat rack, walks straight up to the batters box, faces Steve Carlton without taking a practice swing. Puts his hands above his head and Julie had this distinctive batting style where the hands were way up and Carlton goes into the wind-up and swoosh—strike one. Julie steps back and steps back in, hands up and swoosh—strike two. Still didn't get the bat off his shoulder. Third pitch—Carlton winds up, throws it, swoosh—strike three. Jerry turned around, put the bat on his hip, he knocked it down like Chi-Chi Rodriguez does with a golf club and marches back to the dugout. Jim Frey looks at him and said, "Julie—what the hell happened to you?" He says, "Skip, you can't hit what you can't fuckin' see." That was funny.

I did have some opportunities to stay in the game of baseball after 1986. I had some offers with the Cubs to stay in their minor league system. I had an offer from the Milwaukee Brewers and I had an offer from the San Diego Padres. I didn't really want to travel and make the commitment to travel, being away from my family, as I had for so long. That, plus the fact that there really is

178

not enough money or security in the game of baseball at the minor league coaching level, and I wasn't ready to pay the dues in the minor leagues to wait to get to the big leagues again. I'd done that and I know that it's a very risky proposition. I just didn't feel that that was something I wanted to do. I wanted to take the time to do other things in my life. To see what other talents and skills that I might have in the business world and try to be successful and take some of the values I learned from sports and apply those to another discipline. So I left the game of baseball in 1986.

I've been with GTE in sales and marketing in the mobile communications business since 1987. Have been a local account manager. Have been at the corporate level, in a staff position, in the marketing department, and am now back in Santa Barbara, California, as a sales and service manager for a couple of counties.

It's a tough, tough job in a tough, tough world and I can say that my time in sports has prepared me for life after baseball. I know some people aren't prepared for it when they get out of the game, but I think being an extra player and having to fight for everything you get, and having to go to 13 spring trainings and make the team each year, I think that background was able to provide me with the skills and the discipline that I needed to be successful in the business world.

One of the things that I really regret is I left junior college in '73 to go play. In the first years of the minor leagues, I wasn't able to come back and go to school 'cause I didn't make enough money to go back to school. I had to work. Because in the minor leagues, you make $500 a month, you only make it for four and a half months, and, you know, I had to...I had to sustain myself through the rest of the time since I didn't get a signing bonus, so I had to work. By the time you get to Triple-A or so, I had to go to Venezuela or Puerto Rico to play in the winter. So consequently, I wasn't able to finish my education.

And, boy, I'll tell you. It's a tough one right now. I've been real fortunate to be able to continue with some promotion with the company in spite of not having the four-year degree. I'm going back right now, but I'll tell you, it's really a tough deal to go out in the business world without a college degree. It's becoming more and more important every day. So, that's one regret that I do have from the game that I wasn't able to, in the 13 years, find the time to get back to school.

I'm thankful I didn't stay in the game, 'cause it's nice to be home at night. Got family. I've got kids to raise and I enjoy the winning and losing just like I did with baseball in the business world. I mean it's competition and I enjoy that and I'm able to re-place some of the things that I miss from the game, because I'm in the competitive environment. I can see my sales people hitting for a higher average every month. Or having a tough time and coming back out of it. Or closing a deal, or us as a team having a good month. Or competition trying to get some of our business. It's a good environment to be in and a good business and I'm thrilled to death.

In 13 years you meet a lot of people. Travel to a lot of places. I traveled all across America and traveled with guys six months out of a year. Some guys I was with four or five years. There's acquain-tances and friends that go back 20 years and the regrets that I have are that you don't stay in touch with the people that were part of your life for many years. And there's things that you shared to-gether, that you have memories of and you don't stay in touch with the people that have been a part of your life. You lose touch and that's something that I do regret. It's just something that happens in the game, that people go their own way and you don't keep in touch. So I regret that. There's a lot of people that I would like to visit with and share some memories with.

He had to work hard to stay in the majors. He was a little guy who had a lifetime batting average of only .213.

He was a Cub from 1976 through 1980. He said that the 1977 season, "was really the most satisfying and the most enjoyable season I think I've played in the major leagues."

I got traded to the Chicago Cubs in the winter of 1975. So my first full season with the Chicago Cubs was 1976.

1976 was an interesting year for us. Jim Marshall was our manager. He was a former major league player and also played in Japan and was an interesting character. It was fun playing for him and we had a pretty decent ball club. We finished fourth that year, but we had some interesting things that went on during the course of the year.

One of them being the Rick Monday episode of saving the flag at Dodger Stadium when he scooped the flag up at short-center field as two fellows were about to light the flag in front of about 55,000 people. It was like he saved the world and he got a standing ovation. They wouldn't sit down. And what we had to do when we got back to Chicago was get him an extra locker to handle all the incoming mail and trophies that he had received and was to receive for the rest of the season—from organizations as the Veterans of Foreign Wars, fire departments around the country, police departments, civic community groups—everybody you can imagine was sending mail—fans, kids—it was just wonderful and it was quite an experience.

What do you remember of the '77 season?

I remember spring training in Arizona and we got rained out a lot. It was a very poor spring training as far as the weather was concerned. And our team wasn't really highly touted. I knew we were going to have a pretty good club. Buckner was going to be a big addition and DeJesus was given a really good shot at shortstop and actually played ahead of me in '77 at shortstop. We had a good club. We also picked up Steve Ontiveros from the San Francisco Giants in a trade for Bill Madlock.

181

Bill Madlock won the batting title in '76. On the very last day of the year he won the title, he beat Ken Griffey out and he went 4 for 4 on the very last day of the year to win the title, which was extraordinary. Unbelievable. But he was traded to the Giants that winter. The Cubs made a lot of moves to really help our club and we got third baseman Steve Ontiveros and Bobby Murcer for Bill Madlock. It was a big deal. So, now we traded Rick Monday and Bill Madlock, two stalwarts off our '76 club away. And we got Steve Ontiveros, Ivan DeJesus, Bill Buckner, and Bobby Murcer. Four guys on our '77 team that would play every day. Were in the starting line up. So it was a good trade. It was a very good trade and then '77 was probably the most exciting year that the Chicago fans in general, the Cub fans, and the South Side fans of the White Sox enjoyed because both teams were in first place at the All-Star break.

The Cubs had an eight-and-a-half game lead, eventually to lose it, but really throughout the whole course of the season, it was one of tremendous feeling and almost heroism. I mean it was just an unbelievable situation. You know, there would be standing ovations before every game. People wouldn't sit down after the National Anthem was played. They'd be up for 10 minutes. You couldn't hear yourself think. It was just the greatest feeling in the world. My most memorable, really, in 15 years of playing professional baseball. And even though we didn't win it, and I did play on a division winner, which was exciting too, later, not in Chicago but in California with the Angels, '77 was really the most satisfying and the most enjoyable season I think I've played in the major leagues.

I think the Chicago fans are the best fans in baseball. They're very sophisticated, they're knowledgeable, they're diehard. There's a lot of adjectives you could throw at the Cub fans, and they're all good.

The Bleacher Bums were great. A lot of familiar faces and I still see some of them at spring training to this day.

The ones that were the Bleacher Bums when I played in the '70s still come down. They're still Cub fans. They don't sit in the bleachers anymore...but they're still Cub fans and they still come to spring training and they still go to the ball games.

Herman Franks was hired after the '76 season. He replaced Jim Marshall. Herman Franks took over our club and it was the first time I'd really gotten a chance to see and get to know Herman Franks and he was quite a fellow. Quite an individual. Quite a character. From the old school. Tobacco chewing...rough and tough...gruff type of individual that was a joy to play for. The type of manager that you could play for. All you had to do was give him 100% and he wouldn't say boo to you. Which is the kind of guy you like to be with. And would talk to the players very open and his door was always open.

He was a throwback to the olden days, for sure. This guy could talk to the umpires and chew and spit and throw tobacco all over the umpires with the best of them. He would put on a show. You'd pay your money to see Herman Franks come out on the field and get thrown out of the game. He became a real fun guy to play for in Chicago and the fans really liked him too.

I played for some good managers. Gene Mauch and Sparky Anderson and Ken Boyer. I mean I played for some good managers, but for a character and a guy that was fun to be around and had a different light on the game, because he was from the older school, he brought that part of the game to our ball club that was neat. And guys had a real rapport with Herman Franks.

And I'd like to mention Peanuts Lowrey, who was really an institution, a fine baseball player in his day, was our third base coach. To this day, I think Peanuts Lowrey was one of the best third base coaches of all time.

He was an ex-Cub and played on the '45 Cub team that went to the World Series. The last team that had been to the World Series. But Peanuts passed away a few years ago, but just a neat fellow and a great baseball man.

Getting back to the 1977 season. The Cubs were a fast starting club. We had an eight-and-a-half game lead by July—the All-Star break—and the race was really tightening up and we were losing a little bit of ground, the intensity and the competition from the other clubs was at...it was at a real high and going into August with the Phillies and the Mets and Pittsburgh...we had some drag out fights and some knockdowns that were beyond compare that year. There was a lot of them late in the season.

And a couple of them that stick out in my mind...one was with the San Francisco Giants with Jim Barr, who was really known as one of the "headhunters" in the league. He'd knock you down just as soon as look at you. He was tough. Tough pitcher. He'd pitch inside and he'd knock you down. One day we had about three or four different fights at San Francisco involving Jose Cardenal, Jim Barr, Bill Madlock and everybody else on both teams. And we were out there on the field about four different times in San Francisco with numerous ejections and Madlock and Cardenal and Barr getting severe fines, suspensions...but that was a typical day running down the stretch drive of the '77 season.

I had a fight with Dave Kingman, who was with the San Diego Padres. We had a knock down...this was August 7, 1977. We were playing the Padres at Wrigley Field. And it was a knock down, drag out, all day long. Bob Shirley was on the mound for the Padres and Steve Renko was on the mound for the Cubs. Renko's about 6' 6", 240 and, you know, Kingman's about 6' 7", 225. Players were going down on both sides all day long. The sixth inning or something like that, Renko decided that was enough. We'd all been on the field a couple of times already. He plunks Kingman in the shoulder and Kingman gets up and runs down to first base and doesn't say a word, doesn't charge the mound. I often wondered why he didn't go charge the mound. Renko was 6' 6", 250, I think that was why. Buckner was playing first and I was playing second and DeJesus was at short. The next hitter up hits a ball to shortstop, deep in the hole to DeJesus and I'm coming to the bag and DeJesus gives me a good throw, a good feed, I turn over the double play and I release the ball and there's Kingman about six feet from me running as hard as he can standing straight up, right in my face. I was wide open with my release to first base and he just lowered his shoulder and he buried me right in the side of my ribs and picked me up about 10 feet and put me past second base and that was it. I got up and we started fighting and I was on his back like a little monkey. I ended up flipping him. There was a pig pile. There were fights...I found out later...all over the field involving Cardenal and Mike Ivey, unbelievable as I saw the films later. But, anyway, at the bottom of this pig pile...they drug us off and there was blood all over the place. Alvin Dark was bleeding and George Mitterwald. The Swisher was down there with me...looked like a dog on all fours, dirt in his face. He was chewing dirt...and...just an unbelievable situation, but this was typical of the '77 stretch drive.

Did you get the ball off to first?
Got the ball off to first, the runner was safe. Kingman got

thrown out of the game and I got thrown out of the game. We both got fined $250 apiece and I was off to the hospital with five bruised ribs, a severe charlie horse, and a wrenched neck that didn't heal for about six months.

That winter, Dave Kingman was a free agent and who signs Dave Kingman but the Chicago Cubs. And now we've got a problem with the media and the press and the fans, 'cause they remember what happened in August of '77. So, we signed Dave Kingman and he comes in and I get a call from Bob Kennedy. I'm at home and he says you gotta fly in—you gotta fly in. We gotta cover this —we've gotta patch this thing up. We've got a big press conference comin' up and I need you to fly in. So I do it. I go back and we've got Herman Franks and Bobby Murcer and Bruce Sutter and Ray Burris and Dave Kingman and myself and there's a big press conference downtown at the hotel. They've got Kingman and myself shaking hands and taking pictures and...it was just too much. It was really funny. We had to kind of smooth this thing over so, you know, we could accept Dave Kingman coming to the Chicago Cubs.

Dave never apologized and we became—funny thing—we became pretty good friends. In fact, we became real good friends —as close as you can get to Dave. He's kind of an aloof type fellow, but that's just the way he is. But I got to know him pretty well and we enjoyed each other, but I never did get any apologies for what he did. He said it was just part of the game. And I found out later that Billy Buckner was playing first and he said when Kingman got to first base, he said, "I'm going to kill your second baseman or shortstop if I get the chance." And I said, "Well, Buck, why in the hell didn't you tell me he was going to kill me? Might have been able to do something."

The Chicago fans never really warmed to Kingman.

I think they liked Kingman for what he did on the field, but they didn't...I don't think they really warmed up to him. He put up some big numbers in '79 that were quite awesome. He played well. He played extremely well and then he kind of wore out his welcome. Too bad. I don't know really why 'cause he really had Chicago infatuated with him and he had that kind of power and he did some exciting things. And in '79, you know, he put up like 48 home runs, 115 RBIs, he hit .290, made the All-Star team. He just did some great things. He played hard. He really did play hard. And it was a pleasure to play with him.

Somebody sent me a T-shirt. It said "King Kong Killer." It was a blue Cub T-shirt that had the logo on it "King Kong Killer," so I used to strut around the locker room and I'd pound my fist—I'd run down by his locker and go (clapping) like that and George Mitterwald would be over there saying, "Kingman, don't fuck around with Kelleher. He's going to flip your big ass." People would laugh.

Herman Franks ended his tenure as the manager of the Chicago Cubs in 1979 because of a situation with a sportswriter at the very end of the year. The tendency for the years that Herman Franks was our manager—'77, '78, and '79—we got out of the gate real fast and were in first place all three of those years and characteristically would fade at the second half of the season—usually in August or September, which fed right into the old adage that the Chicago Cubs can't win playing all day games. And I didn't believe it, but I did realize it was tough to play day games and it really did catch up with you, especially during hot seasons in August and September. But anyway, getting back to how Herman Franks resigned as the manager in 1979. We'd just gotten back off the road from Montreal, I believe, and a sportswriter came into him and said everything was off the record and they were just talking back and forth as the beat writer was with us all year. Just casual conversation, is how it went I understand, and completely off the record. Well, anyway, the next day everything that Herman had said in the "off the record meeting" with this sportswriter was in the front page of the *Chicago Tribune*. Herman felt he was compelled to resign, he was embarrassed and was really done a disservice by this sportswriter. In all honesty, what he said was the truth, it just didn't sound very good at the time...very unfortunate..and Herman Franks ended up resigning before the 1979 season was over and Joe Amalfitano took the reins the rest of the way as we finished the season.

SHOW BIZ

*One of the all-time Cub nuts—and not a bad comic. He has some
very interesting insights on the Cubs.*

*You are from Harvey, Illinois—the southern suburbs. Why are you
a Cub fan?*

Well, my grandfather was a Cub fan and my father was. I grew
up as a little boy listening on the radio. You know, hearing the
Cubs on the radio as a little boy and through family passing it
down. Although I lived in a neighborhood of White Sox fans. So
consequently, we had a lot of conflict. They talk about baseball
rivalry around the country, about one city vs. another city. I have
never seen a more intense rivalry in my life than the Cubs and the
White Sox fans.

There were two guys in my neighborhood named Muzanski.
Bobby and Teddy Muzanski. They're brothers. One was a Cub fan
and one was a White Sox fan. They had literally fist fights over this.
Finally, Bobby was getting married and he wouldn't invite his
brother Teddy to the wedding. And his mother cried and carried
on and said, "You've got to, this is family and what are we going to
do." And he said, "Mom, he's a Cub fan and I'm not inviting him,"
and so forth and so on. So the mother cried and finally she said,
"You have to have your brother there. He has to stand up," and so
forth and so. He acquiesced and to make a long story short, he
stood up at the wedding and as his brother was coming down the
aisle and he was standing up...you know how the guys all stand in
tuxedos—the bridal party? He reached in his back pocket and
pulled out his Cub hat and put it on as his brother was coming up
to the altar. Now, anger...nothing was said. At the reception that
night, it was the greatest fist fight you ever saw in your life.

Where I'm from, Cub fans and Sox fans hung out at different
bars, because the arguments would be violent. I wrote a joke one
time that ended up getting me a quote of the year and they donate
$50.00 to your charity. I did it on the "Johnny Carson Show." I
said, "When I was growing up in Chicago, I used to pray that the
Cubs and White Sox would merge so Chicago would only have

one bad team." That got into a magazine called *Sez Who* and it became a famous quote.

I used to shine shoes in taverns from the time I was six years old until I was 12. I mean, I had eight brothers and sisters and we were really, what they call, shanty Irish poor. Five of us slept in one bed. We had no bathtub and no shower. We were so poor...we lived behind a factory by some railroad tracks. And I would take my little shoe shine box and I would shine shoes in taverns every night and I would bring my money home to my mother to help feed my brothers and sisters 'cause there were eight of us. But my mother would keep a nickel out occasionally and she'd put...she had a little cracked cup up in the cupboard. She would keep it until it got enough and then she would let me go down to Wrigley Field. I would take the IC, the Illinois Central. The IC from Harvey, downtown, and then I'd take the elevated over to Wrigley Field. Then I would go sit in the bleachers and root for my Cubs.

It was in the early '50s. There's something about Wrigley Field that is so nostalgic because you go to Wrigley Field and you're going to sit in the seat that maybe your great grandfather sat in. And your grandfather sat in. And your father sat in. And now you're sitting in it. And your son's going to sit in it. And maybe his son. And for a moment, no matter how bad things are in your life —you know, no matter how many bills you can't pay, or how many pressures you have on the job, or whatever you're going through in your life—for a moment, time stands still. Because you're in a place that your great grandfather was and they're playing the same game that your great grandfather saw. And for a moment time stands still.

I was the first president of the Diehard Cub Fan Club. Several years ago at Wrigley Field, a guy named Bing Hampton, who's now very ill with Lou Gehrig's disease, was the vice president in charge of marketing. Bing Hampton, a very nice guy. He saw me on the "David Letterman Show." I had gone on the "David Letterman Show" and gave Dave a Cub hat. And this is around 1982, I think. I think the Cubs were in last place and I said to Dave, naturally we were in New York, right? And I said, "Dave, here's a Cub hat." And he said, "How are your Cubs doing?" 'Cause Dave is a friend of mine and he knows how much I love the Cubs. And I said, "I'm glad you brought that up. Here's a hat. The Cubs donate it to you." He says, "I'll always treasure this." And he threw it on the floor. Of course, the whole audience went wild. So I got up and threw a chair toward the band and damn near killed Paul Schaeffer. I said, "Where I'm from, when you throw a Cub hat on the floor, it's like throwing the American flag on the floor."

The next day, they ran it in the papers and Kups column in Chicago and Bing Hampton called and asked me, when I was in Chicago the next time, he said, "We're thinking of starting something called 'the Diehard Cub Fan Club.' There are so many fans in America like yourself, that are just diehard. They're not Cub fans, they're diehards. And we'd like you to be our first president." So I was the first president of the Diehard Cub Fan Club, where I actually would go on radio shows and television shows and tell people how they could join. It cost, in those days, $6.00 and I got nothing for this. It was just out of my love—but, they would get a big 8 x 10 package with a subscription to the magazine with a big certificate that said "When you became a Cub fan," etc., etc. You get a card for your wallet, which people still show me wherever I go around America. People show me their card.

Later on Bryant Gumble was the president of the Diehard Cub Fan Club. Ernie Banks. They had different people. But I was the first. And the first year over 21,000 people applied. Today, there's over 120,000 card carrying members of the Diehard Cub Fan Club.

You incorporate the Cubs in your act.

Well, depending on where I'm at. I don't always do it, but I will always work on material around the Cubs. The routine that I used to do went like this:

"In the year 1908, the Chicago Cubs won the World Series. At that time, there were 45 states in the Union. Teddy Roosevelt was President of the United States. The worlds oldest living president, Ronald Reagan, wasn't even born yet. Two years later, Haley's Comet came through Chicago. Haley's Comet has been back and the Cubs still have not won the World Series. But we fans believe that this is the year. We'll always believe that this is the year. A fan is not someone who goes to the ballpark when the team is in first place. A fan is somebody who is at Wrigley Field—last game in September—the Cubs are 102 games out and you think they still have a chance. I've been there—45 people in the whole ballpark. The crowd was so intimate, instead of the National Anthem, we sang 'Feelings.' One vendor—I said, 'Can I have a hot dog?' He said, 'I've only got one. Just take a bite.' In the fourth inning the announcer would say things like, 'Would the lady with the lost nine children, please claim them. They're beating the Cubs 11-0.'" That's the kind of stuff I do.

Now, something else came from this. Having dinner one night with Jim Frey, Jim Frey said, "How long have you been a Cub fan, Tommy?" And I told him the story about being a little boy, shining shoes in taverns, etc. I said, "I used to sit in the bleachers and fantasize that I could be a bat boy. But I always thought it was rich kids from the North Side who got that opportunity. People whose fathers were prominent. Never took a poor kid off the street." And so Jimmy said, "Well, maybe we can fulfill your childhood fantasy." And he let me be bat boy for four days at Dodger Stadium. And they lost the first three games and I went into the office after the third loss, and I said, "Jimmy, I don't think I'm bringing you guys any luck, so I think maybe I better step out." He said, "Tom, you stuck with the Cubs all your life, maybe we can stick with you one more game." They won that game. And Ryne Sandberg signed the ball and got every member of the team to sign it for me. I still have that ball. It's like the Oscar to me.

But since then...since they won that game, I started being bat boy once a year and they started winning more often when I was there. In fact, for Zimmer I had like a 12-5 record or something like that. And, of course, they would pretend that it was not whether I was there or not, that made them win. If Zimmer lost the game— he'd say, "You know, we better not lose two in a row or you're out of here, pal." Jokingly, you know. I've been bat boy six years in a row. In fact, I'm supposed to do it again this year.

In the dugout, I wanted to show these guys that I knew something about baseball. 'Cause I still play ball in the show business league, in the fast pitch softball league. So, now I'm in the dugout with all these major leaguers. The leadoff hitter for the Dodgers gets a single. Now I want to let these guys know that I know a little about the game. And I'm hollering, "Shoot the deuce, guys. 21 now. Shoot the deuce." And I'm saying, double play—right? I said, "Shoot the deuce, guys. 21." And the whole dugout turns and stares at me. Shoot the deuce? They say, "Groundball, double play. Groundball, double play." That's what we said in little league. They say groundball. They don't say any of those fancy things that we who are outside of baseball say. They say, "Pop his ass up, pop his ass up." We're doing all these, "Shoot the deuce. 21 now." And they don't talk like that. They talk very basic, so it was so funny. The whole dugout got quiet and they all looked at each other and they said, "Shoot the deuce?" I thought they'd think I was very hip.

Rick Sutcliffe says to me, they're always doing shit with me. Like Sutcliffe is a clown. He'd say, "Tommy, got to wear the hard hat, right?" And I came in from getting a bat. Well, Rick had bubble gum and he'd get behind me and put the bubble gum on top of my head with a blown bubble. He'd say, "There's a bat out there." Somebody would throw a bat out there and they'd say, "You forgot a bat." I'd run out there, get it, and, naturally, the bubble on top of my hard hat—all the fans started laughing and pointing at me. Now, I think they recognized me as a comedian, so I'm laughing and waving back at them. I'm thinking—they're pointing and laughing—oh, yeah, they must recognize me as a comedian. Well, it's this big bubble on top of my head that Rick had put there.

This other time he says to me —in between innings—when they were raking the infield. He says, "Go out there and tell Frank Pulli, the home plate umpire, Tom, that Rick Sutcliffe says that he thinks that Pulli is the greatest umpire in both leagues." So I ran out there and I said, "Mr. Pulli, Rick Sutcliffe said..." He said, "I don't give a shit what he said, you get your ass back in the dugout. I don't wanna see your ass out here again unless you come out here to pick up the bats. You understand that? Get your ass back in that dugout." I go back in the dugout and I know that Rick set me up, see. So he says, "What did he say?" I said, "He said he thinks that you're the best pitcher in both leagues." And Rick said, "Oh, oh." Son of a bitches. I knew what they did to me. They set me up.

Why do you think the Cubs exert such a hold on people in Chicago? It's a dynamic you really don't see any other place in America.

Well, basically, they represent what we are. It's a blue collar town. We're working class people. I think the Cubs represent life, if I can. They fall short an awful lot, but they keep coming back the next day. The weak fall short in life. You know, we get up in the morning and we try to make ends meet and sometimes we can't. Sometimes it's 40 below zero in Chicago and you get up and you can't get the car started and when you finally get the car started, you gotta shovel off the driveway and when you shovel off the driveway, you get stuck on the Dan Ryan bumper to bumper. And now you get to work and you've got pressures and problems there. You come home at night and, you know, maybe you have a second job. Trying to make ends meet. You don't always make it. And you fall short. Even though you're doing the best you can with what you've got. And when you turn on the Cubs—that's what they're all about. They're doing the best they can. No one's throwing the game. They're trying as hard as they can and you can forgive that.

We all hope we're going to go 15 rounds in life and I'm making the analogy to life, 15 rounds. We only hope one thing, that we finish on our feet. I don't know that I'm going to knock anybody out and I'm not so sure that I'm going to win the crown. I just want to finish on my feet. And that's the way the Cubs are. They finish on their feet. And you know what—no matter how bad things got, how bad things go—they're there the next day. To give us a little more hope. And maybe one day you come home and everything's gone wrong that day, but you turn on the news and the Cubs won in the 14th inning. Holy Cow! I can go to bed with a smile on my face. Cubs won today. Things aren't so bad, are they?

I made a lot of jokes about the Cubs. I believe that history will show we have less suicides among Cub fans than any other fan. Because see, every year, we think this is the year that there's going to be a World Series in Wrigley Field and we want to be there. I fear that the day the Cubs finally win the World Series, that the following day some 20,000 people will dive off the Tribune Tower. 'Cause what the hell is there to live for once they win the World Series?

ELMER BERNSTEIN

One of the truly great movie composers of all-time. He won an Academy Award for Thoroughly Modern Millie. *He has also written the music for movies such as* The Magnificent Seven, The Man with the Golden Arm, The Ten Commandments, Trading Places, My Left Foot, *and many more. A longtime Cub fan who would trade one of his big hits to play a season of major league baseball.*

I went to my first baseball game in 1935 when I was 13. The Cubs won in the very late innings, which was thrilling for a first game.

Oddly enough, I didn't have trouble understanding what the game was about because my father had taught me enough about the game. I knew what to expect and I found it very thrilling. It was a great year to get involved in the Cubs because, of course, they went to the World Series that year.

There was one other attraction in being a Cub fan which I kind of enjoyed. I think, it's part of...it goes into one's personality...I liked the idea of sort of being a rebel, so to speak, among my New York friends. It made me really special to be a Cub fan. And I really stayed with it.

The first time I ever got to Chicago was right after the war in 1947. I was giving a concert at the university. Of course, the first thing I did was to go to Wrigley Field. I don't remember the game but I do remember the atmosphere. It was very interesting. Absolutely an indelible atmosphere.

For an old Cubs fan, getting to Wrigley Field for the first time, you sort of thought you'd died and gone to heaven. It was kind of that feeling. You were getting there right at the heart. The atmosphere came from the crowd. It was an amazing crowd. I can't describe it except to say that they were there to enjoy baseball. The weren't there to go to the snack bar and they weren't reading a newspaper and you didn't have the feeling that families were talking about what they should do at home. They were there for baseball. It was a tremendous feeling. It's interesting that it overpowers the game itself. I can't even tell you what team I was seeing that

193

day. Of course, by 1947 the Cubs were in much less good shape. That was the beginning of a very bad period for the Cubs.

I went in the Army in '43. Still a Cub fan, you know, very much a Cub fan in '43. With the war on, it was very hard to pay a lot of attention to what was going on in baseball. I wasn't all that easy to get news when you're in basic training in North Carolina.

Nashville was the Cub farm team. I used to go to those games. I was stationed in Nashville and I used to go to see that Nashville team. And that was as close as I could get to the Cubs.

After Nashville, I was writing Air Force propaganda broadcasts which originated from New York City. So, actually, it took be back to what was then my home. I saw many, many baseball games, because in those days, of course, it you're in uniform, you got in free. I went to Giants games a great deal in those days. The games were laughers. I mean, they were funny. I knew enough about baseball by then to realize that the games were just funny. They had one or two good players who, for one reason or another, didn't have to go into the Army or couldn't get into the Army. Where you saw the game very different was in fielding. You saw plays which you would have considered to be absolutely automatic—nothing was automatic. In a funny sort of way, it made the game fun. You never knew what was going to happen.

It would be fascinating to talk to players who played at that time. I'm not at all sure that perhaps they weren't having, in a sense, more fun than later, because they knew they weren't pros. I mean, I'm sure a lot of those players knew the minute the war was over their big league careers were going to be over.

It was fairly clear that the war was going to be over, and by August it was. August of 1945. I remember topping it off with the fact that my Cubs won the pennant again in 1945.

I remember the World Series that year. Listening to the World Series—the Cubs and Detroit—on the radio. I remember Claude Passeau pitching. I think he won, 3-0. That Series went to seven games. I remember Hank Greenberg, who had just gotten out of the service at that point, seemed to singlehandedly wreck us. Every time he came to bat, something terrible happened as far as the Cubs were concerned. They just couldn't stop him.

As a Cub fan, it was a great way to come out of the Army, and look forward to peace time with the Cubs as a National League pennant winner again.

I would like to feel that anybody who gets interested in the game would really give a great deal to be able to do things they see their heros doing on the field. I remember in particular Red Smith, a sportswriter for the now defunct *Herald Tribune*, wrote a book called *Baseball* many, many years ago. At the beginning of the book, he describes the atmosphere in the older parks, the small parks, the smell of the old wooden benches, the sun, you know, the whole feeling of being around baseball. I think that we've all had that.

I've had some success...some good success in my career for which I am very, very grateful. But I think if I could take one of them, something like the *Magnificent Seven*, and trade it in and be able to do in baseball what Sandy Koufax could do...I mean, be out there at the center of the action for a time and make that kind of contribution, I think it's a tradeoff that I would happily have made.

You'd give up writing that song to play a season the way Sandy Koufax did?

Yeah, yeah, I think so. There's something about baseball to me that is so much part of my life. To me, it gets to be much more a part of my life than any other sport. I don't know why. It's something about the whole atmosphere around the game. It's a beautiful game, even in this hi-tech era, of people basically having fun. People really loving the game. I would have given a lot for part of my life to be part of the game.

You can take the boy out of Chicago, but not the Chicago out of the boy.

I grew up outside of Chicago in Wheaton, Illinois. I went to school at Wheaton Central High School. I went to the College of DuPage in Glen Ellyn, Southern Illinois University in Carbondale, and then the University of Illinois, Chicago Circle.

Well, I think why I got involved with the Cubs is I got involved through Cub Scouts. We would come down to Wrigley Field and Jack Brickhouse would always say, "Well, the Chicago Cubs would like to welcome Den 10 from the Cub Scouts in Wheaton, Illinois"...you know? So it always made me feel part of the Cubs.

Never spent time in the bleachers. No, I was always in the stands. When I would go to Wrigley Field...and I would always go up to the box and say "hi" to Mr. Brickhouse and he would always say, "Well, it's a great day in baseball when Jimmy Belushi comes to Wrigley Field. You know the Cubs are going to win. Jimmy, how are you? And how's that Second City doing?" So, he always made me feel part of the Cubs.

But Harry Caray was, as you know, ill and there are a lot of us actors that are pulling for him so I took over with Steve Stone the San Diego Padre game in San Diego. And it was actually really difficult for me 'cause, you know, I'm much more of a spectator than a numbers man. And I found that when you call a game you really have to know the numbers. And Steve would call the numbers first, but every time a play would come I'd look at my notes and before I could open my mouth, Steve Stone would say everything. So, actually Steve gave me a little bit of a hard time.

I remember one time they told me to call the color. Through the ear plug in my ear. And, there was a big hit. It went in the outfield and an outfielder comes under and catches it. Well, they show a replay of that and in my ear the guy says, "Jim? Jim, we're showing replay." And I say, "Okay." And I watch the replay. Just like a spectator would. The guy goes, "Say something." I went, "Oh, the ball is, ah, going, and it's caught." I didn't know what to say.

Did you find that harder than reading lines in movies?

It was the most difficult thing I've ever done. Those guys—I have so much respect for Harry Caray and Steve Stone and Brickhouse and all of 'em for being able to just rattle, you know?

Well, I had some research with Marc Janser and a couple of my friends and we had all the players and listed little stories and things that they were known for. Their batting average, what they did last year, and where they're from. So any time Stone would mention someone I could go to my notes. Well, Joey Cora was playing second base for the Padres and Marc Janser said, "Well, Joey Cora is known for his speed. He's very fast. He steals a lot of bases," he says. "But an interesting thing," he said, "is that when he was in training camp," or in the minor leagues, I can't remember which, minor leagues, I think, "he was mugged at the bus stop waiting for the team bus." And, so my joke was, "Well, I guess he's not that fast, huh?"

So Steve says, "I see Joe Cora's at second base." I said, "Joey's pretty fast, isn't he, Steve." He goes, "Yes, one of the fastest in baseball." I go, "Well, I understand when he was in the minors he got mugged. I guess he's not that fast, huh?" And Steve Stone turned and said, "He was knifed across the belly and they were afraid that he would lose his life let alone worry about him playing baseball ever again." And I went, "Oh, Jesus, I didn't know that." I didn't know it was so serious. I felt really bad, you know.

The great thing about that game was that at 5:50 they had batting practice, and I went into the Cubs lineup. I had Billy Williams coaching me. He'd say, "Don't kill it, Belushi. Don't try to kill the ball, Belushi. Just meet the ball." Oh, I had a great time.

Mark Grace did a movie called *Taking Care of Business.* It was supposed to be another baseball team winning the World Series. When I met on the movie, they said, "Are there any changes you'd like in the script?" I said, "Yeah, you should make it the Cubs." And so they changed it to the Cubs. And they got Mark Grace to hit a home run in the World Series with the Cubs vs. the Angels. He hit the home run and I catch his ball in the movie. I told the producers, I said, "Look, if you want my character to really root for a team, you gotta pick the Cubs."

BEHIND THE SCENES

An ex-Bleacher Bum who has risen to Director of Baseball Administration for the Cubs. Not all dreams have to necessarily come true on the field.

    First game I went to was on my birthday in 1961. My dad took me to a Cubs-Braves game, Milwaukee Braves at the time. And it was a cold day. There was about 6,000-7,000 people in the stands and he got us some real good seats right behind the Cub dugout. As the day went on, it got colder and greyer and snowier. And the game ended with Al Heist, the center fielder for the Cubs, hitting a grand slam home run to beat the Braves, 9-5. We went to a few games every year, but always on my birthday in early April was a big day and my dad would always find a way to get us some seats for that game.

    I started sittin' in the bleachers in about 1966-67. From where I lived, it would take a train and then two buses to get to Wrigley, and then a bus back to the end of the line and someone would come and pick me up. I was about 20 miles from the ballpark.

    But in '68 and '69, I started attending as many games as I could, just because I loved baseball. I loved going to the bleachers. The bleachers at that time were—I believe they were 75 cents. Might have been a dollar by '69 or '70. It was obviously a very economical way to watch a ball game, since I wasn't working at 15. Didn't have a care in the world. My biggest care was who the next day's starting pitcher was. I just, you know, always loved baseball. And always loved going to Wrigley Field and the bleachers. I've been to a lot of ballparks and there's no place like the bleachers at Wrigley Field —for view and for personality.

    I can remember going out there at 1:00 o'clock and sitting anywhere you wanted and you could sprawl out on the bench for that matter. But as the 1969 team took hold, it became a tougher and tougher ticket. I can remember being in line for Billy Williams' Day, which was in June of that year. I must have got to the park at about 7:00 in the morning and the line was already almost wrapped all the way around the bleachers and there was this tremendous thunderstorm the morning of that game. And nobody left the line. I mean, everybody was just standing in the rain and it came down for about 45 minutes. It became a very popular place to be.

And the people who hung out there...I mean, there was a mix-match of all types of people. I mean, you had kids from white collar backgrounds, some blue collar backgrounds, it was a place for every walk of life to gather. And as you can recall, at that place in time, the late '60s was a bit of a changing time in America, what with Vietnam going on and the Democratic Convention in Chicago in 1968. You had the guys with the real long hair and you had like your hippie group and your radicals, as it were. I mean, you had a mix-match of just about everything.

The Bums were a group of basically older guys than I. I mean they were all of legal drinking age. The would hang out at Ray's Bleachers at the corner of Sheffield and Waveland—right in the shadow of the center-field scoreboard, which is now Murphy's Bleachers. And they hung out there and Mike Haley tended bar there as did Ronnie Grousl, because everybody kind of quit there jobs—they quit their jobs that summer to keep coming to Cub games.

Were the Bleacher Bums officially formed in '69?

No, I would say earlier than that. There was a lady named Ma Barker, who came out there one day with this big bed sheet, with a hole cut out of it that said, "Hit the Bleacher Bum." And what happened is Ronnie Grousl stuck his head through there one day and he had a raccoon hat on and they picked it up on television and the wire service photographers picked it up and it became the thing. The group to be with—to be around. There might have been 60 or 70 Bums in all. Not everybody attended every game. But it started with that big a following.

Grousl was the leader?

Right, he was the president of the group. Mike Haley, as I recall, was like the vice president and, I mean, it wasn't a strictly organized group, but it was pretty well organized. The headquarters were Ray's Bleachers.

They'd actually have meetings?

Well, more or less. I mean, the ball game was the meeting. I mean, they'd gather there in the morning and they'd all walk over to the ballpark together, watch the game, and then all walk back and have a few beers and spend most of the evening together. And go to sleep and do it again the next day.

All you guys had a reputation for riding a lot of opposing players pretty hard. Did they give you reason to do this?

Well, anybody who wasn't a Cub gave us reason to do it. And I would say Willie Davis was one of the prime targets. Rico Carty of the Braves, although Rico would always just smile and wave back. We're not sure if Rico understood what we were saying or not. But he was always a good guy towards everything. And there was no vulgarity. There was nothing like that going on. It was good, clean fun. Pete Rose was one of the best. You know, when he played the outfield for the Reds, you'd get on him and he'd get right back on you. And Mazzilli when he first came up. Lee Mazzilli from the Mets when he first came up—he was another big target. Oh, a couple of other guys were Curt Flood and Lou Brock. They got on them real good.

What are your thoughts about 1969?

Well, that team was an interesting team. Most of the group of Bums had grown up watching that team come together. They had seen Beckert as a kid, and Kessinger as a kid, and, of course, Williams, Santo, and Banks as either rookies or, little bit later on in their career, and they saw Holtzman as a kid in 1966 and Jenkins...so everybody comin' together. Hundley, Hands...and as time went on, I mean, the team got better and better and better. Nobody will ever forget '69. I mean, you've got Willie Smith hittin' a home run on opening day to beat the Phillies. I mean, Ernie Banks hits two home runs that day. And just day after day after day there seems to be something magical happening. You have to remember that this team hadn't had very many .500 seasons since winning the pennant in 1945 and this was something special. And it just kept goin' and goin' and as fall came, as people started going back to school and as the weather got colder, it all started to unravel. It was like a ball of yarn in your hands. It just started unraveling.

The game that a lot of people point to is the game against Pittsburgh in late August, when the wind is blowing in from right field, blowing in a ton, and the Cubs are playing the Pirates and Willie

Stargell comes to the plate against Phil Regan. There's no way a guy can hit a home run on this particular day. But Stargell hits a home run to tie the game and Pittsburgh goes on to win the game.

And they left on a road trip at that point and I think everybody left the ballpark that day feeling like, boy, this is going to be a struggle from here on. And later on in that month, the Mets—they won a doubleheader, 1-0, 1-0, with both starting pitchers driving in the winning run. Steve Carlton with the Cardinals strikes out 18 Mets one day, but Ron Svoboda hits two, two-run homers and the Mets win, 4-2. There was just no stopping it and we were going one way and the Mets were going the other way.

You feel that was the turning point?

The game against the Pirates—there's no question. I've talked to a lot of guys who played on that team and when I prompted them, they all point to that game. It was a Sunday afternoon and it was a game that we had won all year long. The wind was blowing in and we had a lead and here comes Phil Regan, who was our best relief pitcher, to face Willie Stargell—certainly a great hitter, a Hall of Fame player as it turned out—and you know Willie Stargell is going to try to pull it. And he looks to the flags in right field and they were as straight as can be. I mean, they were coming in real hard. But he still got it. He got it up in there and hit it on the street.

What were your thoughts when the Cubs did not win it?

Oh, we were devastated. I can remember sitting in study hall in high school looking at the paper after the last game of the season. Just shaking my head...I could not believe it. Because you know, the Cubs did not finish two or three games out. I mean, they were eight games out when it was over. I mean, it wasn't even like it was a race at the end. They just swept right by us and we had no chance to ever right ourself and continue on. And if you look in that whole stretch from about the first week of August on, the Cubs and the Mets played four times—two times in New York and then the last two games of the season, which were of no consequence at that point. So, it wasn't like there was a pair of four games key series that, you know, if we can beat them two out of three here, or three out of four here, we got a chance to get back on. We had no chance.

When did you leave the Bleacher Bums?

Probably 1972, I went away to college and had to find a job in the summertime. I mean, I would still go but I would probably go 15 or 20 times a year instead of 40 or 50.

Your life changes a little bit when you've got other responsibilities. I mean, those days in the late '60s, those were the greatest days 'cause you had no responsibilities...no worries...you had nothing.

What do you think is the make-up of the Bleacher Bums now?

Well, I'm not sure. It looks to be just as much fun, but the one bad part about my job is that I don't even get a chance to go out there. I haven't been in the bleachers for a game since...probably 1981.

I see every game. I miss about 10 games a year. Home and the road.

I was the PR director and working the public relations department from 1982 until this past November. Then I took this new job in November. I worked the PR side to the baseball players.

When I went to work, the offices were pretty small and cramped. The whole area of the game has changed. I mean, our highest-paid baseball player when I first got there, I think, was Bill Buckner, who made about $400,000 a year. And when you look at today's salaries, I mean, there's not too many guys that are veteran ballplayers making $400,000 a year. So, I mean, that's changed drastically.

I travel with the team now, this will be my 10th year, and I mean, you see a lot of different things. You see all the ballparks. You see all the cities. You see all the different fans. You see our team go through stages of triumph and of struggle. And you see players go through triumph and struggle. I mean, you kinda know when a guy's in a slump, but you don't feel it as much as you do when you're workin' with them and you're a part of the daily grind. And it is a grind. I mean, it's a great grind. It's a beautiful grind. But to say it's not a grind is misleading. It takes you from Valentine's Day to Halloween, almost. And there's very little time in any of that for anything but baseball.

What's been your most exciting moment watching the Cubs?

One is the day that we clinched the division in Pittsburgh in 1984. I mean, it's just a beautiful moment. We celebrated in that clubhouse for probably four or five hours. It was the end of a long, long, long dry spell. The ballpark that night ...Three Rivers had about 7,000 or 8,000 in it, which in that place is not very many. But it still had a certain electricity to us. I was in the dugout for the last three outs of the ninth inning and it was almost deafening. There were so many Cub fans there—even in that big ball park—it was so loud and such an electric moment...it was really, really something special.

A second one would be during the '89 season when we were playing the Cardinals on a Sunday afternoon in Chicago. And, we're struggling at this point. We go into the game a half a game up and we're losing this game...this is Saturday, I'm sorry...and Luis Salazar, who we just acquired, hits a ball down the right-field line to tie the score. And we end up winning that game. That was probably the biggest game since I've been here in nine years. That is probably the biggest game because we were hanging by a thread of gettin' beat and having somebody overtake us and once that happens, you lose so much momentum that you may never come back. And that was the biggest game of the year for us. Salazar was terrific and the next day, Steve Wilson struck out 10 Cardinals in five innings and we win that game. From then on we were rolling.

And then, of course, the third would be clinching the division in Montreal two days after the St. Louis series. That was just a real key victory for us. Especially, since we had to play the Cardinals three games at the end of the season—in St. Louis. Had we gone into that weekend without having it clinched, there's no telling what could have happened.

Were you hurt more by the inability to take it in '89, or did '84 hurt more?

I wrestle with that all the time. I don't think you ever get over getting that close and not having it happen. For different reasons and they both are real special.

'84 we were one win away from doing it. When you really get down to it, we were eight outs away from doing it. And when you get that close and not do it, and know that if you would have played Detroit, you would have had a chance of maybe winning the whole thing...it's painful. It's tough to take.

Then you think about 1989. And 1989 was such a miracle-type season. Everybody started jumping on the band wagon in July and early August and we were still, as a group, trying to win as many games as possible. I mean, the division wasn't even part of the thing, even though we were leading it. We were just trying to hang with it and win games because it was a club made up of young players. We had Wilson and Girardi and Walton, who had never played Triple-A baseball, who were contributing mightily to the cause. It was just a special type of season. Maddux was just coming into his own. Bielecki, who had great promise, had suddenly become one of the best pitchers in the league. Sutcliffe, who had come back from injury after injury after injury, turned in a great year. And there's Mitch Williams saving 36 games. It was a group that...when it was put together in spring training, I mean, hardly anybody knew anybody. But as time went on, it became a very, very close knit group. And to have the miracle dashed out within moments, practically...you know, through five games only...was stunning and staggering.

After I got out of school...I graduated in 1976 from NIU and I was a journalism major. 'Cause as a young person, I wanted to be involved in sports in some way and I knew that I wasn't going to be a professional baseball player, professional hockey player, professional basketball...I knew that wasn't going to happen. So I decided that I loved to write and I decided I was going to pursue that avenue. I can remember listening to Vince Lloyd, Lou Boudreau doing the games on radio on the road, and dreaming about being on the road and writing baseball.

In 1976, I got out of Northern Illinois and I got a job on a newspaper and I covered high school stuff, high school sports, and then I ended up after four years, I ended up being in Philadelphia and covering professional hockey...covering the Philadelphia Flyers. And, as the Tribune Company bought the Cubs in 1981 in June...by November of that year, Dallas Green, who had been the manager of the Phillies was coming to Chicago as the GM. Actually, in October. And a friend of mine, who I worked with at the paper, was hired as the PR director. And the paper I was working on...the newspaper industry was going through a real tough time and the paper I was working on was about to fold and he called me up and said, "Would you like to come back to Chicago and work for the Cubs?" He says, "I'm not from Chicago. I don't know that much about the Cubs. You'd be a great asset for me, plus it would give you a chance to come back to Chicago."

'Cause as life would have it sometimes, you go through these rough, rough periods and at that point in time, my son was just born—he was about two months old—I was about to have this newspaper fold from underneath me, and in the meantime my dad was back in Chicago dying of lung cancer. So, I relished the idea of coming to Chicago and working for the Cubs. And that's how it all began and I started as the assistant PR director from '82 through '84—actually through '85. And then beginning in the winter of '85-'86, was promoted to PR director and did that until November of 1990 when they decided that it was time to move me to the baseball side to give me some more responsibilities. And that's what I'm doing now.

Right now, during the wintertime, I negotiate our player contracts. And during the next couple of years, I'm responsible for orchestrating a computer system, analytical system that will take all our scouting reports of all our players and all other professional players and all the medical histories, salary history, and statistical history of every player and put them in a system that we can get information on any particular player at the push of a button. I also continue to travel and will do some leg work for Jim Frey as far as, you know, when I'm on the road, if he's got a player he's interested in with another team, I'll go to the GM and see if that GM has any interest in (a) trading that player and if he does (b) who is he looking for from our club or if we've got somebody we're trying to move, try and do that. Plus, I'm responsible for all the baseball rules...the waivers, the outrights, the assignments.

I enjoy it tremendously. It's...I never forget—I mean this from the bottom of my heart—when I walk into Wrigley Field...and I do it probably 200 times a year...when I walk in that building, I never forget where I'm at. And I never forget the aura that it still has for me and, when I'm on the field, I mean...it's still something real special after now...probably 1,500 games or so. I've probably been at 1,500-1,800 Cub games in my life and it's still a real special thing for me.

I've been tremendously blessed and it's something that I'll never forget or ever take for granted.

V.P. in charge of Scouting and Player Development for the Cubs. He thinks pitching at the college level is "pathetic" because of the aluminum bat. They try to fool the hitter too much because of their fear of the bat.

I was general manager of the Mariners. I got fired in August of '88, and then came over here in November of '88.

When you took over in November '88, what shape were things in?

It wasn't in bad shape. I think they had some players that were right on the verge. As I recollect, there wasn't a whole lot in Triple-A. The players were at the Double-A level, the Girardis, the Waltons of the world. Lancaster had been up and down maybe once or twice. Dwight Smith was at Double-A. I'm trying to think who else would have fit into that particular...Wilkins was still down in A ball. Berryhill had come up a little bit the previous year, I want to say. Dunston was already here. Grace was already here. Dascenzo was up and down a little bit. So, they had some guys like that. I think, in all honesty, the '88 draft and maybe the '87 draft was not very good for the Cubs. Particularly the '88 draft. And I think the lower levels were kind of dry.

I've kind of incorporated the associate scout program, which is a bird dog program, a little bit more. As a staff, I think we have about 21 free agent scouts and three scouts who do strictly major league work. We have about 25 part-time scouts who do free-agent work. We have a network of about 100 scouts. So I have kind of stepped that phase of it up. I'm a big believer in that. I'm a believer in tryout camps, and in the last year and a half, we've tried to really get a little bit more involved in those kind of things.

Will you get prospects from a tryout camp?

Sure. Guys who did not play high school or college baseball because schools didn't have it, or because they had to work and couldn't play or because they simply weren't good enough to play in the eyes of the particular coach, and who have athletic ability.

You get a lot athletes—football players—who didn't get a chance to play baseball.

If you have enough camps, you'll have a turnout of anywhere from 75 to 100 people. There may be exceptions where you'll have much fewer or much greater numbers. But in the tryout camp, we try to gear it up to get names and addresses and ideas for guys who will be eligible for the draft for the following year. And at the same time, you do keep your eyes out for the guy who was overlooked in this particular draft for some reason, who was not in school or whatever the case may be, who can be signed. I'm a funnel theory guy. The bigger the funnel, the more names you put in the hat coming in, the more players you're going to get out the bottom.

What would you say of the fellows that you have in the minor leagues. What percentage were from the draft and what were just, for lack of a better description, walk-ons that you just signed?

Well, currently, 95% are drafted players. Because we've just instituted this tryout camp in the last year, year and a half. Now, when I was at Kansas City, the Marvell Wynnes of the world, we got...Brad Wilman was a drafted player. I think Mike Kingery signed out of a tryout camp in Wisconsin. You get some players. We get one out of 100, something like that. I have a theory that you could field an entry-level club, a rookie league club, with guys signed out of a tryout camp. If you do it over a period of time, you'll get a major league player or two.

Since you've come on board, who do you see in the farm system that will be comers?

Well, I think you start with Gary Scott and Lance Dickson. Scott was an '89 draft. Dickson was a '90 draft. And then we have a boat load of pitching at the A level, Double-A level. Ryan Hawblitzel, who is a '90 draft at Winston-Salem. You have a guy like Troy Bradford, who is a 1990 draft. He's at Winston-Salem. Tim Parker is a right-handed pitcher, who's at Charlotte, which is a Double-A club. He was a '90 draft. Earl Cunningham's still in Peoria, but he missed most of last year with a broken wrist. He was our first pick in '89. We have a couple of Latin kids—Rafael Soto, who's at Peoria. He signed last year from the Dominican. There's a young outfielder who just signed—Pedro Valdez from Puerto Rico.

So your strength right now, which is what the Cubs need, is in pitching?

I think it's our strength in the minor leagues. But again, see, the '89 draft we isolated and kind of honed on some hitters. That's why we took Cunningham and Scott. In 1990 and in '91 we really honed in on pitching. For example, I think in 1990, of the top 20 we took something like 16 or 17 pitchers. This year, we took another 15 or 16 pitchers of the top 20. We took some high school kids who will just take some time. But I'm a believer in pitching. I think you have to have not only quantity but quality.

Are you happy with the managers and coaches in the system now?

Yes. Billy Harford runs the minor league system on a day-to-day basis. For the most part, he has hired all the people that we have and most of them have been with us now for a couple of years.

What are the factors that will hurt a young prospect from making the big leagues?

Lack of ability. It's still the primary thing. I think a second factor is the lack of emotional stability. These kids, for the most part, and again there are exceptions, most of them haven't understood that you really have to work at this game as a career. And the dedication and the priorities that you have to have to become a successful player or pitcher, whatever the case may be.

Does that come under the heading of attitude?

I think so. I think we, in the last two years in our drafts, have dealt with a lot of high school kids. The more high school kids you get, the more that you have to understand they're young kids who need to mature mentally, physically, but emotionally also.

Say you signed a fellow out of the University of Arizona which has a good program. He's 22, four years of college. Is he going to be more intelligent than a high school graduate and have a better attitude?

Well, you'd like to think so, but that's not always the case. You cannot assume that. It's a big, major mistake to assume that.

Why?

Because the college baseball programs—there are a lot of good ones, but it's not the same. You've got the metal bat. It's a different theory. Winning and losing is a much more accepted thing. Pitching, particularly at the college level, is so backwards it's pathetic, because of the aluminum bat.

Most college pitchers try to fool hitters. Curveball, curveball, curveball-type mentality. And pro ball is vice-a-versa. It's fastball, fastball, use your breakin' ball. I don't care whether you throw 80 miles an hour or 90 miles an hour—you've gotta throw your fastball. At the college levels, you throw breaking ball, breaking ball, and maybe mix in a fastball. It's just back-ass backwards. A lot of that is because of the aluminum bat.

What are some of the better baseball conferences?

On a given year, the Pac-10 is good. On a given year, the Southeast Conference or the Southwest Conference is good. Then the ACC or you come up with some independent program—I don't think there's a predominant one. I really don't. And then you always have some small schools in the NAIA or Division II that are constantly producing some players who can play the game.

Your organization has a uniform system of play. Do all major league teams?

I think that's an assumption on some people's part that that's the way everybody does it. I am a strong believer in that. And I think it adds to easy development or easier development and it makes the player more comfortable in knowing what's going on.

But there are organizations who don't believe that. They do it differently based on the quality and the caliber of players that they have. And they make those adjustments particularly in the cutoffs and relays. Particularly when you get to the third basemen's and first basemen's stronger arms and less stronger arms and more agile athletes vs. less agile athletes. I don't believe in that.

We do a lot of work on our manual. I mean, we publish a manual for our staff and players. We have diagrams. We have written instructions and we go over this stuff. And we expect to have it done the way we go over it.

Kids have many more things to do today than play baseball. And I think that's why we don't have the number of kids playing today that we used to. I think soccer has taken a big toll on the young player and taken potential baseball players out of circulation and put them in soccer uniforms and on soccer fields. And I think that's just an example.

Kids today have many more things to do than play pick-up games on a summer day in the back of the school in July. They go to the beach. They go down to the mall. They've just got a hundred other things. And I think that's why they don't know the Ernie Banks. That's why they're not going to know the history of various players. There is still a certain segment of the young player who know all of that. The baseball card industry has created some of that because statistically they know these people. Most young people today just haven't spent the time to research and to have enjoyed doing that type of thing.

Will the Cubs be a dominant team in the '90s?

Well, I like to think that we're going to be good. But it's tough to say that one organization is going to be that far superior to the other 25 and, well, the other 27 now, I guess. I think it runs in cycles. I think there are certainly those clubs that were consistent in the '70s and were consistent in the '80s and will be consistently competitive in the '90s. But for me to go out and say we're going to be the best, that would be foolish on my part.

I think we've improved ourselves and our pitching. I think pitching's the name of the game. And I think as long as you continue to sign pitchers and get pitchers who are quality guys, you're going to have a running chance.

You played eight years in the minors—never made the big leagues. Any regrets?

Oh, no. I'd do it again. And I got nothing. I signed out of a tryout camp and got not one dime to sign. Those were the best eight years of my life. I was single. I had no responsibilities and I enjoyed the game. I just enjoyed it. It's unfortunate the kids today who get a chance to play, either don't sign because they didn't get enough bonus, or they didn't try hard enough once they were signed to prove themselves. It's a sad scenario.

[*Publisher's Note: Dick Balderson was fired as part of a structural reorganization of the Cubs in August of 1992.*]

BILLY HARFORD

Never played minor league baseball, but is the Director of Minor League Operations for the Cubs. He has helped develop the Cub minor league system to a point where it is considered one of the best in baseball.

You didn't play organized baseball, but you're in charge of the system. How did all that evolve?

Well, I played college ball and after college, Bob Kennedy was the general manager. He worked for the Cubs in '79. And he hired me at the time the farm director was C. V. Davis. He hired me to work in the farm system and I've been here ever since. Been through some changes so, I've had a chance to learn from a lot of people. My background is one of learning from the front office end of it, as opposed to the playing end of it.

I worked for C. V. as his assistant for about two years until the change was made when Dallas Green came into the organization. I then worked for Gordon Goldsberry. I scouted for him, did a little bit of everything. In '87 I was named Director of the Minor Leagues.

I went to Franklin & Marshall College. A Division III school in Lancaster, Pennsylvania. I played baseball there for Don Warden, who played for the Tiger organization. And then came to work for the Cubs. I worked a little bit for C.V. Worked for Alvin Dark for an instructional league. And then Dallas came in and Gordie came in. I probably worked directly for Gordie more so than Dallas, but I enjoyed Dallas. I thought he was a great leader. He was great for me. I mean, a lot of people are very wary of his tirades, if you will. But he was a great guy and very helpful to me and very influential for me at a younger age. And then Jim Frey, of course, has come in and been very fair to me. Has given me some responsibility and a chance to grow.

I guess what I'm proudest of is the people that we have in the organization. I've worked with a lot of these guys for a long time. Our organization—our minor league organization really has remained intact. There are a lot of people that have worked for us now for a considerable number of years.

211

Mick (Kelleher) is one of them. He's worked for us, I think, five or six years. Richie Zisk has been with us about four or five years. Jim Essian was manager and assistant for a long time. Jay Leviglio has been with us a long time. Rick Cranitz has been with us about seven or eight years. Brad Mills played for us and worked for us. So, I'm very proud of the job our people on the field have done and I think it's been reflected in the success we've had of putting our own people, if you will, into the big leagues.

I think today there are 15 or 16 that have come through the system, signed by us and developed by us, that are playing for our big league club and, if I'm not mistaken, according to a *Baseball America* poll, I think we lead all of baseball in the number of players signed and developed that are now playing in the big leagues.

You have 25-men squads now?
Right.

So, 15 out of 25. Nearly two-thirds of the squad.
That's a credit to a lot of people. That's a credit to the scout. Really, in my job and in the job that the field people have, I think we play a very key role in the success of the organization. But really, we are given a hand.

The scouts sign the players. They've gotta go out and get the talent —the players. Once they get them and sign them, they become the development's property and it can be difficult. A good or bad draft or an injury here or there and losing a blue chip if you will, can be very detrimental to a development system.

But I think the beauty and the success that we've had is there have been a lot of players that were signed by the Cubs that maybe were late-round draft picks or free agent picks that our field people and our teaching staff have done a terrific job with and gotten to the big leagues. That might not help your big league club win a World Series, but I think it reflects very well on the kind of job that your field people are doing in the field.

Some consider the Cubs' minor league system one of the best in baseball.
I do too. And, of course, I guess you'd have to speak to other people about that. I've seen Bob Kennedy as a GM, Herman Franks as a GM, Dallas Green as a GM, Jim Frey as a GM. I'm very

proud of what I've been involved with, but more importantly, what we've been able to accomplish and the success that some individuals have.

When you see a Shawon Dunston start in rookie ball. Mark Grace come into the organization. Dwight Smith, Dascenzo, Maddux, Girardi, Berryhill, Lancaster, Harkey, Boskie—you know, it just makes you...you see these kids struggle. You have tough times with them.

In my job sometimes it can be even more difficult because I'm also involved off the field with them as far as their salary and what level they're going to play at. That all rests on my shoulders with the help of our teaching staff. It's a very rewarding job in that manner. To see them go on and mature, have success and do well. And that's really, I think, what most of our people are in this industry for.

You take a guy like Mick Kelleher, a guy like Richie Zisk—they don't really need to stay in baseball. They're very well-to-do people. They've done very well in their professional career as a player. They've invested their money wisely. They have interests outside of baseball. They do it because they like the game of baseball. More importantly, I think they like to help young kids. Teach them how to play the game, the right way. A lot of them felt fortunate when they were coming up in baseball that they had people there. I think that's what they're here for.

There are a lot of intangibles that come into play when you're talking about developing a human being. That can happen in any business. There are a number of factors that come into play there. Personality can be one. Ability to retain what people are trying to teach you can be another. Ability to accept failure or to accept success the right way. These are all factors that come into play and all factors that, in my position, I'm concerned with.

That's why we have an educational program. That's why we have an English as a second language program for our Latin players. That's why we have an employee assistance program to help kids overcome problems that all of us are going to go through when we're grown up. I'll be 36, but you look back when you were 18-19-20-21, there are things that you did at that time that you wish you could go back and change.

I think what we all have to realize is not everybody playing in the big leagues today is going to be a great guy or a smart guy. But he's a good baseball player. The Lord blessed him with great talent. I think talent will overcome most of the other deficiencies but sometimes those other deficiencies are so grave, that even the greatest talent in the world can't overcome it.

Unfortunately, I don't know the boy, but you look at Albert Bell with Cleveland. You look at some other characters in the game. Their outside influences weighed so heavily on them, and were such a factor, that even the great ability they have wasn't good enough. That's an unfortunate thing.

We in baseball try to make it better just as I'm sure anybody else does who's a salesman or whatever business you're in. There are factors—sometimes alcohol, sometimes drugs, sometimes just...the guy just can't get along with people, but is a terrific salesman. It's written so much about in baseball, but I think it's certainly prevalent in other industries as well.

On an average, how many minor leaguers will make it to the Cubs every year?

We consider ourselves successful if we can place two players a year, two to three players a year, onto our big league club every year. We have between 150 and 160 in our minor league system now. So those percentages are very low. It's a tough business, but the rewards are great. That is written negatively about our industry; that the success ratio is not too good. You're getting into an industry where you're really going to have to struggle and hope things go well and get lucky to get to the big leagues.

I sort of disagree with that premise. I think any industry—to get to the top—is difficult to do. In any business you're in. As a player, you have an opportunity to make $100,000 a year stepping on a major league baseball field, have a pension plan that's second to none, medical and dental plan that's second to none, revenue sharing that is equivalent of about $30,000 a year and up. I mean, go at it like anybody else would go at their job.

What is the average stay in the minors for a man who doesn't make the Cubs?

Three to four years.

What is the average salary at Triple-A?

Well, it can range. A lot of Triple-A players are on a "40-man roster." But I would say the salary of Triple-A ranges from $2,500 to $6,000-7,000 a month, for about 4.75 months.

The lowest minor league classification is what?
    Our lowest is rookie ball.

What would they make?
    $850. That's mandated by baseball. When you sign a professional contract, your salary is $850 a month.

Would you rather sign an 18 year old or a college graduate?
    I would prefer to have the 18 year old that is taught by our people and taught how to play the game our way. I'm not taking anything away from the college programs. There are some terrific college programs and some coaches at those levels that are terrific teachers. I just happen to believe that if you're a good baseball player and by a good baseball player, as an 18 year old, I would think you're drafted maybe in the top 10 rounds.
    If you can play, if you can throw, you can run, you've got some ability and you go to rookie ball, you're going to play 72 games. You're going to have maybe one or two days off from the time you sign in June until the end of August. If you're a good ballplayer, we'll probably bring you to our instructional league, which starts mid-September and runs through the end of October. You're going to learn how to play baseball day-in and day-out. Just as you're going to have to do when you get to the big leagues. And one of the biggest adjustments that players have to make is learning how to play every day. Learning how to make adjustments when things aren't going well. And I don't think that comes from playing baseball a couple of times, maybe four times a week.
    I certainly think if you're going to go to school, I think you should go to school to learn. I don't think you should go to school to play baseball. If you're going to be a plumber, there's nothing wrong with that. You want to be an electrician or a carpenter—you don't necessarily have to go to college. If you want to be a baseball player, you come play baseball. Now that doesn't preclude that you can't go get your education in the off season. You can get your education while you're playing through correspondence classes and we encourage that. But I just think that if we get an 18 year old that hasn't been taught bad habits, we can teach him how to play the game to be successful at the major league level.

Are you optimistic for the Cubs in the '90s?

I'm very optimistic. I feel very fortunate. We have Dick Balderson in our organization now as the Scouting Director. Mick Kelleher, I think you know the kind of person he is and he is certainly, I think, a reflection of the kind of people we have in the minor leagues.

So, I'm encouraged about some individuals in the organization, but, more importantly, it's the people that we surround our young players with and the Cubs have, and the Tribune Company have, dedicated money to the minor league system. We're paying our people well. I think we've got people that can teach and develop these kids hopefully into big league players and, if they're not, I hope that some of the extracurricular things that we have for them will enable them to go on and be productive citizens and they'll feel that their time spent in the minor leagues has been worthwhile. Worth something.

[*Publisher's Note: Billy Harford was fired as part of a structural reorganization of the Cubs in August of 1992.*]

PAUL GERLACH

Manager, Event Operations/Security at Wrigley Field. The Joe Friday of Cubs baseball, he keeps the lid on. Trying to maintain peace and calm with 35,000 people most every game is no day at the beach.

Describe your job and what you do?

Manager of Event Operations and Security. I manage the event operations personnel for the ball club, so all of the ushers, crowd control, security personnel are recruited, interviewed, hired, and trained by me and they work for me.

I started with the Cubs in 1983 as a seasonal part-time crowd control supervisor. I worked seasonally for the Cubs from 1983 through 1985 and at that time I was promoted to Crowd Control Coordinator. At that time we did only in-house security and crowd control. Then in 1987 when we went in-house with the ushering, I got the title that I now have when we went to a complete proprietary crowd management system.

I used to cut school and go to Cub games and figure out how to break into the place without paying.

Have you seen a change in the makeup of the crowds in the last few years?

I think since the *Tribune* has purchased the Cubs, you've seen a lot more season ticketholders. So you do have a lot more corporations. On day games, you will see a lot more of the corporate type. It's still a family ballpark in that we have all the general grandstand seats. You will get a lot of people coming from businesses, from offices.

Mid-week games, day games, you'll see a lot of children's groups. We do a lot of season ticket sales, but we also do a lot of group sales, which affects the nature of the crowd.

The bleachers have changed. We don't sell tickets on the day of the game anymore. We sell them in advance. I would say the bleachers have changed very much; you've got more of an influx of families out there, because it is one of the cheaper seats in the ballpark. You're getting families that will buy tickets in advance.

You always had the young crowd, whether you want to call them yuppies or whatever you want to call them. The 18 to 30 age group that sat out in the bleachers for as long as I've known the Cubs. That was always the place for the young people to sit.

I think the bleachers are probably the calmest they've been as long as I've been associated with the Cubs. Each year it quiets down a little bit more. We're constantly taking a look at the bleachers. I know that many of the bleacher regulars—I'm not a real popular person with them, they think it's all my fault—but we have to take a look at the fact that not everybody wants that type of behavior where they're sitting. At the same time we get complaints from the bleacher regulars that it's not fun anymore, that it's too restrictive. We've got other people saying that the language out there isn't good. That there's problems. That they can't bring their children.

But, all in all, the bleachers are probably the calmest they've ever been. We have set certain restrictions. We've got more man-power working out there per capita than anywhere else in the ballpark. And we try to maintain kind of a controlled chaos out there.

I've been in the entertainment business pretty much all my working life and I would compare it to a general admission concert. No one has a specific seat. There's a lot more mobility. There's a lot more freedom of action and motion, so to control that you're trying to keep people within a certain bounds of behavior and action. We've managed to bring the bleachers under control. By no means are we completely happy with where we stand anywhere in the ballpark, nor the bleachers. But I would say it's the calmest it's ever been.

In the box seats and in the main grandstand, everybody's got a ticket, an identity to a certain place. We do things in the boxes and in the main grandstand that you just can't do in the bleachers. With the ushers, you've got control levels in the grandstand that you don't have in the bleachers, 'cause no one has a particular seat.

What's the most common problem at the ballpark?

I would say people that have had too much to drink. In terms of crowd control, that would be a major issue.

When do you cut off beer sales?

Day games at the eighth inning. Night games at the seventh inning or 9:20 P.M., which ever comes sooner.

It definitely does help. You know there's always the give and take here. I would like to have beer sales cut off sooner. I would like to see it done at the bottom of the seventh for all games. But then again, there's revenue that you have to take into consideration. It helps that we're not selling beer right up to the end of the game as we did when I first started working here. Right up until the game ends and actually after the game ends, the beer vendors were finishing off their loads. And that becomes an issue because some one who was just served a fresh 16 oz. beer doesn't want to leave the ballpark, I understand their point. If I've just gotten this fresh beer five minutes ago, I'm not necessarily going to leave.

The troubled drinker, the guy who's going to drink to get drunk, is going to do it anyway. So, it's really not controlling them so much. But I think the drinking issue just in America in general, we're seeing a lot more responsible drinking. Where people at one time might drink until they couldn't drink anymore and now I think that they're looking at the issues of driving while drunk or who's going to drive and their behavior in general. I think that's had a major effect.

What's your most serious problem at the ballpark?
Medical is one of the biggest issues. We really try and train our people on what to do in a medical situation. And it's not necessarily giving first aid. Depending on what type of medical problem you have, more often than not, our role is to secure the area and make sure that we can get expert medical personnel there as quickly as possible.

Heart attacks, falling down and twisting an ankle or breaking a bone or something like that. Being hit by a line drive. But that just fits in line with our general overall theory of how we do crowd management. What's different about Wrigley Field is that we are a totally proprietary system. We're under one management for ushering, crowd control, and for security. This is not true in most ballparks or in most stadiums you would go to. Most stadiums have policemen working security and possibly another security agency doing crowd control and another agency doing ushering. So you have a division there and the communication level isn't as strong as we feel we have.

We will do plain clothes-type people on occasions, very seldom. Mostly we use our uniformed personnel. We also have a very sophisticated closed circuit television system. We're one of the first—I think we were the first major league team to develop one. And we presently have a 15-camera system and it's become a real useful tool for us in being able to monitor behavior, monitor fans, and what's going on.

We use eight off-duty police officers every day, but they're wearing a uniform. Sometimes when I've got a specific problem, I will put people out in plain clothes. We haven't done nearly as much of that recently because our approach to crowd management has changed a little bit in the last couple of years. It used to be we really tried to...oh, my term was "babysit"... you know, if you had a problem group, like four or five guys who were really loud, rowdy, acting up a little bit, we would warn them and then we would actually place a guard right there who would babysit their behavior.

We changed our approach a little bit. And we let the patrons know that. If someone is doing something that is outside the bounds of what we consider acceptable behavior, we will give them one warning. This is the only warning you're going to receive. If your behavior doesn't change, we will take this one step further. If we have another problem in that area, if we have a problem with those people again, they are removed, and asked to leave the ballpark.

So a few years ago, our ejection rate, the number of people we ejected in a season, increased dramatically. We've also noticed that the number of violent incidents where fights—patron against patron fights—that type of thing, has decreased dramatically. Also, the number of times we actually have to arrest someone has decreased.

We're always dealing in the business of lost patrons. People getting separated from their groups. We especially have problems on certain days. We'll have groups from hospitals, senior centers, especially homes for the retarded, that type of thing. It doesn't matter how many monitors they bring with them, these people have a tendency to get lost. Back...I think it was during the '84 season...you get the call over the radio, "lost patron," and most of the time it's a 10-year-old boy named "Johnny" wearing a Cubs hat. That could describe anyone of 3 or 4,000 children at the ballpark.

But we had a call come over the radio about a lost patron. He was quadriplegic, blind and mentally retarded and tended towards violence. So they were trying to tell us to be careful. He was never found. To this day I don't know if he was ever found. We searched the stadium and finally a lost person report was done by the police, by the people from the hospital. But, it always strikes me as funny in that how do you lose a mentally retarded blind quadriplegic? This isn't a guy who just wanders off to the bathroom by himself.

Trying to get a ticket to a Cub game is not always easy. Next time, call Frank.

My title is Director of Ticket Operations for the Chicago Cubs. Basically what I do is administer the distribution of all the tickets to all Cub games. That includes the season ticket aspect of it. Of course, we're trying to sell season tickets. I oversee the sales effort and then also the distribution of the season tickets. We also have the day-of-game tickets. In other words, the tickets that are not sold to season ticketholders are sold at our box office. They're sold on telephones, through Ticketmaster, they're sold at Ticketmaster outlets, and I basically oversee that operation also. We have a work force that I have to supervise. Plus, a myriad of other things. Prepare budgets for the ticket operations, prepare planning. I have to input every year what our planning is going to be for tickets for the next year and prices—all types of things. I submit those to our board that runs the ball club. Answering customer complaints. We're always getting complaints and that type of thing. So, quite a mixture of duties. I represent the ticket department to the media anytime questions are asked; television, radio, printed media, whatever.

How did you get the job?
I was offered a job selling paper, really. And, through a mutual acquaintance, I had a chance to talk to Andy McKenna who was in that type of business and I was going to talk to him, really, to just discuss this other job opportunity I had, just to see what he thought of it, because he was in the same line of business. But the same day I went to talk to him about that, by the time we were done with our conversation, he asked me if I thought I'd like to work for the Cubs. He threw me for a loop, because he said, pick up the paper the next day. And sure enough, the very next morning it was an announcement the Tribune was going to purchase the Cubs. So, it was just a mere fate of circumstances, of timing.

Actually, I didn't go to work for them right then and there because I still had to go through the general manager aspect and then they named a general manager a few months later, which of course, was Dallas Green. I started working for the Cubs when the Tribune took over in October of 1981.

What were you faced with back in the fall of '81?

Well, when I first got the job, I was Director of Group Sales. So, basically my job then was to spearhead sales efforts and particularly large groups coming into the ballpark. At that time, of course, attendance was nothing like it is today. My first year, we had just come off the strike season. That was the big, long strike season that went for about a month or six weeks. We had about 2,000-2,500 season ticket holders at that time. And we literally got on the telephone cold, calling businesses, churches, what have you, trying to get people to purchase group tickets or purchase season tickets. We actually had a sales force that went out onto the street. We'd hire young guys, send them down Michigan Avenue, trying to sell season tickets, trying to sell group tickets.

At that time, the all-time Cub record for attendance was set in 1969. The record I think then was 1,679,000. Well, at that time, in my wildest dreams, did I ever dream we'd come up to that mark. I mean, I thought it would take a tremendous team and all of that to come to that mark. So that went on for my first couple of years and we did increase every year. We made some real nice increases on a year-by-year basis.

But it was really 1984 that changed everything. In 1984, when we won the division, the year after that, going into the '85 season, is when the explosion occurred. Because our season ticketholder base just took off. We went from a 2,000 season ticketholder base to 21,000 or 22,000 tickets that year. It was fantastic and it just turned around to the point that no longer did we cold call anybody. We couldn't handle the calls that were coming into us. No longer did we go out - send people out into the street. We had a tough enough time just handling the business that was coming into us. And, it's been pretty much that ever since. We've operated with that strong base and, of course, we've gone over 2 million several times. I mean, right now, the old record would be considered a poor year for us in ticket sales.

Do you have any box seats available on a walk-up basis...on a day-of-game basis?

Well, occasionally. Basically, all our box seats are pretty much season ticketholders. But, I mean, there always is a possibility. We have to hold back tickets for the players' families, the visiting team, that type of thing. Sometimes if they don't utilize all those tickets, there may be some scattered box seats available on a daily basis. But, it's very few and one would be very, very fortunate to come across them.

Your job has changed then?

Well, we're not selling—that's true. Now we've got the tremendous job of getting these tickets out to the public, like season tickets. I'm no longer in sales. I'm the head of the operation and so now we have to mail these out. Input them into the computer...we became computerized in '84. So we have to get all these into our computer system. The nature of the job has changed. There is no doubt about it. Now, my job is much more service-oriented than sales-oriented.

If the Cubs fielded a terrible team, do you think you'd still do over 2 million?

Yes, I do. I think we would. I mean, if we fielded a terrible team for several straight years, we might not. But I think the Cubs are unique in that we are one of the few franchises in sports that can draw very, very well with an inferior product.

I think part of the reason is Wrigley Field itself. So many people come here just to come to this ballpark. That's the big difference. I think there are many other franchises that just have to win because the park is nothing special. But this is probably one of the—if not the most special park in baseball—certainly close to it. And that's why I think we'll always have that base. But if you get too sloppy and lose too long, it'll drop off.

With that kind of attendance, does that cause an increase in ticket prices?

Well, you know, you're caught between a rock and a hard place. You're caught between a rock inasmuch as this has always been a family franchise, they try to keep costs down here. We don't want to see our costs get to be like basketball or hockey or football. It's still by far, I think, the best sports bargain around, but at the same time, as salaries are escalating in tremendous proportion to these players, the money's gotta come from somewhere. So, we've tried to keep it down. It's a fine line—you're walking a tight-rope. You're trying to keep it down so the average guy can bring his wife and his kids to the ball game. But at the same time, you've got bills to meet. So, it's kind of a fine line.

Obviously, television has helped us tremendously in that respect. Without the income from television, prices would be out of sight. And that's why I think many people in our industry are fearful that if that television well ever dries out, something drastically would have to give. In other words, these salaries would have to drop dramatically, or ticket prices would have to increase dramatically.

Well, that could happen in 1993. CBS' contract is up at that point and they're reportedly not happy with it. If CBS doesn't go for it or another network doesn't pay at least as much for the renewal, the major leagues would have to increase their prices or do something about the salaries. One or the other.

Oh, I would definitely agree with that. But whether that will happen or not, I don't know. But see, that's part of the difference between our sport and basketball, or hockey, why prices are so high. They don't have the television revenue that baseball has.

Have you felt the recession at all?

Not at all. No sign. We see no sign of it. Again, I think it's because from an entertainment aspect, we're still one of the cheaper buys. You can get a ticket to the ballpark for the same price or less than a movie theater. We haven't seen any signs of it, so we've been very fortunate.

What is your cheapest seat in the ballpark?

Six bucks.

And that's the bleachers.

Bleachers and the upper deck reserved is also a $6 seat. The most expensive is $15. It's lower deck, box seat. There's an $11 seat. There's an $8 seat. The $8 is grandstand. The $11 is upper deck box seat, or what we call a terrace box seat—which is on the lower deck.

Have you ever run into counterfeit tickets?

Yes, we have. Not too frequently, but we have. Most of the time they're pretty easy to pick out. If the guy at the gate can spot it, we can authenticate it very quickly. But, we change it around enough so it's pretty hard to do. I mean, nothing's impossible. We're very fortunate in that our park is sold out so often that if there's a counterfeit ticket, logically speaking, someone else has the real ticket for that seat. So, it generally shows up in the park and a guy is unable to keep that scam going for too great a period of time.

What is sold-out attendance?

I don't have the exact number at my fingertips. We have 37,000 something seats in the ballpark. But, to be honest with you, we rarely sell out. What we call a sell out—that's when we have no more tickets. But we sell standing room almost on a daily basis. And usually, from around the end of May until the beginning of September, we're in a standing room situation. Generally, we sell no more than 2,000 standing room. Usually, we always have standing room available when somebody comes to the ballpark.

One of the interesting phenomenas that has happened in baseball the last few years—another interest factor—is what we call "the no-show factor." Because the season ticket base has increased so dramatically, we have 24,000 season tickets here. A lot of those people buy those tickets just to insure certain dates. A lot of corporate people, for example, do that. So, almost every day when you hear Cub attendance, you hear 31,000 paid, 32,000 paid—we've probably sold anywhere from 38,000 to 40,000 tickets.

So that figure is just who is in the ballpark, not tickets sold.

There's a difference between the American and the National League. Any National League figure is who is in the ballpark. So consequently, that revenue is only shared with the visiting team of who is in the ballpark. The American League is the opposite. The American League is the tickets sold for the game.

In other words, if you had 37,000 tickets sold at Wrigley Field and you had 30,000 in the ballpark, the visiting team doesn't get that other 7,000.

But it's equal, because it's the same for all teams. It isn't necessarily a great situation because those 5,000 or 6,000 that didn't show, although we're not paying the team on those tickets, we're losing that revenue that they would have spent on concessions and that. So, we would rather have everybody here.

What is the all-time attendance record for one game?

It's back in the '40s or '50s. And see in those days, if you re-member, the center-field bleachers were open. The all-time record here, I think, was 46,000 something. When we were kids, there wasn't that greened-out section out there. Plus, the park has been remodeled in different respects. When they put in the sky boxes, for example, they lost some seats. So, it's been remodeled. We have less seating capacity now than we did in the late '40s or early '50s.

FRANK CAPPARELLI

As Supervisor of Stadium Operations Facilities, Frank is responsible for keeping Wrigley Field the most beautiful park in baseball. Most will agree, he is doing a great job.

My title is Supervisor of Stadium Operations Facilities and that entails the overseeing of the cleaning of the ballpark and also the ground maintenance. With the ground maintenance, I have a field foreman and four other men that work with him. And in cleaning the ballpark at night, especially after a ball game, I have a night foreman that oversees the cleaning and makes sure the park is ready for the next morning for a game.

I received this position in the middle of July of 1982. This is my 32nd year at Wrigley Field.

I knew an old-timer that had worked here a good number of years and there was a few openings back in '59 and so I happened to be kidding around with him one time. I said, "Gee, I'd like to work at the ballpark. I'm not doing anything now." And so he inquired for me and it's a union job and so there was an opening and I went in to apply and I received a job in March of '59.

You could almost say there's something being worked on throughout the day, which is an eight-hour day. You always have a man working on the vines. It takes sometimes at least three days to trim them and also for the grass to be cut every other day. Watering. And the same thing for working on the runner's line. And the mounds. And home plate. The bullpens. The cleaning of the dugouts. The photographers' booths. Sometimes they have to do edging to make the field look neat. There just always seems to be something that you have to do, plus your batting range inside under the bleachers.

Do you work on the field much after the season's over?

Well, yes. For about two weeks, we'll do our re-sodding. The men usually get two weeks after the last game before they get laid-off. And in that period of time, we'll do whatever is necessary to do our re-sodding, usually like from dugout to dugout because that's what you call the heavy traffic area. Behind the infield. Plus, whatever we have to do on the infield in front of the mound or home plate, which gets sort of cut up during the season. And then after that, the majority of the men get laid off.

When will they come back to work?
Normally, the second or third week of March, depending on what week we'll open up in April.

Do you have a fast or slow infield?
Having day ball here, and not as many night games as the other parks do, I know a lot of players may not realize this, or even fans, but having as much day ball as we have with the hot sun and the wind, our infield seems to dry out much faster and it gets harder. So, that takes its toll sometimes and that makes it a fast infield. But as far as the grass goes, we keep our grass longer than the majority of the parks. But this also is called upon by who's ever managing. If he feels he likes to have the grass longer, that's what we do. To accommodate the teams.

Will management ever come to you and say we want shorter grass, longer grass...?
Well, normally management wouldn't, but the manager would. He might confer with his coaching staff and if they feel they've got the type of hitters they want a fast infield for that ball to get off the grass, they'll want it cut shorter. But sometimes maybe they want to help the pitching staff out and so they'll want the grass longer.

Is there a league rule regarding the length of grass?
No, not to my knowledge.

Some teams have watered around first base.
I think the Giants tried that, always against the Dodgers, when the Dodgers had Maury Wills, a great basestealer. And a few other teams and they would water down first base quite a bit so a good runner just couldn't get a good foot hold and take off for second on them.

Have you ever done anything like that?
No, sir.

229

What type of grass do you have at Wrigley Field?

It's called Kentucky Blue. We also seed throughout the summer. We try to seed in the fall after the season, we airify the field, we over-seed it, and we fertilize. Then we'll try to do it in the spring if the weather's permitting and we try to airify at least two times a year.

How do you maintain the vines?

Well, it's just like any plant. You hope for warm weather. Mother Nature's gotta help it along. The sun. Plus, you have to water it if you don't get any rainfall like now. As you probably know, there's quite a bit of drought here in the Midwest, especially here in Chicago. We haven't had rain in God knows—a good rain for a long time.

Maybe, twice a year we'll fertilize the dirt. But trimming them is also another thing. You know, try to get rid of the broken branches and then sometimes you have to try...ones that break off, maybe you can tie them back in. And if you get any bare spots, you hope to try and fill them in.

What's the most unusual thing you've ever witnessed at Wrigley Field?

Right during a ball game. In a way it was pretty comical, but it was unusual. The Cubs had a tie game, I believe, I can't recall the year. I think it was Randy Hundley at bat and he hit a home run to win the game and as he was rounding second, one of the men on the crew got pretty elated and everybody was just cheering and he ran out and took third base out. I guess the coach and everybody just started screamin' at him and the poor person was just so embarrassed, but he did catch himself and put the base back in.

It's Not Just The Game—The Fans

DAN PETERSON

Grew up in Evanston, Illinois. A sports nut with a sharp mind and keen powers of observation. After coaching basketball in the U. S., including head coach at the University of Delaware, he became one of the foremost coaches in Europe. He lives in Milan, Italy.

My first game? No way I could forget that! We all have dates that are stamped on our brains. Take Pearl Harbor Day. I wasn't quite six when it happened. It was a Sunday morning. I was playing in front of our standup radio when my dad said, "Quiet!" He leaned forward, listened for a moment, and said, "We're at war." That was December 7, 1941.

Then there was Kennedy's assassination. I was freshman basketball coach at Michigan State University at the time. One Friday afternoon, the two biggest jokers on the coaching staff, hockey coach Amo Besson and track coach Jim Gibbard, came in our office to tell us what had happened. We thought they were kidding. That was November 22, 1963.

Then, there's a third date, between those two: the day I saw my first major league baseball game: The Cincinnati Reds vs. the Chicago Cubs, Wrigley Field, Chicago, June 9, 1945. I was nine years old. The game itself? I can't remember a single play. I recall something else but, before coming to that, I think I should explain how "innocent" I was.

It may be hard for some people to understand but, in those days before television and sports magazines, I had no idea major league baseball existed: I had never seen a major league game; I had never heard of names like Babe Ruth, Joe DiMaggio, and Ted Williams; and I'd never heard the name of any major league team, not even of the Chicago Cubs.

We didn't exactly live in a vacuum up there in Evanston. We played softball—12" and 16"—from sunup to sundown. No 9" ball, though. One foul tip and we'd have been paying for a broken window. When we played "hardball," it was just "catch" or a little "pepper."

231

Every Sunday, we'd go down Mulford Street to see the cream of Evanston's 16" slow-pitch league play. They were our heroes. Had you told me, back then, that some guy named Babe Ruth was the greatest power hitter of all time, you'd have had an argument. To me, the all-timer was Carl Hertz, MVP of that 16" league, a guy whose line drives just handcuffed infielders.

For 12" games, we'd head for Boltwood Park, taking the No. 2 bus to Main Street, then transferring to the No. 3. We were there in 20 minutes. It was worth it, as we could watch the finest fast-pitch softball pitcher anywhere: Bill Mlekush of the American Legion team. He was unhittable. He was our hero at that level, no question about it.

Boltwood Park was also where we could see 9" games, on Sundays, between our local Bill Erickson Boosters and whoever was scheduled that day. It was always a big game when they played the next-door Skokie Indians or—look out!—the invincible Cole-Lenzis, from somewhere out in the western suburbs, who were respectfully called "semi-pros" by the older fans.

I had no idea what "pro" meant, much less "semi-pro." Little did I know but the "pros" were less than 45 minutes away. Then, one day, a teenager from across the street, Jack Walls, asked me if I'd like to go with him to see a baseball game at "Cubs Park." Not Wrigley Field, but "Cubs Park." My parents said OK but I had no idea as to what to expect.

We took the No. 2 bus southbound to the end of the line at Howard Street and then took the "L" train southbound into Chicago. Twelve stops later we were at Addison Street.

My first look at Wrigley Field didn't throw me. I'd been to our 55,000-seat Dyche Stadium, the home of Northwestern University. So, I'd seen a lot of people in one place for a sports event. I'd also seen ivy on walls there, in addition to pennants flying, a modern scoreboard, and all of the trimmings that go with a big game.

Once inside, the first thing I noticed during pre-game warmups was that one team had "clean" uniforms while the other team's were "dirty." Jack Walls explained that in the major leagues, the home team wears white, while the visiting team wears "traveling grays." That was the first time I'd heard the term "major leagues." I started to sort all of this out.

Just about then, a visiting player came close enough for me to read the lettering on his uniform: CINCINNATI. I said to myself,

"Cincinnati? Wait a second! I know my geography! Cincinnati is in Ohio! If they came all that way to play, well, this must be a very important baseball game!" Then...it happened!

A voice cracked through the air: "ATTENTION! Attention, please!" No jolt of electricity could have shaken me more. This voice ricocheted through the ballpark like those amplified rifle shots in TV westerns. It told me, in that fraction of a second, that this was the very top, like an injection of instantaneous total under-standing.

That moment is fixed in my mind forever: 1:25 P.M., just five minutes before game time. What's more, I have no doubts as to his exact word:

"ATTENTION! ... (hammered out, then a pause)
Attention, please! ... (normal tone, then a pause)
HAVE YOUR PENCILS ... (a direct order, then a pause)
and scorecards ready ... (almost a whisper, then a pause)
AND WE WILL GIVE YOU ... (all business, then a pause)
The correct lineup ... (back to normal, then a pause)
for today's ball game." (downshifted)

About the same time I had my pencil ready, Pat Pieper was giv-ing the lineups. His sequence never varied. It was one of those constants in life. It was the same every time I heard him, always giving the batteries—which he called "batt'ries"—first. Here's the way it went for that very first game I ever saw:

"BATT'RIES! ... (high-pitched, a pause)
for cincinnat-uh (sic!) ... (low pitched, a pause)
BECK and unser ... (a shout, a whisper, a pause)
For the Cubs ... (back to normal, a pause)
WYSE and livingston." (a shout and a whisper)

In order to fully describe the impact Pat Pieper had on me, and most of my friends, I have to move on to subsequent games. Above all, those played against the truly great teams the Cubs faced in the years just after World War II, in particular, those against the two perennial pennant contenders of the era: the Brooklyn Dodgers and the St. Louis Cardinals.

Take the Cardinals. We didn't need any pictures drawn to tell us who they were. We knew them alright: Veterans of many a

World Series, a team of fighters that simply refused to lose, that would battle on every pitch, every time at bat, every relay. They were a tremendous team and Pat Pieper's voice just seemed to underline that.

Not that Pat Pieper changed anything for the Dodgers or the Cardinals. He'd bark out their numbers, names, and positions as he'd do for a last-place team. It was those names, given by that voice, that told us the Cubs were in for a ball game. We'd listen with awe as he'd give us the lineup of the St. Louis Cardinals, almost all with single-digit numbers:

EIGHT! Moore! center field.
TWO! Schoendienst! second base.
SIX! Musial! first base.
NINE! Slaughter! right field.
ONE! Kurowski! third base.
FIVE! Walker! left field.
FOUR! Marion! short stop.
EIGHTEEN! Rice! catcher.
THIRTY-ONE! Brecheen! pitcher.

As each player would come to bat for the first time, Pat Pieper would announce him. Once through the order, he'd back off. None of this announcing every batter, as is common today. I liked that. He didn't overdo things:

"NEXT BATTER! ...
for the Cubs ...
Forty-four ...
PHIL Cavarretta ...
first base."

Pat Pieper also had a way with nicknames. He knew when to use them and when not to use them. I have no idea what yardstick he used to determine when not to use a nickname but I never disagreed with him. It was never "Slats" but always Marty Marion. It was never "Frenchy" but always Stan Bordagaray. It was never "Country" but always Enos Slaughter.

It was the same when he'd use a nickname. Again, I can't say why but I always had the feeling that his every choice was a perfect fit. It was never Harold but always "Pee Wee" Reese. It was never George but always "Whitey" Kurowski. It was never Albert but always "Red" Schoendienst. And, of course, it was never Harry but always "P-Nuts" Lowery!

Pat Pieper would come back only to announce changes: pinch hitters, relief pitchers, pinch runners, defensive changes, and the like. Every sub became an important player just because he announced his entry into the game. That pinch batter might be hitting .219 or that relief pitcher might have an ERA of 6.87, but Pat Pieper's voice made him a major leaguer!

Pinch hitters hadn't attained the "specialist" status they now have. Dusty Rhodes, Smokey Burgess, and Manny Mota would come later. At this time, with rare exceptions, a pinch hitter was a benchwarmer, a so-called "humpty-dumpty," not good enough to crack the set eight-man lineup. That is, until Pat Pieper told us who he was and that he was coming to bat.

We'd see that pinch hitter come out of the dugout and take his spot in the on-deck circle, swinging a couple of bats—the "dough-nut" hadn't been invented yet—and we might not react. Then, Pat Pieper would boom his name over the PA system—twice!—and we'd sit up and take notice. Going back to that very first game in 1945, here's one I remember well:

"ATTENTION! ...
Attention, please! ...
ERIC Tipton ...
batting for Bosser ...
ERIC tipton."

Relief pitchers were much like pinch hitters back then. Whereas a pinch hitter might be a player that couldn't break into the regular lineup, a relief pitcher was often a man that couldn't break into the starting rotation. In many cases, he was nothing more than a "mop-up man," brought in to take a pounding in a game that had been given up for lost.

In those days, I never heard of the term "save," much less "middle man" or "set-up man." And, only a few teams had real "closers." They were, of course, the better teams. The Yankees had Joe Page, the Phillies had Jim Konstanty, and, Lord knows, the Cardinals had Ted Wilks. When he came in for the eighth to hold a lead at Wrigley, folks just headed for the exits.

If an outstanding pitcher was coming on in relief, things really heated up for us. Pat Pieper's voice lifted that player's ranking from star to superstar. Unfortunately, those great firemen were always playing for the other team, almost always a contending team, a "plus" for them, which seemed almost "unfair." Who cared? Pat Pieper was back, working overtime!

As always, we wrote nothing on our scorecards until Pat Pieper gave his announcement. Forget that we saw the man warming up in the bullpen, saw the manager signal for him, saw him walk onto the diamond, saw him give his jacket to the batboy, saw him take his seven allotted warmup pitches. He wasn't "official" until Pat Pieper's voice made him so!

The one thing you didn't want when you went to a Cubs game back then was for Pat Pieper to call in sick. On those days, the "voice" of Wrigley Field was that of "Whitey," the head Andy Frain usher, who was the PA man at Comiskey Park. He was alright but he was not, in any manner, way, shape, or form comparable to Pat Pieper.

The only time Pat Pieper was out when I went to Wrigley was in the early '50s. I wanted to ask for a refund. My friends said I was out of my mind, that they gave rain checks for bad weather and a refund only for some official reason. That was my point! To me, the game was just not "official" unless Pat Pieper was at the mike.

Going back to the first game in 1945, the only two facts I recall are that the Cubs won, 5-1, and that the winning pitcher was Hank Wyse. Only in future visits would I define "my" players—Stan Hack, Andy Pafko, and Phil Cavarretta—and build the backlog of memories typical of every Cubs fan. The only thing clear in my mind of that game is Pat Pieper.

Old as he was that day, Pat Pieper was with us another 30 years. We lost him in 1974. To me, though, he'll always be there at Wrigley Field, seated in his folding chair, just to the left of the backstop, a bucket of new baseballs at his feet, scorecard in one hand, microphone in the other. Every time I go back, I expect to hear his voice.

His uncle, Bill Sianis, put a hex on the Cubs during the '45 World Series because they would not let him attend one of the games with his goat. Sam finally lifted the hex in 1984.

Back in 1945 when Billy Goat put the hex on the Cubs, I was back home in Greece, so I came here bit late. But my uncle told me how he did it. He always kept a goat at his tavern which was across the street from the Chicago Stadium. He had a goat as a pet. In 1945, when the Cubs played the World Series, he took the goat to Wrigley Field. He had two tickets to go see the game. But when he got to the gate, they stopped him from going in. Asks why, I got the tickets. So one guy comes up and says, "Well, we don't allow the goats in here." He says, "Why?" "Because the goat smells." Then, Billy Goat left, went back to his tavern. Later on the Cubs lost. Lost the World Series. And he sent a telegraph to Mr. Wrigley. He says, "Who smells now?"

Since then, they never won. In 1973, myself and Dave Condon, he used to write a sports column for the *Chicago Tribune*, we decided to take the goat to the Cubs game. It was sometimes around July and the Cubs that day, I remember, they were winning, 2-0, third inning. And they were seven games ahead. So, one day with the goat—I had two tickets—same way what Billy Goat did. We had a sign made already, "Let's forget the past and let me lead you to the pennant." And we got to the gate, you know...I rent a limousine. And went there with the limousine, the guy comes out with the red carpet there, and me and the goat comes out, go by the gate there, and stopped me. Go around to another gate, they stopped me. And next I know, there was about 15 security guys around follow me, so I can't get in with the goat. Jenkins says to me, "Bring the goat in."

Who is this now?

Ferguson Jenkins. He was by a small door where the players go in. A side door. He asked me to go in with the goat. I said, "They don't let me." He said, "Go on, bring the goat in." So, when the security follow me, he's told them go back and he closed the door. So, the Cubs are being unfair to the goat, who left to come down here. There was a big article in the paper with my picture with the goat in the paper.

And I left—I went back home to Greece for a month. When I came back, the Cubs—I came back around September 10th—and the Cubs were about 10 games behind. So, other people were calling me up and giving me all kinds of names, you know, for not lift the hex.

So in 1984, they invite me back to take the goat when the Tribune bought the Cubs. So, they invite me to go there opening day. So, all the news got it, we had all the—Channel 9, 5, 7, and 2—they all wait. I brought the goat out. They interviewed me with the goat here and they follow me all the way to Wrigley Field. So the gates open before the game. Jack Brickhouse was on the mound and he did a speech. He say about the history between the goat and the Cubs and Sam Sianis, the nephew of the Billy Goat, he's willing to take the hex off so we can have some winning team in Chicago. So, after all...when all this happened and the doors open and I walk in with the goat, you know, I lift the hex off. I walk around and around. They took pictures there by the mound with some players. It was a big deal. Then I left. The Cubs win the opening, then they won the division. In 1984. They won the division.

This was the opening game of 1984, you took the hex off?

Yeah. Then they won the division. So when they won the division, they came down here to ask me to the game. They had four tickets for me to go to take the goat there the open day. So, Channel 7 was here and Channel 5, I think. They interviewed me about that. They said, "What do you think?" I say, "I guarantee I'm going to win two games for them here." So, we went to both games and they won here, but after that they went to San Diego, but they didn't invite me to go there. So then the Cubs lost. Lost the pennant. But, they won the division.

Then, I got mad 'cause I think—not only me, but a lot of people do—Jim Frey, he's the one who lost the pennant for the Cubs. Any other manager, he would never lose that pennant because he left from here with two games to nothing. Went to San Diego. He was worried who's going to start in the World Series before he got there. That's the problem it was. He should have started the best pitcher. The best pitcher that year was Sutcliffe. He was the best pitcher. Opening day was Tuesday here. He only pitched six innings because they were winning 13 to something and took him out. So he had Wednesday off, Thursday off, Friday off. They should have let him pitch Saturday. He didn't let him pitch Saturday. If he was pitched Saturday, you know, he would had him right then, he didn't. I was real mad that time. Everybody was mad.

Well, now, after that, the Cubs didn't invite me back to the game. A couple of years ago when we won the division here again, they was San Francisco. All the papers came down here and interview me on TV, live from San Francisco, all that. And say to me, "What do you think?" I said, "Without my help, they're not going to work." That's what happened.

And they didn't win.
    They didn't.

Grew up in Winnetka, Illinois. Played professional football with Baltimore, Chicago, Oakland, and Minnesota. He was one of the founding members of the Right Field Bleacher Choir.

I grew up in Winnetka, Illinois, and went to New Trier High School. After graduating from New Trier I went to Michigan State University and fortunately graduated. Played football at Michigan State. Subsequently, and again fortunately, I was drafted by the Baltimore Colts. Played with them for four years and then was traded to the Minnesota Vikings. Played with them for a year and then with the Chicago Bears and the Raiders for a couple of years. After not being able to hold down a job, I just got out of football.

What was your first involvement with the Cubs?

Well, it probably goes back to some games with my dad. He didn't have Cub season tickets, but he had Bear season tickets and he was also an avid baseball fan and we'd go out to the Cub games from time to time. But what I remember more vividly is when I started going with my high school pals.

As we wound down high school—we had a very close knit group in high school. A lot of good guys. We went to a lot of games together through high school and to the best of my recollection toward the end of high school, we started having these Sunday evening clubs. Some right at the end of high school, some all the way through college. And we'd get together all summer long and just renew friendships and spend the summer together and it was always on Sunday nights and what they were was just beer-drinking marathon barbecues. I mean, some went to dawn. A lot went to dawn. As the night wore on, we'd start singing. And as the night grew really old, we started thinking we were pretty good.

To the best of my recollection, this group was "Wampa" John Peters, Denny Wright—who, by the way, was a pretty good musician and singer and had written a couple of songs that had been on an album by the folk singer, Bob Gibson. "Poopsie" Schweitzer, "Red Dog" Olerich. Wade Fetzer. "Rat Mouse" Morrison. Bill

Chambers. Jay "Bagle" Pollack—who was an aficionado on the "fart arm." There was Todd Stadheim. John Jeffers—who had to be constantly bribed to not sing and only mouth the words. He was the shittiest singer I have ever heard in my life. "Buzz" Gross and Ben Harris—and if I've forgotten anybody, I really apologize because I had to tax my memory on that group. But we got to the point where, seriously, we weren't too bad.

We started going to ball games as a group—again to keep that friendship alive from our high school days. We started singing at the ball games and, as I recall, it got to the point whenever we showed up, about the fifth or sixth inning, they'd start bugging us to sing. We always sang at the seventh-inning stretch. But we'd get bugged. Sometimes we had to sing in the second inning because we'd get bugged by so many people.

This Clark, I can remember vividly, this Clark and his sidekick would drive us crazy. "Come on and sing, guys." And then people would start joining in. Actually, as the years went on, they all knew the words. It was a sing-a-long.

How long was the Right Field Bleacher Choir in existence?

I would say, probably, from '55 to '65 with me kind of phasing out of the operation because I went on to play pro ball. I was in other places, but I wasn't the biggest baseball fan that ever lived anyway. My reasons for being there was the camaraderie, the fun, the beer-drinking, the party angle, and so on.

Any stories?

Those games where I would be the designated pusher for the keg wheelchair, with "Rat Mouse" Morrison being the guy sitting on the wheelchair with the blanket over him and sneaking the pony in underneath. That was always the biggest hysterics for me, because I did not keep a very straight face, anyway, and getting by Andy Frain usher, after Andy Frain usher, was unbelievable with "Rat Mouse," who is really a classic character, and he would try to get me to break up. Try to screw up the deal and we'd inevitably get in there.

There were certain games when we did a rope lift of cases of beer up over the right-field wall. I mean, here were cops and ushers everywhere, and we'd be pulling cases of beer up with a rope. With a lookout.

But I remember the silly things, not being a huge baseball fan. I remember Hal Jeffcoat coming in from center field and pitching, because he had a gun for an arm. I remember Eddie Waitkus getting shot by his girlfriend. I remember Lou Brock when he first came to the Cubs, he was the world's worst fielder and we were out there in right field and we just gave him shit—I'm surprised he didn't retire. When our group heard that he'd been traded to St. Louis for Broglio, we threw a party. Of course, as we all know, it's rated as one of the worst trades in the history of baseball. I remember the famous cliché—"Miksis to Smalley to Dugout." That was the big deal back in our days. I was really impressed that Chuck "Rifleman" Connors could both act and play first base. But the catch was he couldn't play first base. And really not that great an actor. Those were the kind of things that I remember. It was a party to me. It was getting together with my pals, going to Wrigley Field.

What do you think the Cub appeal is?
I think it's the ballpark and, you know, this sounds kind of silly —but, the ivy on the walls. I think it's the neighborhood. I think it's the fact that, certainly in our day, a very low crime area. I think everybody felt comfortable going to the ballpark. It's like the family going to a Denver Bronco game today. It's a family event, because it's a nice area. It's not a high crime area. Everybody went out there. Everybody enjoyed themselves. It was a good, inexpensive way of spending the day. And it was always during the day. Again, not only was it a low crime area but it was always during the day. There was never any night stuff. The parking was lousy, but no one cared. Part of the deal was walking 10 miles after you parked the car—or the "L" went right by the ballpark. You just jumped off the "L" and you were at the ballpark.

After I started playing pro ball, I kind of got away from the Right Field Bleacher's Choir routine, but it was just about that time that I was still living in Chicago during the off-season and through a real pal of mine, who was not part of the choir but was around that group back in the old days—a guy by the name of Al Viola—I got to know Jack Quinlan very well, who was the Cubs' announcer back in those days. Jack and I used to play golf—oh, my goodness, I bet we played golf four or five days a week in my early Colt days back in '60, '61, and '62. I've never been known for my smooth temperament on a golf course, but I'll tell you what, Jack took it to another dimension. I mean, he was something else. I think he taught me the art of throwing a golf club. I remember those days well. Playing golf at Wilmette Country Club every day. Whoever was around would join us on the course, because they all loved Jack.

Through Jack, I met people like Jack Brickhouse, Vince Lloyd, and Lou Boudreau. Ironically, many years later I was one of the people involved in putting a golf tournament together in Phoenix, Arizona, which is still called the "Lou Boudreau Golf Classic." I play in that every year and a lot of players come back. A lot of guys—old ballplayers—participate in that golf tournament in Phoenix every February. Including other than ballplayers, Vince Lloyd, Jack Brickhouse. Of course, Lou and Ronnie Santo and Glenn Beckert, a lot of these old players come to play for Lou every year. And it's been a great situation for me because, by knowing Jack, I met these other fellows. They're all great guys. It's been a lot of fun for me.

*One of the original members of the Right Field Bleacher Choir.
They placed a keg of beer under a wheelchair, put Morrison in the
wheelchair, covered him with a blanket, and got special attention
from the ushers to enter the ballpark.*

*You were part of the original Right Field Bleacher Choir. How did
that all evolve?*

We were out there one Sunday for a doubleheader and it
started to rain. People scattered for the exits and we had a few
beers and just decided to stay there. For some reason, we started
singing. The rain eventually ended and the game started again. I
remember the next time we were out there we started singing
again. Somebody came up with the name "Right Field Bleacher
Choir" and that's how I remember it starting. That had to be the
late '50s sometime. I mean '56-'57. We had a bunch of guys that
all went to high school together. And some days we might have 20
guys out there. We just had a good time.

There were a lot of days when nobody was there. There were
days that I remember you could actually yell at the players and they
would hear you. In fact, we had one of the guys bring what he
called a "loud hailer" out there. He would zero in on these players
and they would actually, you know, their heads would turn around
because they could actually pick that voice out of the crowd.

What is a loud hailer?

It's a thing the cheerleaders use. In fact, shortly after that, I remember Pat Pieper coming on the PA system and saying that artifi-
cial amplification devices were illegal. So we didn't bring that any
more. We used to pick on all of the guys and especially the opposing right fielder was in for a lot of grief.

You'd ride some Cubs too?

Oh, yeah. Yeah, when they needed it. Which was, you know,
pretty often in those days. Those were pretty bad teams.

I can remember being out there on one of those days when

there weren't too many people there. The most exciting thing that day was a standing broad jump contest in the bullpen. These guys would stand on the rubber and see who could jump the furthest. You know, there was just so little happening in the games. Actually, I think that's why some of the players you kind of forget about, because there just weren't any stars. I mean, Banks was playing at that time and then Billy Williams came in in probably '60 or '61. And Billy was a great player. But we had Walt Moryn playing out there and he had his problems on the field.

We started bringing our own beer. Then the authorities got a little tough, so it became a real challenge as to how you could get beer in there. Everybody in those days wore a raincoat. One of these tan London Fog-type raincoats. What some of the guys did was to sew pockets on the inside of those things and you could carry maybe a case of beer in one. We used that a lot. There used to be some doors on Sheffield that were just bars. Sometimes you'd send a couple of guys in and then two guys would just roll cans underneath the bars until you got a couple of cases of beer in there. We kind of prided ourselves on being able to sneak beer in.

Then we decided that we needed another challenge or just to have some fun we decided we'd try to sneak a quarter barrel in. How could you do that? So somebody said, "Well, how about a wheelchair?" So, we decided that would be the way to go and a quarter barrel fits just perfectly underneath a wheelchair. I happened to be the guy who was inside this thing and they just put a blanket over my lap and we met over at Ray's Bleachers and got outfitted. Put the keg in. Got the blanket on me. Wheeled me across Sheffield and, of course, I couldn't fit through the gate so the usher had to open a special gate for me. I was a little bit embarrassed about the thing. But we were having a few laughs. These guys pushed me up the ramps and got me to the top of the bleachers. We didn't want to blow our cover right then. We were in the park kind of early so they started to push me down the stairs. A couple of other fans came over and helped me down. We got down into about the fourth or fifth row and I just hopped up and took the blanket off, we took the keg out, and we tapped it. Of course, these fans couldn't believe it. But we managed.

I remember we were having so much fun with this keg that we ran out of beer. So we decided we were going to go out and make a beer run. So I hopped back in the wheelchair and they wheeled me over to Ray's and we bought probably a couple of cases and I put them between my legs and up on my lap. Put the blanket over me and they're wheeling me across Sheffield and the blanket caught underneath the wheel. And I'm out in the middle of Sheffield and Waveland with two cases of beer on my lap, exposed, but nobody saw it. Covered it up and again had to go through a special entrance. And the ushers were very nice. They wanted to take care of this poor guy in the wheelchair.

For some reason, we used to do a lot of singing. After a few beers, we got hooked on this and got a name for ourselves, we just enjoyed it. Singing between innings or whatever. You kind of got to know the vendors and you just got to know a lot of people.

There were a couple of guys that used to come every Saturday and Sunday. And one of these guys looked like a poor man's Clark Gable. We used to yell back and forth to Clark—he was always there. I really don't know what his name was, but to us he was always Clark Gable. He had the mustache, you know, and there was a lot of yelling back and forth—good natured.

It seemed to me there were a lot of empty seats out there. It was a great place to watch baseball. Seventy-five cents. It was really the best bargain in sports at that time. You could walk across the street five or 10 minutes before game time and not have a problem finding a seat.

When do you remember breaking up?

When people start to get married and that kind of thing. Probably early '60s. I imagine we were going out there for four or five years anyway.

You never really had a good ball club, did you?

No. Never did. I can remember being out there one opening day when, I think it was Willie Smith came over from Cleveland or some place. He hit a home run to win the ball game. All these guys are sitting around at Ray's at that time. Someone went out and grabbed ahold of him and dragged him into this bar, put him up on a table...and hey, I'm sure he couldn't believe what was going...

You're a native Chicagoan. Covered the Cubs all these years. What's the appeal?

I've often wondered about that. I mean, I grew up as a Cub fan and it kind of got reinforced with my high school friends going out there. They were losing all the time, so you couldn't have been following a winner. And there must have been some appeal in that. But Wrigley Field, it's just a great place to watch baseball. You're right on top of it. But, it's a very strange thing that people are so loyal to them after all these years of losing baseball.

The first night game. What was the feeling?

Well, it was just electric. It was kind of like an opening day crowd. I mean, I don't know what a World Series crowd would be like, but it was that kind of...there are certain sporting events that are just exciting. There's something in the air. I've always felt that opening day at Wrigley Field is like that. And maybe it is in every park, but it's a special day. And that was too. That was exciting and everybody kept saying, somebody up there doesn't want the Cubs to be playing night baseball and that's why it's being rained out.

I took my kids out there—used to take them for their birthdays. We were there...we didn't know it at the time, but it was the last game that Billy Williams played as a Cub. He hit one into the seats and the guy in front of us caught it and he looked at me—I had my son and five or six of his friends at a birthday party. He just looked around, he flipped the ball to me. And then Billy was traded to Oakland that winter, so it was really his last...you know, his last home run as a Cub. I still have the ball.

*He saw his first Cub game in 1958 and was forever hooked. Be-
came one of the original Bleacher Bums and raised some hell out
there.*

When did you first get involved with the Cubs?

No doubt about it—watching the games at a young age on
WGN-TV and Jack Brickhouse and that's, of course, P. K. Wrigley's
brainstorm of putting games free on television where everybody else
in the country was afraid of TV, wouldn't televise any games. I can
remember at age four watching ball games—day games on TV, putting my nose up to the TV set. My parents thought I was nuts. Nei-
ther was that much involved as a fan. I just enjoyed this ball game
and Jack Brickhouse and his enthusiasm. So, by the time I was seven
years old in 1958, I badgered my parents into taking me to "beautiful Wrigley Field," as Jack used to call it on the TV all the time.

The Cubs were tied with the Milwaukee Braves in July of 1958
for first place. Maybe they were a game out of first. And, unbeknownst, you know from the suburbs, we didn't realize it was going
to be that crowded. So, we drive in the car before expressways were
even built and we get in this tremendous traffic jam around Clark
and Addison and, walking up to the ballpark, the Andy Frain usher
on the PA system, I'll never forget, was saying, "All seats sold out.
Standing room only. However, plenty of bleacher seats available."
Which is ironic. Nowadays, it's the bleacher seats that sell out first
and the rest of the park is available later. Back then, the bleacher
seats were evidently the last seats of recourse that anybody would
even want. So we trudged to the bleachers and sat up a couple of
rows under the old scoreboard there.

In my first game, I'll never forget, Ernie Banks hit a home run,
Hank Aaron hit a home run—two pretty good names. Also, Moose
Moryn for the Cubs and Joe Adcock for the Braves. So, the Cubs
win the game, 5-4, and there were 43,000 fans at Wrigley Field, it
turned out, that day. Half of Wisconsin came down to watch the
Milwaukee Braves. It was the biggest crowd at Wrigley Field since
1948 when, I believe, Jackie Robinson made one of his first appear-

ances. So, from then on with the combination of TV and seeing that exciting first game, I was hooked on going to Wrigley Field and being a Cubs fan.

What was it like going in that ballpark for the first time?
The first thing I remembered was after watching only on black and white television, was how huge it was when you walked in and how green everything was. The vines, the grass, and it was just like Brickhouse had said. It was indeed, you know, beautiful Wrigley Field. It was just bigger than you could imagine as a little kid having watched on a small, little black and white TV set for three years prior.

When did you get involved on a day-to-day basis with the Cubs?
It was that summer of '64 when my parents would let me and a few of my buddies hop on the suburban train, the Burlington. Take it down to Union Station, we'd hop on the CTA train and be at Wrigley Field. I can remember we'd leave with like $2.00 and a couple of sandwiches. The train was, let's see...the train was $1.60 roundtrip. The "L" was a quarter each way. And 60 cents to get in. So, whatever that adds up to. We'd come home with no money and no sandwich left. We went three or four times a week that whole summer. Every week.

And the beauty was, I think that also got me hooked on the Cubs, that those were the dark days. Those were the days when the Cubs would, you know, finish in eighth place or ninth place where, of course, by 1966—10th place. When all 10 teams were in the National League with no division. Of course, Leo Durocher made the famous statement in spring training, "This is not an 8th place team." And he was right. It was a 10th place team. So what was fun, you'd get out there and there'd be no fans. The average game would be 2,000-3,000 fans. So you get out there when they opened up the park—which was two hours prior—now it's like an hour before. Back then, you'd get there two hours before the game, there might be just, you know, 50-80 people in the entire ballpark. We'd be out in the bleachers, maybe a dozen fans. And during practice the balls would come flying up. You'd catch three or four of them with your Wilson A2000 and put them in your pocket and pretty soon you can only carry so many baseballs. We would actually play catch during batting practice in the bleachers with Billy Williams down on the field. We'd throw the ball. He'd play catch with five or 10 of us up in the stands. It was a last-place team. It was August. You never nowadays see someone playing catch with the fans before the game.

When did the Bleacher Bums evolve?

That's the correct word—it evolved. We cannot organize something and have it be a success. It's gotta happen spontaneously. And, in 1966, as I mentioned, the Cubs finished in 10th and there were literally maybe 10 or 15 fans every game out in the left-field bleachers. That's all. The entire park might have 800 fans at a game...1,000. So, after coming out day after day, you start seeing the same few faces, if you know what I mean. You know, I know that guy. I know that guy. And, pretty soon you say, "I'm Bob, I'm Mike," you know. And there's about 15 of us. And most of them were city kids or some were from the suburbs—it was a melting pot. Different ethnic and nationalities. Just like Chicago. But what happened was, in 1967 the same 12 or 15 of us arrived there but all of a sudden, the Cubs start winning. They start winning. The team starts jelling. All of a sudden by May, Wrigley Field is the place to be.

The Cubs go into first place around June or July of '67 for the first time, probably, since 1945. Other than maybe like an opening day, you know, opening week. Now, the same 15 of us that had been out there—we're all sitting together now and we're sort of a bunch of...bunch of fun loving, wild, eccentric sort of chaps and we have chants and songs and we know most of the players, 'cause we used to play catch with them the year before when nobody wanted to come out. I have my bugle. I bring out some of the bugle calls and the charge...ta-ta-ta-da-ta-da...and we're out there. We dance along on the wall. We get the crowd fired up. The players like us. And, all of a sudden with four daily newspapers in Chicago at that time, the *Tribune*, the *Sun-Times* are still here. But there used to be the *Herald American*—which became the *Chicago Today*, the *Herald American/Today*, and the *Daily News*— there was a rivalry with the four papers 'cause the Cubs were the hottest story. The editors are sending out every writer to cover the Cubs. Get an angle. Get a story. The feature writer's out there. The movie critic's out there. The food-home cooking editor's out there. They're sending everyone to get an angle.

Well, at this time, a husband and wife from Morton Grove,

"Ma" Barker and her husband, "Big Daddy," they used to bring bedsheets out there with whacky slogans and phrases. You know "Pizza Power" when Santo would come up. Randy Hundley, you know, they'd have a rebel flag they'd wave. One of their bedsheets, and Lord knows what they slept on at home on their mattress 'cause they always had bed sheets with them. Spray paint. But one day they cut a hole in the center of a sheet and simply wrote—"Hit the Bleacher Bum." So, our leader, Ron Grousl, would stick his head through that sheet meaning, what greater love does a fan have than to sacrifice himself for a home run by his beloved Cubs. Well, lo and behold, an AP wire photographer snaps a picture of this from first base—the old catwalk underneath the upper deck. The photographer's catwalk? Well, this picture not only runs the next day in all four Chicago papers, it's picked up by the wire services and literally every newspaper in the country within the next few days ran a picture of this goofy guy's head sticking through a bedsheet which said, "Hit the Bleacher Bum." From then on, we were the "Bleacher Bums." We never sat down and said, "Hey, let's organize a group and call ourselves the 'Bleacher Bums' and get a lot of publicity." You can't do that.

June of '67. The Cubs went into first place—sometime in that time frame—maybe early July was when the Cubs finally beat the Cincinnati Reds, in a doubleheader. At Wrigley—on a Sunday. And you know how the flags up on the yardarm, on the mast above the scoreboard dictate the standings. Well, the Cubs were the second flag, the blue flag, and Cincinnati started the day No. 1. Well, when the doubleheader's over, there's maybe 42,000 fans there—and the Cubs win the second game to go into first place.

Well, all of a sudden, we Bleacher Bums start chanting, "Change the flags! Change the flags!" In other words, we wanted to see that 'cause they were going on the road the next day on a Monday. We wanted to see, for the first time in our lifetime, the Cub flag up at the top. Well, the only problem was, the old fella up in the scoreboard, the grounds crew member that runs the scoreboard, had taken the flags down as he'd done for 30 years. Left the scoreboard. Locked the little hatchdoor. Gone down that little ladder and had already skiddadled out of the park. 42,000 fans picked up on this chant, "Change the Flags!" No one would leave the park. One of the Cubs' front office guys had to finally go —I don't know if he used a crowbar or had a master key, but he finally unlocked it. Went up there and 15 minutes later was finally able to just run up a single—the Cubs flag—to the top. Everyone cheered and finally went home. I think the people would have stayed all night.

1969. What do you remember of that season?

Well,'69—that the Cubs get off to the tremendous start, of course. In '67 and '68, you could see that this team had something going. In fact, they made runs for the pennant in those two years. '69 the year when Willie Smith hit the opening day home run and things just started snowballin'.

The Bleacher Bums—we would rent Greyhound buses and 50 or 100 of us would take off and go to Pittsburgh. We used to go to Old Forbes Field and stay in the Cubs' hotel. We'd go to old Crosley Field and stay at the Netherlands Hilton Hotel where the Cubs would stay. We went all over the country and P. K. Wrigley one day, owner of the Cubs, around May—called Ronnie Grousl up to his office before the game through a security guard. We thought, "Oh, boy, are we in trouble now." 'Cause we did a few wild antics out there. Well, Grousl comes back and we said, "What is it, Ronnie? Have we been kicked out?" He goes, "No, it's the opposite. P. K. Wrigley is so enamored with us, the Bleacher Bums," and he pointed out that the Cubs had been using on their advertising on radio and TV, "Come to Wrigley Field. Sit with the Bleacher Bums," etc. "He wants 50 of the Bleacher Bums—the 50 top Bleacher Bums that come out the most—P. K. Wrigley is going to fly us, all expenses paid for a three-day road trip, to Atlanta."

I'll never forget this. We meet at Wrigley Field on Friday morning. The bus is there. The traveling secretary—just like we're ballplayers. You put your luggage in the bus. You never touched it again. The bus to the airport. On the airplane. You land in Atlanta. A bus takes you to the hotel. You get your keys. You go up to your room. Your bags are delivered up there. The bus took us to the ballpark Friday night. We had our tickets out in the bleachers near Chief Nakahoma in left field at Fulton County. The bus back —the whole three days—the whole shot—paid for...and that was a lot of money back in those days for an owner to do that. So, it was just a great season.

The players, they'd hang out with us on the road trips, 'cause they didn't have a lot of money back in those days and there

252

weren't 10,000 fans in the hotel like you'll see nowadays where you run for your life. Back then, there was 30-40 Bleacher Bums. We'd sit down in a tavern and have beers with Glenn Beckert and Ron Santo. Leo Durocher would walk by and throw a $20 bill on the table and say, "Here, guys, drink on me." And you gotta remember, beers were like a quarter. You'd drink—$20 bucks! We didn't have a penny to our name, the Bleacher Bums. We were all students or, you know, college kids in the summer or high school. And a guy like Leo would flip $20 bucks. That would be like $200 in today's money.

So, we were, of course, very disappointed when they...the Mets got hot and the Cubs cooled off, 'cause they were friends of ours more than just ballplayers. It's something that will never be created again with the high-priced salaries of the players. Today's players look at the fans as a nuisance that they wish they could, you know, brush aside.

What about the snake dance the last game of the '69 season?

Yeah, yeah. I wasn't there. I was a freshman in college and I was down in Southern Illinois University the final week. Though it didn't matter 'cause they were out of it. But, I'd have been back if they were. But, well, the fellows sent me movies and the pictures a few times. About 50 of the Bleacher Bums snake danced, like you say, in the last inning from the bleachers—which you can never enter the box seats—but the guard let us through. And, led by, you know, our leaders and the big rebel flag for Randy Hundley. Marched around the ballpark box seat area. All stood on top of the Cubs' dugout and sort of waved goodbye and it was very touching. It was a love affair not just with the fans and the players, but the players loved the fans, too, in that era.

Was there ever another season like that for you?

No, that disappointment to the team, more than even the fans, I think just killed those guys. They were in the running in '70 and '71, but if they'd have won in '69 and the players all say that there's no doubt they would have won for three or four more years in a row. It just tore everything apart and Leo was getting old and crotchety. And he had a lot of bad points as far as managerial maneuvering and the way he dealt with players on a personal level — interpersonal level.

What about some of the stories?

Well, we used to find out true facts, such as Willie Davis' Chicago girlfriend was a Playboy bunny named "Ruthie." We knew that her name was "Ruthie" and, in fact, we were told this by some of the Cubs players. We were encouraged to get on the guy. He's got a short fuse. So, we'd spend the entire game out there, you know, "Willie and Ruthie, Willie and Ruthie," chanting in unison or "Ruthie's got (he claps)," meaning she's got VD. You know, "Ruthie's got the (clap, clap, clap)." In fact, one night one of the Bleacher Bums sneaked into the ballpark. They had left one of the gates open on a Friday night when the Dodgers were in for three games and went into the visitor's dugout and, again, one of the bedsheet signs—"Willie and Ruthie" and attached it to the back wall of the visitors' dugout. In the morning when the players came in, they all got a look at this. Then Willie, he'd give us the finger and back and forth. You see, he didn't know how to play us.

Certain players, like Rico Carty, we'd try to get on him and he'd smile and wave back and within a few innings, you know, you liked him and then you cheered him. We weren't out to bury every visiting player. Rico Carty, just a fantastic Latino guy that had the big smile and would wave at us and we liked him—"Rico, Rico"—we'd cheer him like we cheered Billy Williams 'cause he was a fun guy. We just got on the people with the short fuse.

How did Davis handle it?

Oh, badly, badly. Yeah, he'd give us the finger in front of 40,000 people. In one game, he sort of got back at us. He lined an opposite-field home run, right into the midst of the Bleacher Bums at left center, above the 368 sign. And he went around the bases pointing the finger at us. All the way around the bases. If you did that nowadays, you'd be suspended by the league president. But, the funny thing was watching the WGN-TV news that evening, where they replay everything. The great Jack Brickhouse calls this, okay? Back, back—home run, you know. Now, the camera—Arne Harris, the producer or director of WGN, zooms in as he usually does right about when the home run guy is rounding second. That's the standard shot. Well, here, right on the camera, right on the big screen as I see it, Willie Davis pointing at us, back and forth, gesturing a hand pump with the middle finger at us. Well, what does Brickhouse say without missing a beat—the pro that he was—

"Well, I see Willie Davis is gesturing left fielder Billy Williams to play a little deeper next time." One of Jack's best ad libs.

Pete Rose was our favorite target. We'd get on Pete Rose and he'd literally, you'd think, was going to climb up the vines. Once, a fellow tried to climb the vines to get up at us, to physically confront us. It was a little before the Bleacher Bums. He tried to go after Ronnie Grousl. Leon Wagner...was with the Giants.

And Lou Brock we used to get on quite a bit, simply because, you know, he was the worst trade ever and we just didn't like him. We didn't need a reason. It was the Lou Brock deal. And I'll never forget—we had heard from one of the Cubs that Lou Brock is scared to death of mice. So, the big game's coming up and the Cubs and the Cardinals on "Game of the Week," which was rare back then, 'cause New York didn't think much of Chicago and drawing people, you know. So, it's the "Game of the Week" on a Saturday, NBC. Ronnie Grousl, somehow on Friday night, procures 12 white laboratory mice. Sneaks them into the ballpark in a shoebox. So, here we are in the bottom of the first inning as Lou Brock trots out to his left-field position, right? We all quick grab, in the last row of the bleachers, the live 12 mice and on the count of three, like a handgrenade, 1-2-3, we all loft about 20 feet into the air—you're already 20 feet high back there—from 40 feet comes lofting down all around Lou Brock 12 live white mice. Bouncing off—I'll never forget—bouncing off the beautiful grass which is quite spongy and lush at Wrigley Field. So the mice didn't even really get hurt. They'd like bounce like two-three times...boom, boom, boom. Like they're on a trampoline. All around Lou Brock. Well, it backfires. Lou Brock, it turns out, is not afraid of mice at all and turns around and starts chuckling and laughing at us. Well, the mice run around in circles for a minute or two. The Cubs go three up, three down.

Now, this day Willie Smith was in left, not Billy Williams. He was in right that day. Willie Smith, the Cub left fielder, comes running out in the top of the second inning. He's scared shitless of mice. He won't go out there. And the sight to see was the grounds crew running out with cardboard boxes, chasing 12 mice around for 10 minutes trying to catch 'em, while the NBC "Game of the Week" is delayed and the announcers must have been going "What the hell is going on out there?"

Another great Bleacher Bum disruption of a "Game of the

Week." This is in '68. 42,000 people. Well, Ronnie Grousl stands, gets up—and this is again spontaneous—he stands up in the middle of the game, you know, two out—man on second—sort of quiet...and he stands on top of the wall, which you could do then - they put a cement pyramid in '71 or 1970 to prevent us from standing on the wall during the game—Ronnie Grousl stands on the wall and he yells. Shag Crawford was the ump. You remember him. "Shag, Shag, Shag. Timeout. Timeout. Ball on the field." Well, that's the secret words for an umpire. Ball on the field, stop everything. Dead. You've seen that. Well, Shag Crawford says, "Timeout. Timeout." And he's in his final season, he's old and very fat. And he starts jogging out. So, he's jogging out towards the 368 sign. Plodding. Boom...Boom...Boom. "Shag, ball on the field." Boom...Boom...Boom. He gets out there. Gets to the warning track. He's looking up at Ronnie Grousl. He goes, "Where's the ball?" Then Ronnie makes that universal sign, like pumping your inner elbow. He goes, "Hey, Shag, fuck you. There's no ball on the field." At which point Shag Crawford collapses to his knees and starts a laughing jag for 10 minutes. Crawford is doubled over laughing—on the warning track. Finding there's no ball on the field. Ten minutes before he could finally collect himself and I gotta wonder to this day what Curt Gowdy and Tony Kubek said for 10 minutes while Shag Crawford's on his knees out by the warning track.

When did you leave the bleachers?

Well, no one really left them. Some guys got married. Some had families. Some moved away. The team went into the doldrums by the mid-'70s. But we still see the same faces, maybe once or twice a year. We hang out in the same tavern. Bernie's Bar over at Clark and Waveland. It never really broke up. It's just like your college friends or your wife's old card club, you know. People move, people change, but you still stay in each other's memory forever. And we still get together. I formed a reunion—a 20-year reunion in 1989 and we had over 100 people show up in the bleachers with their kids, their wives, and people came from Connecticut, Utah, Los Angeles, Florida to reunite with their friends for one weekend in 1989. So, everyone's still there. It's just, you know, people change. But you never forget your friends.

I go to the bleachers all the time when I go to Wrigley Field. Only because it's $6.00 and I'm too cheap to pay $15.00 to these prima dona ballplayers. I go there 'cause it's the cheapest seat.

Why do people follow the Cubs so faithfully?

I think it's a feeling that grows on you, partly because of the ballpark. Partly because of Jack Brickhouse and how Harry Caray's developing a whole new generation. One of the reasons the White Sox don't have the love affair is their ballpark was horse shit. And they never had much free television during the daytime to cultivate the young kids. I think the main reasons that people are hooked on the Cubs is the ballpark and the daytime television and Jack Brickhouse and Harry Caray's salesmanship/persona.

MARGE MEYER

Wife of Ray Meyer of Ray's Bleachers, a bar located across the street from the bleachers at Wrigley Field. She helped her husband build the business which coincided with the resurgence of the Cubs during the mid to late '60s. This was the meeting place for the Bleacher Bums and before them, the Right Field Bleacher Choir.

We got married in 1953. He had another little tavern at the time, which he sold and then he was working in a little factory, but he always wanted his own place. This bar came up by Wrigley Field and so we bought the bar in the fall of 1962. The first games that we serviced with food, and of course the bar, was the Bears. I had never served food before and I was bumping into everyone. I must have said "I'm sorry" a thousand times that day. My size 10s was in everyone's way. It was unbelievable money that I couldn't fathom, 'cause nothing like that had ever happened.

It was successful right away?
Oh, yeah, but that wasn't because of us. It was just that there were, you know, Bear fans.

What was the name when you bought it?
Eddie's Bleachers.

And you changed it to what?
Ray's Bleachers.
Well, then the seven days of the Bears was over and now it was really bad business. There was nothing around here. No factories to depend on.
And so then opening day was just another fantastic day like the Bears. We had a lot of people that day take off of work to help us —be bartenders, you know. The next day everyone was going back to work. So Ray and I got there and we were frantic—how were we going to handle this? So we were going to let it be an honor system. I went there early and I cooked piles and piles and piles of hot dogs and stacks and stacks of hamburgers. And I think

that the day brought in about 600 people. And I had to throw all this out because the hot dogs, from being cooked, they reduced in size and it looked like I had a whole big pile of cigar butts. They turned brown.

I thought that every day was going to be like the Bears games and like that opening day was. Naturally, we found that we could handle it. I had another job at the time so I used to come in and help Ray 'til the game started and then I would go to work. And he could finish the day. That's how little business there was. And then it would just pick up, you know, on the weekend.

Your business improved as the Cubs did in the '60s.

Yes. Well, when we first got there, the group calling themselves the Right Field Bleacher Choir was in place already. I mean, they had been coming in there. They were a very fun loving group. They sang. They had a roll-up sign that they would unfurl in the park. They would unfurl it in Ray's. They would sing. Then they had a pre-opening day party for themselves. They were very integral in Ray's although, you know, the place was open to everyone, of course. It created a lot of fun there from the get-go with that group. And they were very, very fun loving and intelligent and it was great. Then as the years went on you were seeing less and less. Getting married, or going into business or moving.

In the meantime, the Cubs was improving and now this other group was forming. But yet, it wasn't meant to be a club or anything. They were just fans that would go out there every day pretty near, or as much as they could, and they would see each other there. And they all started doing things. Chants and...I guess maybe about '67 you start seeing a little bit of them coming in. And '68 and them of course '69 was THE YEAR.

You're speaking of the Bleacher Bums?

The Bleacher Bums, yeah. They were so much fun. Every day you were just prepared to laugh. I finally quit work because business had really steamrolled by then.

This is June of '69?

Yes. They had some sign. A kid put his head through the sign that says, "Hit the Bleacher Bum." Then they were getting articles in the paper and it was being in the right place at the right time that

259

they began calling Ray's Bleachers the home of the left-field Bleacher Bums.

Did the Bums only meet at Ray's?

Right. As far as the Cub days, yes. And then even without Cub days, they'd come in because there was always something happening. There were more and more newspaper men coming to observe and find human interest stories. There were articles in the paper always. Of the group or an individual. My son and a lot of the Bleacher Bums became great statisticians. They used to talk what should have been done, you know. Road trips, going to St. Louis They were going to St. Louis and different places. They had been going to spring training. But as far as Ray and me, we began doing that in '69. But some of them from the Bleacher Bums, they were doing that already.

In '69, everyone would run up to the window—how can I be a Bleacher Bum? They were making up things to say. Well, if you do two road trips, you can be a Bleacher Bum. If you come every day.

Who were some of the ballplayers that came over to your place?

Fergie, Ron Santo, Banks, Williams...Beckert stopped a little bit. Selma, Hank Aguirre, Larry Biittner, Steve Stone, Pepitone, Harry Caray had come in. Vince Lloyd. Guys from the grounds crew, Jack Brickhouse, people from the ticket office, other office people. Because it was just something to see, you know. Ray used to put on different costumes and wigs and stuff and he would just make people laugh. It got to be like going there and see what's happening.

There was a newspaper man who was vindictive against somebody in the bar. One of the Bleacher Bums. And he came in one day with a photographer and he said he'd like to line up "A Day at Ray's." So we said, "Yes, that would be wonderful." And he came in with this photographer, but that particular day nothing much was happening. They were walking around, they were taking pictures of different memorabilia, things on the wall, but really nothing happened.

So, anyway, Roberto Rodriguez was a pitcher. Roberto Rodriguez was a dancer. He would dance with himself, with the chair, with anything...he was just rhythmic. The Duncans—well, Ruth Duncan was "Ma"—"Ma" Duncan, everyone called her that.

He knew her and he come in and he went over and he kissed Ruth. But that didn't mean anything. It was like kissing your mom. And they took a picture of that and the article the next day went like this: "There was some planes hijacked somewhere in the Mideast. Nobody cared about that. Nobody in Wrigley Field cared about that. The Bleacher Bums didn't care about that. Robert Rodriguez didn't care about that. Maybe if Roberto Rodriguez would care about anything, they might have won the game. But instead he was in the bar, dancing and kissing women and..."

That same man one time in Ray's sat in the front and he was watching the television and then the article the next day in the paper was as if he had been sitting in the bleachers. Spent the whole day by Ray's. But we didn't want to say nothing because the pen was mightier than the sword. This man could really do you in if he so desired.

Fergie Jenkins used to come over and arm wrestle Ray, didn't he?

Oh, yeah. Everyone just loved him. And he was just aces. He signed autographs. Never complained about that. If it was 50 people, he would do it. And so everyone got to really love him. And we used to send over, when he wasn't pitching, sandwiches for him. Polish sausage...he would call up and say, send over...I think he was ordering for a couple of his buddies, too. The game would begin and they'd take over sandwiches for him. But when he wasn't pitchin'.

Well, in the bleachers, they used to call us up and order drinks and we'd get them ready and then pass them through the gate to the people. The Right Field Bleacher Choir, they call, the word was "a coup." One time had a man in a wheelchair with a blanket over him and, in so doing, they got him in with a quarter barrel of beer into Wrigley Field. And they took movies of that, which I still have the film if anyone is wondering what happened to it—8mm.

When did you sell?

Our last year there was through '79. We were out of there in January of '80.

Did you see the Bleacher Bums starting to fade away in the '70s?

Yes. There was no more group that started up. Wrigley Field became a little more strict. Because they were walking on the wall, they were invincible they believed. And the chanting and all of that, well, that has ceased. You can't do that now. The minute you want to start anything there now, it's all security. So that began happening about '75. And who got married and who had to get a job and settle down. It was over. It was fun while it lasted and that song by the Beetles or McCartney—"those were the days my friend, we thought they'd never end." Ended. But it was fun while it lasted, let me tell you.

When did Ray die?
    Ray died in 1985. He died from cirrhosis of the liver. He had 36 hospital days. He died on 7/11. But he had a really great life. He really enjoyed it. And drinking was part of it. But it was great and everyone really loved him. Oh, gee.

Why did you sell in '79?
    Well, because we never used the money to fix the place up and it was sort of crumbling. It was like, it was time to go.
    Ray is buried at Graceland Cemetery and on the day of his funeral there was a ball game with the Dodgers and his policeman friends, they—well the funeral home was really close by. It was at Cooney's. And the policemen, instead of going with the cortege around your house, they had it go around Wrigley Field. Traffic was stopped and there was Ray going around Wrigley Field and everyone was waving at us. We went all around Wrigley Field with all kinds of salutes and waves and then to the cemetery.
    When I made the arrangements for the cemetery, they said, "Well, it's pretty well crowded here. We could give you room by the 'L.'" And I said, "Well, we had the 'L' going by us all the time. We couldn't hear on the phone if an 'L' went by." I says, "He would love it there." And so that's where he's at. And on his tombstone...well, Ray always used to—whenever he had a drink—he'd go, "First one today." Well, that's what I put on his gravestone. His name and date of birth and death and "first one today." You'll always know you're looking at Ray.

What are you doing now, Marge?
    I've got a little part-time job. I have met a gentleman who's a widower and we're seeing each other. I've a sister that lives in New England that I visit.
    Now we all hang out at Bernie's. It's a bar called "Bernie's."

We do not hang out at Murphy's Bleachers. Well, he made Ray's beautiful and it's quite a legacy, you know. But it isn't Ray's.

Do you miss it?

Uh...yes. Yes, I sure do. I see very few people anymore. That's like 20 years, you know.

Any regrets?

Any regrets? Well, I just think it could have...well, maybe if Ray didn't drink...well, no. No regrets. Everything is fine. I believe it just turned out that way it was supposed to. I mean, you know, that's like your whole lifetime. When you put it all together, then that's what's supposed to happen. So that's that.

He saw his first Cub game at age five in 1944. They have been a big part of his life ever since.

I grew up on the north side of Chicago, Montrose Avenue across from Graceland Cemetery. I went to grade school at Stockton on Montrose. I went to high school at Senn. Went to the ballpark walking on the railroad tracks behind Graceland Cemetery.

First memory I have of being in the park was sitting under the scoreboard and Phil Cavarretta was playing right field in place of Bill Nicholson. I remember seeing Nicholson there 'cause he was one of my early favorites. Cavarretta, the name "Philabuck" and the fact that he went to high school in my neighborhood, or not too far, always led me to favor Cavarretta. I was going to Lane Tech until I discovered what girls were all about and I decided to go to Senn instead.

Every Saturday that I could scrape together 50 cents, I would pack a lunch and go to the ball game.

What are your memories of the '40s teams?

A lot of futility, but a lot of excitement there. Bill Nicholson, as I said, Johnny Schmitz, Roy Smalley, a classic looking shortstop. He had a scatter gun arm and hard hands and he liked to strike out a lot. But the main memory of the '40s, I guess, was the visiting teams. That was '47-'48 when Jackie Robinson came into baseball and followed by Campanella and Joe Black when the Dodgers came to town. It was just electric. You could cut the excitement in the ballpark. It was just really something, especially sitting on the steps on the upper deck on the day that they had the all-time attendance record. Still to this day stands: 47,000 fans.

Early '50s, the pitching staff strikes me. Bob Rush, Warren Hacker, Paul Minner, Turk Lown. I remember Dee Fondy, a first baseman. Wasn't that great a hitter but he could lay down a drag bunt better than anybody I've seen up to this point. I remember Chuck Connors playing on the team in the early '50s. He had good power. He was a good ballplayer.

Then Ernie Banks came into the league in '53 and I had a paper route about that time and I used to go from one building to the next building delivering my papers, knocking on doors and asking people if I could just watch Ernie bat.

Bill Serena played third base and he was the host ballplayer on a day when I was in what they called the "Knothole Gang." They had a couple of kids compete for a baseball prize. I was on TV there in the early '50s. He was the third baseman so we were both supposed to take the plays the third baseman made. I came in second. That wasn't bad except there was only two people on. I got an autographed glove and a baseball out of it and it was a great experience.

Mid to late '50s are kind of a blur in my memory 'cause I went in the service in 1956 and made a career out of it. So my baseball memories of Chicago—'56 until the mid-'60s anyway—were from newspapers and when I could pick up KMOX out of St. Louis and KDKA in Pittsburgh and a Philadelphia station on clear nights on the coast when I was stationed there.

I came back during my military career. I was stationed at the Naval Air Station in Glenview from 1961 to '64. That was a unique time in the Cubs' history because they had some success there and they also had some tragedy. They lost one of the best young second baseman that they ever had in Kenny Hubbs in a plane crash. And the following spring, I believe it was, they lost the best broadcaster they ever had. Sorry, Harry. Jack Quinlan, who was just a fine, fine talent, really made baseball enjoyable.

Those were the early years of the development of the Cubs with Santo and Kessinger and those guys. And after I left, Durocher came along and before you knew it, it was '69 and they were for real.

I made two trips back in '69. I was stationed in Virginia at the time, but I had to be there. So a couple of the long weekends, I came back and spent the three days each time in the bleachers with my family, who was then firmly entrenched in the Bleacher Bum organization.

I don't really have any strong memories of the '70s. I was not near Chicago. I didn't go back as much as I had in the past and I kind of drifted away from focusing on the Cubs, although I always looked at their box scores and followed what they were doing. But they never had a team...they were in transition, I guess. Letting the old guard go...Jenkins and Williams and Banks faded out...the new group just didn't grab me.

Early '80s, they started to really play good ball again and the '84 season was the first year I had cable television here in California that picked up WGN. I think that was the year they had the long strike and I was so mad at them for having that strike. But then when they finally came back on I forgave them 'cause the Cubbies came on and clinched that pennant in 1984 and I packed up my brother that week and went back to Wrigley Field so I could be there the first time they stepped on that field in my adult lifetime as division champions.

What was that feeling like?

Very, very special. I was goose bumps, tears in my eyes, bumping in my heart.

Were there other people with tears in their eyes sitting around you?

Oh, yeah. It was about a 10-minute standing ovation when they came out.

Won the first two in Chicago. Went back to San Diego...

I was convinced that I finally was going to get into the World Series. And, unfortunately, Mr. Mike Royko had to fire up the whole city of San Diego and I was living north of San Diego at the time, in Orange County. But I came down for all three of those games and I want to tell you and Mr. Royko and any other Cub fan that that was the most fired up crowd I ever saw in my life. And I've been in a lot of stadiums over the years.

What was it he did?

He had criticized the San Diego fans about being small town, or hicks, or something, that after the first two games they'd be back to the beach or something. And he did it toward the end of the regular season, when the Padres had already clinched and I didn't see the article myself, I only heard pieces of it. And then when I came down here, 80% of the people going in that ballpark had the circle with the Cub in the middle and a diagonal line. They had those shirts everywhere. I had never been in a stadium that was so electric. And they stayed that way for three days. The second game, the one that Garvey won with a home run in the ninth inning, was probably the most exciting baseball game I've ever seen. Certainly from a crowd reaction point of view. I'll never forget that.

I just walked around the parking lot after the Saturday night game, saying, "Wait'll tomorrow, guys. Sutcliff and sunshine—that's all we needed." And by the seventh inning, my brother and I were so deflated, we got in the car and headed north. We just knew. It was just like the baseball God was telling us it still wasn't time.

What about the '89 season?

'89 season I thought they had a strong team, but I guess when they got into the playoffs, having seen the Giants play the Padres here, and on TV, I knew that the Giants were a strong team. But I knew that the Cubs could have beaten them if they did everything right. Unfortunately, I think they overmanaged a little bit and a couple of key players just had a bad week. But, it's, you know, like that guy upstairs. Just keeps saying "Not yet."

I put my thoughts down about being a Cub fan in the form of a poem. I wonder if you'll just let me read this?

Being a life long Cub fan is more than a state of the heart
It is something very special and it sets us all apart
From other fans and other places, who think winning is the prime endeavor
We Cub fans know that it really is the long wait if it takes forever
From the ivy covered walls of brick to the scoreboard in the sky.
We know we're bound to be there saying "Go, Cubbies" til we die
So keep hustling, you Cubbies, and keep cheering you fans,
yell and holler and shout
For we know that we'll always share a feeling
that others can only write about.

I remember the first night game in Wrigley Field. It was so special. It was something that I was opposed to my whole life, because I, like all traditional Cub fans, just wanted that sunshine to stay there forever. It turned out to be a wise decision. But on that first night, I went to the game in a tuxedo hat and a tuxedo shirt and a tie with my brothers, and we sat in the front row, right behind the Cubs' dugout. It was, again, one of those electric moments, but when those clouds came over that left-field wall, I looked up and said, "Thank you," because it was just meant to be that the baseball God said, "You might put lights in this park, but not tonight."

I stood out in that rain. All three of us, in fact, stood out there for half an hour in pouring down rain. It was above our ankles in the box seats. Just revelling in the fact that somehow, the baseball God said, "Not tonight."

A loop attorney who would rather chase the Cubs than ambulances.

Do you remember your first game at Wrigley Field?

It was 1962. I was sitting in the center-field bleachers which are now blocked off for hitting background. The outfield was Billy Williams, Don Landrum, and Lou Brock—left center and right. The infield was Santo, Andre Rodgers, Kenny Hubbs, and Ernie Banks and the battery was Larry Jackson and Dick Bertell.

I bugged my dad to bring me down to the ballpark as often as possible, but until I really got into my teens, I wasn't allowed to go by myself. My dad used to prefer to take me to see them play the Braves up in Milwaukee. We did that until the Braves moved to Atlanta and then I got him, and whoever else I could talk into, taking me down.

The first year I was allowed to go down by myself was 1969. Of course, you've heard plenty about that year. We used to get on the train in Barrington at 5:15 A.M. Used to take it down to Irving Park and get off at Irving Park and take a bus over to get in line for bleacher tickets, 'cause they wouldn't sell them in advance back then. So there we are in line at the ballpark at 7:00 A.M. The game starts at 1:30. At 9:00 A.M. they open the gates and it's a mad rush to get the choice seats where I then sat in left field in the first couple of rows. There's like 500 people in the park, all in the bleachers, and the game doesn't start for four and a half hours and I'm 14 years old. I haven't even had a beer in my life yet, okay? And so, we wait. We would cheer the grounds crew when they came out —one by one. We'd cheer Yosh Kawano and then when the first player showed up—the place just went up for grabs. Batting practice, the whole thing, the game and then back on the bus, wait at Irving Park, the trains would come about once an hour and then back to Barrington.

What was it like in '69?

It was wild. It's almost overshadowed because baseball has become so popular in general. Back then, it was just like a cult thing. And the Cubs set their all-time attendance record. The Cubs hadn't really seriously contended since 1945. They made a brief run at it in '67 and '68, but they finished like a dozen games back of the Cardinals. They were never really a serious threat after the Fourth of July. And it was just nuts. Let's put it this way. There were fewer people at the ballpark than there are nowadays, but there were a higher percentage of maniacs, which made it all the more fun.

Back then there was a bunch of maniacs like you'll find at a Chicago Blackhawks game even to this day. And so everybody who was there was crazy. Dick Selma leading the cheers from the bullpen and Santo clicking his heels afterwards. And the hatred for the Mets.

The fact of the matter is—my theory—we had the best utility, all-around infielder by the name of Paul Popovich. And Durocher was from the old school and it's like you got a starting eight. The only guy he rested occasionally was Ernie. I think Randy Hundley started like 150 games that year. Something outrageous like that. Anyway, had Popovich played one game a week at third, one game a week at short, one game a week at second—the Cubs wouldn't have lost anything and those guys would have been fresh going down the stretch. But Leo is from the old school. He did a lot of good things, but he made a big mistake on that one. And of course, you've heard enough stories about opening day with Willie Smith and things like that and that's when this incredible hatred of the Mets was born because, not only were they winning, they were mocking the Cubs as they were winning. And then, worse comes to worse, we're out of it and they come in for the last game of the season and win their 100th game at Wrigley Field when everything is all over but the shouting. And they're really just rubbin' our noses in it. And it took 15 years to get that out of my system.

The greatest moment I ever spent at Wrigley Field was August 8, 1984 when we beat the Mets for the fourth straight game and it was a bean ball war for four entire games. There was a single game on Monday the 6th. A doubleheader on Tuesday the 7th and a single game on Wednesday the 8th and I was just beside myself. I just couldn't stay away from the ballpark. So, I was out there and we just rolled along and the bean ball wars and it just got greater and greater and greater and finally we took that fourth straight.

And I'll never forget, I called my best friend who had gone

through '69 with me, who couldn't be at the park. As soon as he heard the noise in the background he knew it was me at one of the local saloons. He said it took us 15 years, but we finally got revenge to which I replied, "and as the Klingons say, 'that is a dish which is best served cold.'" We knocked 'em down, we beat the shit out of them, we came, we saw, we conquered and they left town and were never the same. That was the greatest moment I ever had at Wrigley Field.

What was the difference between the '84 and '89 seasons?

The team in '84, because of the manager, they were very low key. They never got real high and they never got real low. The fans were going nuts, but the team itself kept a very, very even keel and I think that comes from the top on down. Jim Frey is a very, very low key guy. Extremely low key. And he never let the team get too excited when they won or when they lost.

Whereas, the '69 team—it was almost like a manic depressive thing. I mean, when we won, the players, everybody were just ecstatic. And when they lost—and I'm not knockin' those guys. You know, Ron Santo—he's just a guy who wears his heart on his sleeve. You can't criticize that. That's just his nature. And he is, to this day, if you hear him broadcast the games, he's just an extremely emotional guy and he was the leader of that team. Well, the leader of the '84 Cubs was, you know, guys like Sandberg, Sutcliffe...very low key guys.

What about the difference between the '84 and '89 team?

The '89 team was a team that nobody expected to do anything —that had a bunch of kids and, I'll tell you, it just wasn't that big of a thrill because—I mean it was nice, but I had already seen the Cubs win once in my lifetime.

In '84, I'll never forget standing at the Cubbie Bear and watching the game at Pittsburgh. It looks like we're going to win it and there's this sign that somebody's stretching out at Three Rivers Stadium—"39 years of suffering is long enough." And, that's when I and a lot of other people started to lose it.

What about baseball today?

I saw a chart comparing inflation to increases in baseball tickets. Baseball tickets have increased in price at a rate slightly less than that of inflation. Over the last 25 years. I don't know if people are complaining, but every year the attendance goes up. That speaks louder than any complaint anybody would make.

What bothers me is a lack of good fundamental baseball. That's what bothers me. You don't see, and this has to do with free agency, arbitration, and awarding guys on their stats—like hitting to the opposite side to advance a runner from second to third. Well, you don't get a sacrifice for that. You get a ground out, 4-3. And yet it can mean the difference in winning several games. You don't see a lot of younger players doing that.

For instance, we've got a couple of guys now. Jerome Walton is up for arbitration next year for the first time. He's been bitching about his salary ever since he got into town two years ago and now he's like, he's trying to do so much more than he's capable of, to get his stats up there. And the hole he's digging is just deeper and deeper and deeper.

Shawon Dunston turned down a $2 million a year deal for the Cubs for like three years with an option for the fourth, figuring he'd put himself on the open market. Well, on the open market his value is going to go down because this pressure that he's dealing with—he's trying to get his stats up there, he's swinging at bad pitches, he's doing stupid things.

Now, in Andre Dawson, who they brought in in '87—who came in for like a very low salary, played out his option. He came in and just went nuts. He could handle the pressure. But he also was a great team player at the time.

And so what's happened is you have non-baseball people awarding salaries. It's not the free agency. 'Cause the free agency —that's when you're paying for a star. It's the arbitration combined with free agency—because you have people who know nothing about baseball deciding what guys are going to be paid. And that's the big problem.

Do you still enjoy the game?
I'm mainly in the bleachers. And more often than not, since the early '80s anyway, when I got back into it after getting out of college and law school, and etc., etc., started working on my own where I was able to get off in the afternoon, I was a real good, rowdy heckler in the bleachers. Never in a cussing fashion. But just in a way to really get under somebody's skin—without being

racist or obscene or anything like that. To really get after some guy about his poor play—on the opposing team, of course. And what I find now is, it's a little less enticing because almost everybody is younger than me. I'm going to be 36 next month, which doesn't feel old but there's very few players left that are older than me and so I look at these guys in a slightly different light. At one time, they were larger than life. They certainly aren't anymore.

And so what I enjoy, I guess, is the cult that exists in the bleachers at Wrigley Field, whether it's right, center, or left. I'm like a quasi-member of that cult. I work as an attorney downtown, five or six days a week. Things go well, but out there—these people, it's a totally different world. I get on the "L" for a buck and in 20 minutes I'm in a totally different world and these people—the single most important thing in their lives is the Cubs. And being in the bleachers. And being in their particular section for as many games a year as they possibly can. They plan their vacations around the Cubs. They go on the road with the Cubs as often as possible. And so I'm like a quasi-member. I'm not a member because it's not that big a deal to me. But I enjoy that cult, I guess is what I like. Because it's so far removed from my day-to-day life.

One of the few people that is both a Cub and Sox fan. An attorney and partner with the law firm of Pedersen & Houpt in Chicago.

I became a Cub fan as an adult. I know that most people will tell you that there is no such thing as a Cubs fan and a White Sox fan in the city of Chicago. One of my friends says if somebody tells you they were a Cubs fan and White Sox fan, check for your wallet 'cause you're talking to a dishonest person. But I don't think that's true. The truth is that the White Sox were the team of my youth— my childhood. And the Cubs have become the team of my adult-hood. There are a couple of reasons for that, not entirely based on the success of the team.

The Cubs have had two division winners in the '80s that made it very easy to follow. And when I was a child, the White Sox had the '59 pennant and the truth is that I moved with my parents to Chicago in 1959. At that time, the White Sox were winning the pennant in the American League and the Cubs were next to last with the Phillies below them in the National League. And the only thing—we grew up on the South Side—and the only thing that the people there ever said about the Cubs were, "Gee, it's too bad Ernie Banks is on that team because he's a good player and he deserves something better." So, I was a White Sox fan. And, I was also a baseball fan.

I first started going to Cubs games when I moved to the north side of Chicago in about 1978. I first became a Cubs season ticketholder in 1984 and I'd have to say that I was a Cubs fan be-fore that.

But, I was a Cubs fan in capital letters in 1984. I bought season tickets that year for the first time. I personally think that I was re-sponsible for the Cubs winning the division because I bought season tickets. As a matter of fact, we went out, my friend and I that shared the tickets, went out to Wrigley Field and we talked to the ticket agent and before we purchased our tickets, we said, "We'd like to see where these seats are. Will you take us out to the ballpark?" And the Cubs weren't drawing then like they draw now.

And the ticket guy actually had time to go out to the ballpark with us. This is February, there was snow on the seats, and we sat in about eight different places to see what we liked. I mean, you'd never get that kind of attention now. But what was funny about that was, my friend said to this guy, "Now, if we buy these tickets, do we get extra playoff tickets?" And that was considered a joke because the Cubs in '83 had been hopelessly under .500. The guy said, "Sure, if the Cubs make the playoffs, you can have the entire right-field bleachers." We later called the Cubs' office to see if they would give us the entire right-field bleachers. But they didn't remember making that promise. So, I would say I really became a Cubs fan in 1984. As a child, I was a White Sox fan.

I now live on the North Side. I follow the Cubs passionately and have, really, throughout the '80s. You know, the '84 team was great fun to watch. It was agony in San Diego. The '89 team was even more fun to watch. Probably not as good a ball club, but one that really hustled and took extra bases and won on suicide squeezes. Also, an agonizing loss on the West Coast when they lost to San Francisco.

I have a friend who's a Cuban and he tells me that he speaks Spanish and he speaks English. I ask him when he dreams, what does he dream in. He said, "Spanish is the language of my youth and English is the language of my adulthood. If I dream about my parents, I dream in Spanish. If I dream about my business, I dream in English." And that's sort of how it is for me. If I think about baseball in the '60s and in the early '70s, I think about the White Sox. And if I think about after that, I think about the Cubs.

Would you say that you have equal passion for both the White Sox and the Cubs?

As a defense mechanism, I can swing with whatever team does better. I make fun of people that only follow teams when they do well. I follow both teams even when they do poorly. But I reserve my passion for a successful team, just as a defense mechanism. I'm sort of tired of bleeding. My line to most of my friends is ... "In Chicago we don't have enough winners that we can afford to reject one." If the White Sox are going to do well, I will root for them. If the Cubs are going to do well, I will root for them. The Cubs have had two division winners, though they didn't go on to the World Series. So I've certainly followed the Cubs more. You know, this won't go too far before you ask me the question, what would happen if the Cubs played the White Sox in the World Series? That falls into the "we'll cross that bridge when we come to it" category.

You had an opportunity most fans never have, behind the scenes in the Cub clubhouse.

I think this was in 1988. It was when Goose Gossage—he was a great relief pitcher for other teams and not really so great for the Cubs—was pitching for them. A friend of mine, Steve Birger, runs a rib restaurant called "Stevie B's" and a lot of the Cub players go to Stevie B's. They have an outdoor cafe out by Wrigley. He had a jinx for a while, where the players who'd start going there the most were traded. Once Lee Smith started going there, they got rid of him. And then Dave Martinez—they traded him to the Expos.

But anyway, "Stevie B" was popular with a lot of the Cubs and his ribs are great. And he was catering some of the games. One time he told me that he goes up to the Cubs games and caters the clubhouse. I said, "Stevie, you mean you go into the Cubs' clubhouse and you serve them ribs and you sit there and eat dinner with them?" He said, "Yeah." And I said, "Well, what do I have to do to get a job with you." He said, "Carry in a pan of ribs." I said, "I can do that." So, this was like a little boy at this point, I was so excited about this.

I went up with Stevie B. We went in the back way, into the clubhouse and set up. The Cubs at that time were about in the fifth inning. It was a close game. I believe they were playing Philadelphia. Sutcliffe was pitching for the Cubs and he was doing pretty well, but he got tired in the fifth and Frank DiPino came in for the Cubs. He was a little left-handed pitcher. They later traded him. He held the lead until about the seventh or eighth inning and it was a close game, but the Cubs had a couple run lead when Goose Gossage came in. And here we were, sitting in the clubhouse, talking to Rick Sutcliffe, talking to Frank DiPino. They'd come out of the game. They'd showered. They were sitting there in their towels and talking to us like we were old friends. I could hardly keep my eye on the game. The TV was there in the clubhouse, everybody was watching the game, but I was really looking at these baseball players who were my heroes. And, we were talking when Gossage started getting behind in the count and walked a couple of players.

Goose was a fierce competitor and he'd once had a 90-plus

fastball, but he didn't at this point. What happened is he threw a fastball to some rookie that I don't think had ever had a hit before and the guy crushed it, hit it out of the ballpark, and the Phillies took the lead. At which point everybody in the clubhouse got quiet and started watching the TV. I looked around, I didn't know what was happening. I was unhappy about the game, but I didn't know what was going on. Don Zimmer started to walk out to the mound to take out Goose Gossage. I didn't think anything of it until everybody in the room got up and made some sort of excuse or other—they'd been sitting around leisurely, towels, a can of beer, a rib—and everybody got up and just absolutely made the quickest exodus you've ever seen. Stevie B and I were still there. We had all the ribs. We had everything. We didn't know what was going on. We were looking at the TV to see who the new pitcher was going to be, when Yosh Kawano, the clubhouse man came in and said, "Oh, my God, you guys are still here? You'd better leave!" And the panic in his voice set us scurrying.

We didn't know why until, as we were leaving, we heard Gossage coming down the corridor from the dugout to the clubhouse. And, not that we hadn't heard those four-letter words before, but he was throwin' things. He was kicking things. When he got to the clubhouse with the lockers and the bats and the balls and the gloves—things went flying and he turned the clubhouse into a shambles. Apparently everybody knew that this was gonna happen. When Gossage (a) gets taken out of the game, (b) blows a save and (c) lets up a home run to an absolute rookie that had never had a hit before, that was pouring gasoline on the fire. The veteran players all knew that it was time for them to clear out and had we not been rescued by Yosh Kawano, we would have been in the firing line. We went up and watched the rest of the game and the Cubs lost.

I can't to this day see a relief pitcher get taken out of the game without thinking, what's happening right now in that clubhouse. I mean, you don't realize that these guys are fierce, fierce competitors, and they do not like to fail.

He decided to live his fantasy and has gone to three of Randy Hundley's Baseball Camps. At his first camp, at age 37, he actually thought someone might say, "Hey, there's some old guy here who can still throw."

I went in '87, '88, and '89. I used to think I was a good ballplayer. Quite honestly, the first year I thought there was a real good chance somebody might say something like, "Hey, there's some old guy here who can still throw." I mean seriously, that's how far gone I was.

I can throw hard and I thought that, you know, hey—as a kid I never had an opportunity. I really thought I was good. Then I went down there and found out I wasn't.

What was your first inkling?

My first inkling was I went to pitch the fourth inning, I couldn't get the ball over the plate. I ended up going to changeups instead of just fastballs. I felt bad for my teammates in the field because I walked some people. Hundley had said upfront, he wasn't big on having campers pitch. Those of us that wanted to pitch were very upset about it. So, finally, the third day of camp, he said, "Okay, fine you guys. I'm warning you."

Normally, they have a batting machine that handles the games. It's always batting machines. You know, the ball just goes in there and you play. He said his experience in the first two camps was when you have old guys pitching, the games go too slow, they drag and I was thinking to myself, with those guys it did, but not with me. I found out that getting the ball over from 60' 6" consistently was more difficult then I remembered from 20 years ago.

I pitched that inning and I remember Hoyt Wilhelm was standing behind me. He was the umpire. If I fell behind in the count, I attempted to tantalize the guys with an off-speed pitch so they'd go after it. I remember it worked the first couple of times—got guys out on it—and then guys started laying back waiting for it. They started killing it. I remember Hoyt Wilhelm saying to me, "Jeff, I think you better file that pitch for a while."

Hundley always says you don't have to be a jock to go there. I would say half the guys played either in college or played some minor league. But this is 20 years ago, 'cause these guys are 40 and 45 now. At 37, I was a young guy. Because you have to be 35. That's the minimum. So I was on the young side.

There was a 72-year-old guy on our team who played second base and he had a mitt that looked just like the mitts that they used to use in the '30s and '40s.

I played third and I can remember my first time I'd get a groundball and I go to throw to second for a force, I'd see this guy standing there with this little bitty mitt and I remember the first time I took something off of my throw, and he said, "Jeff, throw it." So the next time I got a grounder, I threw it. He caught it. Yeah, I mean it was phenomenal. The interesting thing is when you play with older guys, you can tell they've played.

The hearts were there—the minds were there, but the bodies weren't. Hundley used to grade the ballplayers. And I'm sure I graded out as a pretty good ballplayer. But what bothered me was, sure, I was a pretty good ballplayer, but I was playing with a bunch of guys who, quite honestly, they were going to play baseball for one week and never play it again for the rest of their lives. I play baseball in the summer league that Hundley set up. You know, I'm serious about it. I like to play baseball. So when I think to myself —yeah, you were good among those guys, but that means absolutely nothing.

You'd have some really good plays and then you'd have some really bad plays. He used to grade the ballplayers the first day of camp. And then the next day all the coaches, all the ex-Cubs would sit around that night and they'd grade us and they'd say, "We want so many Grade A players on the team, B, C and so forth." That way everything equaled out.

Who were some of the Cub players?

Billy Williams, Glenn Beckert, Don Kessinger, Ernie Banks, Fergie Jenkins, Randy Hundley, Gene Oliver, Hoyt Wilhelm, Jim Hickman. Bob Will was there one year. God, I'm trying to think— Moe Drabowsky was there one year, Carmen Fanzone, Ron Santo. And Ernie would make guest appearances. You just didn't know if Ernie was going to show.

It was $2,900 total. That included airfare, uniform, and room and board.

I kept my uniform so the next year I went it was $200 off.

Sixty is a full camp. One year I think they may have had 66, but they go with six teams, 10 guys on a team. There's three fields and you've got two teams playing on each field. And it's a round robin thing during the week.

How long does it last?

One week. You get down there on a Sunday afternoon. Sunday night there's a cocktail party where Randy introduces all the ex-Cubs and they all sit around and talk. Then Randy talks about what's going to take place during the week. Then Monday morning at 9:00 o'clock you head out to the ballpark and you strap on your stuff.

The mornings you had your practices. Those guys that wanted to pitch, those guys that wanted to play infield, those guys that wanted to catch, and those guys that wanted to play outfield. He would break you off into different groups. And you'd have individual training in those various areas. Then, you'd move after 45 minutes to the next station which might be hitting instruction. Then you'd move on to the next instruction which might be your second position—let's say that's playing infield. For example, in my case, I signed up to be a pitcher and third base. So, one of my stations was pitching. The other one of my stations was infield. So you did that all morning.

The ballplayers used to tell funny stories. Santo and Beckert roomed together. Beckert was a rookie. Santo tells the story that they were rooming together and he said that year he was hitting .325 and he was really tearing up the league and Beckert, in his first year, was 0 for 22. He was batting .133 and Santo, as you know, has diabetes. So every morning, he used to give himself a shot. Insulin. And he told the story one morning...that he got up and he went into the bathroom. He pulled out a needle. Put the needle in his arm for the insulin shot. Well, Beckert was laying in bed and he could see Santo giving himself a shot. So, Santo tells the story, "We went down to breakfast and Glenn says to me, 'Ronnie, I'm not going to pass judgment on what you're doing. I saw what took place in the room this morning. I saw what you gave yourself. I need some. I don't care what it is. I need some, too.'" And he says, "You idiot, I've got diabetes. Do you want diabetes? That's insulin." He was just so intense about getting his batting average up —"I don't care. Whatever you're taking. I want some of it."

They were talking about the old dugouts at Wrigley Field. When it used to rain, the water used to drip over the edge of the dugout. And Durocher would take the towel and kind of dry off the top part of the dugout. Raising his hand and just catching the drops so they stop dripping in front of him.

They had an outfielder called Johnny Callison. Well, Callison was new to the team and he didn't know where to play. So, Durocher says, "When you get out there, I'll put you in position. You just watch me." Well, he puts him in position and Callison—his eyes are trained on Durocher because if you played for Durocher you just didn't want to screw up. It started drizzling and Durocher is now taking that hand that he was using to signal...he's now using it on top of the ledge to dry off the drips. And he's moving his hand across the side and Billy Williams is in right field and he sees Callison running back and forth in the outfield. He thinks that Durocher is moving him back, then moving him forward—where all he's doing is catching raindrops. So, Williams says, "You just stay there. You're alright."

And one of the years I was there, Billy Williams got into the Hall of Fame. So, the ex-Cubs really celebrated big time.

I went for three and I noticed the third year I was there, I was playing third and I thought about business. And I said to myself, gee, too much. Take a year off. Also, playing at third, you have to be thinking about what's going on. I was getting kind of bored. I'd heard the same stories. The thrill was gone for me from the standpoint of, "Well, there's Ron Santo," and all this. All I wanted to do was play baseball.

I'm hoping to go back next year. But I notice that I just got kind of stale. All I wanted to do was play ball and yet I knew the new guys—the first time guys at camp, oh, they wanted to sit around and hob nob with the ex-ball players and listen to stories. That wasn't the case anymore for me.

Did you see the movie Field of Dreams?

I've seen it numerous times. It was a tremendous movie. One thing it related to me was the fact that I had never gone to a baseball game with my father. I had never played catch with my father. And it didn't dawn on me until I was watching this movie and I'd been playing catch with my son who plays little league, and I'm thinking to myself..."Gee, maybe I could have been good had I been given a little encouragement as a kid." But fathers—at least in my area—fathers when we were growing up, they were working all the time. You know, they weren't into exercise and this type of thing. You worked late. You came home. You got up early. Went back to work. So when he talked about, he didn't get to do this with his dad and how he left things with his father, it got very sad for me especially the ending scene where he finally got to play catch with his dad again. That really hit home with me.

What's your biggest disappointment in life?

That I didn't play professional baseball. My biggest disappointment is I never, ever thought about being a professional ballplayer and being serious about playing even though I loved it so much.

Bill Veeck's widow. A woman of strong convictions. Years ago, Wrigley told Bill Veeck he would have a first refusal on the sale of the Cubs. After meeting Wrigley, Mary Francis told Bill that he would never sell to him. She was right.

People associate Bill with the White Sox, but actually he started with the Chicago Cubs under his father.

Right. His father was president of the Cubs at the time and he was really a little boy. When he was eight or nine years old, he went to spring training and I know when he was around 10 he was a kind of "go-for" at the park.

Bill was always a president/owner/operator of every ball club that he ever owned. There was always this talk about, oh, the money and so forth. Before I knew him and we ever since, always put the big bulk of our money in. That's how we made our living and he had this very strict thing that you did not ask anyone to invest unless you put yours in there. He always had the controlling voting interest. Now, the reason I get into that is because I don't believe there was an owner/operator/president that was grounded so well in the education of how you ran a ball club and a ballpark. So, he started very young and you've heard the history of the vines and the scoreboard which, until they put this new gizmo in, his old scoreboard was still operating.

And, then he worked the concessions, worked the grounds crew. Because he worked them, he knew what had to be done but then he took a course at IIT at night—I think it was Armour Institute, then—in architecture so he would know how to do that.

Then when his father died, he was secretary/treasurer of the Cubs. So, that was a very happy association because, again, he learned another part of it and the only reason he left was, he kind of needed a raise, too. By that time he was married and had a child. But the main reason was the way of young people everywhere. You want to try your ideas. You want to try your new things.

Mr. Phillip Knight Wrigley, for whom he worked, he had great admiration. He thought he was a really nice man. He thought he knew a lot of things. But he was a shy person and he didn't seem to know a whole lot about people. But at any rate, that was why he left. He was just itching to try some of his ideas.

Bill was known as a fan/owner. Most clubs are owned by corporations.

That was a title that was given to Bill by fans themselves and I think some writers picked up on it. I wouldn't go so far as to say that there are no owners that don't care about fans. But, no one cared more than Bill and I think there were very few that cared as much.

You're right—you made the point about corporations and so forth. That, of course, has been happening for a long time. I mean, the old baseball names, the Comiskeys, the Wrigleys, the MacPhails, the O'Malleys, the Stonehams—God, it's terrible to start naming, because then you leave somebody out. Of course the Buschs. I think there's still a Busch involved. But, that was a different time and there are still some of them around. There's a third generation of MacPhails—Andy MacPhail. And, of course, Bill Wrigley was the third generation and the last Wrigley connected. Bill was the second Veeck and our Mike running an A ball club is the third generation. I don't care if it sounds like being a mother, he's good.

I really deserve no part in the Cubs because that was all before I ever knew Bill. I did not meet Bill until September of '49 and so that was in his past. Jerome Holtzman is the one who pointed out that he's the only person that was an executive with both Chicago ball clubs.

Bill spent his later years in the bleachers at Wrigley Field. Why?

He had to get his baseball fix somewhere. You see, any time that we had a ball club, we never had a box. I mean, we didn't have an owner's box or anything like that. We wandered through the stadiums and so forth. But, the last years, he really had to watch the game mostly from the press box. Just the sheer thing of getting around, he couldn't get around quite as much.

He said until we got married that he really didn't know what to do with himself from the end of the World Series 'til the beginning of spring training. I know he loved...he really loved this game. And that is something that gets lost occasionally. And he was a good baseball man.

He didn't want to go to Comiskey afterwards. And so, he went to Wrigley and he knew that the bleachers were great seats. That was just his way of saying, "Gee, what a great way to spend a day." I didn't go with him every time because of things that I was involved in and had to do. But, we went a lot. And he went a lot. And there were a lot of friends. The last opening day of his life, he took all of the employees at Illinois Masonic Medical Center, who were able to go, who had pulled him through when they had to remove a tumor from his lung—he took them all there for opening day. We had a great time.

That was '85. So, ever since then, a lot of us have gone to opening day at Wrigley Field and we all sit in the bleachers. It's all the family and it's not a maudlin thing. I don't think we'll do it every year for the rest of our lives, but it felt good to do and right and there's an awful lot of other people who go whom we never knew until we started going to the bleachers. I couldn't give you their last names, but, we all sort of got to know one another there. And there's a lot of give and take and he loved, you know, he loved conversation.

I'll tell you something else, too. He would never say this, but I really do think Bill made it okay for a lot of people, who would never have thought of going, to sit in the bleachers. It sort of became fashionable, if you will. "Gee, Bill's out there," you know. And so people, you'd see people come—that's when they started developing going back to the old 3:00 ball game. See an awful lot of people would come right from the office, with briefcases, with tie loosened and you know...

Did he try to buy the Cubs?

Well, he would have loved to have bought the Cubs, yeah. He put out feelers for them before WGN bought them. Actually, Phil Wrigley told Bill that if he ever sold them, that Bill would have first refusal rights. Based on a previous conversation with Bill, he didn't think he would ever sell, but if he did, that Bill could certainly have first refusal rights. After we bought the Browns, we were in Chicago and had dinner with Mr. and Mrs. Wrigley. They had a dinner party in their home and that was my first meeting with them. And when we left, I said to Bill, "He will never sell you the Cubs."

I just knew he wouldn't. It was obvious that he was fond of Bill. And the long association with Bill's dad and his father—those were things that meant something to Mr. Phillip Wrigley. He still thought that Bill was this brash young man with these wild ideas. He had respect for him, that I could tell. But, I just didn't think that would ever happen. I knew it would never happen.

What happened when he put the feelers out?

Well, I think it was already a fait accompli that the Tribune was in there, you know.

I have a lot of respect for Mike Royko and he thinks Chicago could become a Sox town.

Well, I have great respect for Mike, too, and I'm very fond of him in addition. He's basically always been a Cub fan. I think maybe that he sees things not working out. The Sox have a good team. The Sox are going to keep building. It's a good ball club. So, I think they're going to do it and the town loves a winner. I think that if the Cubs put it all together—but, of course, that's an oxymoron right there.

I said this first in 1975 and I tried to spread the gospel. Any ball club that is composed of grown men, playing this wonderful game that is known as the Cubbies, ain't never gonna win.

The Cubby-Wubbies. Well, it's true. When you sing "take me out to the ball game." Well, of course it works in the "root, root, root for the White Sox," okay. You don't have to say the Cubbies. You say, "root, root, root for Chicago." When you're in a National League park, you know who Chicago is. And, of course, they were originally named the Cubs as a kind of ferocious, young little bear. So anyway, I'm half in fun and whole in earnest.

Do you think baseball is a different game today than years past?

I have been lucky that I have lived through a fabulous time in history in all aspects. As far as all sorts of artists of every kind have been concerned. I don't believe that there's not as much commitment today. I truly don't. It's like people say, "They don't have as much fun today." Well, who says? Of course they do. To say they're not as committed, I just don't believe that. I think they have other distractions.

But, in another way, it's a little tougher. I think because they're making all this money that there's not as much pure, unadulterated love lavished on them by fans. And that in itself is stressful and looking at it from a young player's thing—you know, he could say, "Hey, don't hate me. I walked in. This is how it is now. And I'm going to bust my tail." But I think that when they incur this animosity, then I also think that the pressure to produce is...it's not as relaxed a game. I think the fact that a lot of companies and corporations own the clubs; corporations and companies produce men who look at the bottom line. What did you do for me yesterday?

I take umbrage at what people say—they're not as committed and that they're not having as much fun. How can somebody my age or your age look at those kids and say, "Well, they're not having fun?"

Her father was called up to the Cleveland Indians late in the season and did not get to play. In spring training the following year, he hurt his knee and was released. He was never the same again. He spent his later years watching the Cubs on television.

She understands the baseball experience but believes following the Cubs is a waste of time.

I grew up in Park Ridge, Illinois, a northwestern suburb of Chicago. Went to Main Township High School in Park Ridge and Northwestern University in Evanston.

Your father played minor league baseball.

My dad didn't spend much time talking about his career. He was called up with Cleveland in the early '20s at the end of the season. Then went back the next season for spring training, but injured his knee trying to steal a base and never played. And it just about ruined his life. He always had that thought in the back of his mind, if he only could have done it. So he spent a lot of time watching the Cubs, which was an enjoyable experience but I think also a frustration for him because he never was able to do it himself.

I think it was one of the greatest disappointments of his life that he aspired to play...like so many other men, and almost made it. And because of an injury, he couldn't do it.

Your dad watched the Cubs on TV for 20-plus years. How did it affect him?

I think it shortened my dad's life because of the frustration. The loyalty to the team and watching in the hope that this was going to be the season—and every year they failed.

What would he say at the end of the season?

Goddamn Cubs...Every year.

Was the '69 season harder on him than the others?

I don't think his frustration that year was any greater than any other year. I'm sure it was because they were closer to winning a

288

pennant, but it just seemed that...I think it was just an accumulation of years and years of frustration with the Cubs.

I think he became used to the agony. He began to enjoy the agony. He loved the game. He had played as a youngster in Chicago what they call "sandlot baseball"—just enjoyed it so much. But not to have a home team that could win once in a while was really sad for him. Anybody who likes to suffer is a Cub fan.

What did the movie Field of Dreams *mean to you?*

When I saw the film, I didn't quite understand the attachment of other men. I recognized it as a good film. But in speaking to men afterwards, there was such nostalgia and men became teary-eyed talking about it. And I never quite understood that and it took me a while to realize that for men and for young boys—this is almost like a passage into adulthood. It's a recognition of a father and son camaraderie. It's not only a physical activity for a son and his father to either watch a professional game, or to go out and play it, but it's the emotional attachment of a son recognizing that he had a father, or that he didn't have a father, who played with him and brought him from childhood to adulthood.

It wasn't until I began thinking about it and talking to other men about how they reacted to the film that I recognized it for what it was. And I think it's because I'm a woman and women don't have, generally, the same attachment to the game of baseball or football, because it's mainly a male sport, of course. It's a father-son sport. Women might have the attachment as a child to remembering going to a ballet with their mother, or a play, or rollerskating, or something like that.

Do you think there are a lot of men who harbor the dream "if only"...?

Oh, I know so. It's not only "if only" but it's a remembrance of their youth. It's so many things. It's the camaraderie of friends. It's the attachment to their dad. Remembering walking in the stadium to watch a game, or remembering their dad taking them out to pitch a ball, or just as a little child to catch a ball. I mean, there's so many things that...so many elements that go into that attachment to baseball. It's not just the game.

289

His grandfather, mother, and father take him to see the Cubs and he plans to take his children. He told me, "I like playing baseball with my dad." Somebody is doing something right in this family. Tom is eight.

What do you like best about the Cubs?

They're really a good team. Sometimes they lack skills at a few positions, but I mean, it's still real easy to like 'em. They've got a lot of stuff that you can associate with them. Bleacher Bums, Wrigley Field...

I think it's a real nice ballpark. I like a lot of things about it. There's really good seats and it's a real pretty ballpark.

Who do you go with?

Sometimes it's just me and my mom and my dad. Or, sometimes we bring along my grandfather. It's better to go with everybody. I like it when my grandfather comes along. He can remember what baseball was like when he was a kid.

When you grow up 20 years from now and you have a son or a daughter, do you think you'll take them down to Wrigley Field?

You bet! Because I think it's good for kids to go to a ballpark. They learn about their national pastime. It's real fun.

Do you play ball with your dad?

On the weekends or really early in the evening—that's mainly when I play ball with my dad. It's real nice. You can talk while you're playing catch, or at batting practice.

Do you think you'll always remember that you played catch with your dad?

Oh, yeah. Maybe I'll play catch with them and tell them about when I did it with my dad.